The Continuity of the Conquest

The Continuity of the Conquest

Charlemagne and Anglo-Norman Imperialism

Wendy Marie Hoofnagle

The Pennsylvania State University Press
University Park, Pennsylvania

Library of Congress Cataloging-in-Publication Data

Names: Hoofnagle, Wendy Marie, author.
Title: The continuity of the conquest : Charlemagne and Anglo-Norman imperialism / Wendy Marie Hoofnagle.
Description: University Park, Pennsylvania : The Pennsylvania State University Press, [2016] | Includes bibliographical references and index.
Summary: "An interdisciplinary study examining the origins of Anglo-Norman views of kingship in idealized interpretations of Charlemagne's imperium. Demonstrates how the idea of "Englishness" developed in the Middle Ages as much as a consequence of the Anglo-Norman imagination and experience as a reaction against it."— Provided by publisher
Identifiers: LCCN 2016010401 | ISBN 9780271074016 (cloth : alk. paper) | ISBN 9780271074023 (pbk. : alk. paper)
Subjects: LCSH: Normans—England—History—To 1500. | Great Britain—History—Norman period, 1066-1154. | Great Britain—Politics and government—1066-1154. | England—Civilization—1066-1485. | Charlemagne, Emperor, 742-814—Influence. | Imperialism.
Classification: LCC DA195 .H685 2016 | DDC 942.02—dc23
LC record available at https://lccn.loc.gov/2016010401

Copyright © 2016
The Pennsylvania State University
All rights reserved
Printed in the United States of America
Published by
The Pennsylvania State University Press,
University Park, PA 16802-1003

The Pennsylvania State University Press is a member of the Association of American University Presses.

It is the policy of The Pennsylvania State University Press to use acid-free paper. Publications on uncoated stock satisfy the minimum requirements of American National Standard for Information Sciences—Permanence of Paper for Printed Library Material, ANSI Z39.48-1992.

Contents

Acknowledgments vii

1 Introduction 1

1 Conversion Politics and the Ideology of Imperialism 18

2 Making Their Mark: The Imperial Ideology of Topography 57

3 Taming the Wild Beast: A New Look at the New Forest 89

Epilogue 112

Notes 119
Bibliography 164
Index 189

Acknowledgments

Considering all of the changes that this book has gone through in the long years that I have been writing it, it is impossible to thank everyone adequately for their support and encouragement, without which I could not have persevered. Primary among these would be the provost at the University of Northern Iowa, whose generous financial support through the Pre-tenure Summer Fellowship Program allowed me time to make the revisions necessary to bring this project to fruition.

My colleagues in the Languages and Literatures Department at the University of Northern Iowa have been a great inspiration to me, modeling the ideal combination of scholar-teacher that I strive to emulate. And this project would have never gotten off the ground if weren't for Rosemary Meany and the other interlibrary loan staff at the Rod Library. I swear they can find just about anything, no matter what remote rock it might be under.

Working in a new field can be an intimidating process, but historians are a gracious and generous lot. I am especially grateful to Paul Hyams, who gently guided my blundering way through this field and whose enthusiasm for the project bolstered my confidence many times over. My thanks also go out to Matthew Gabriele for his support and advice in the project's early stages, and for including an early version of part of chapter 2, entitled "Charlemagne's Legacy and Anglo-Norman *Imperium* in Henry of Huntingdon's *Historia Anglorum*," in his collection of essays, *The Legend of Charlemagne in the Middle Ages: Power, Faith and Crusade*, published by Palgrave Macmillan in 2008.

I would also like to thank my editor at Penn State University Press, Eleanor Goodman, for her extraordinary dedication to the project and for helping me make it the best book I possibly could. I am also grateful to the anonymous readers, whose suggestions have been invaluable to the revision process and have improved it in countless ways.

Many thanks go to Wolfram Keller for his dedication and good humor while we worked on our collection of essays, *Other Nations: The Hybridization of Insular Mythology and Identity*, for Winter Verlag's Britannica et Americana series in 2011, which also contains an early version of part of chapter 2 entitled "*Altera Troia*: Geoffrey of Monmouth and the Creation of Landscapes of Power." Greg Semenza, Leah Schwebel, Kat Tracy, Niall Brady, Mary Dockray-Miller, John Burnight, and Jolene Zigarovich also merit my undying gratitude for their unflagging support and guidance on this very long journey. My sincerest thanks also go to Allen Frantzen for his friendship, patience, and wisdom, as well as for reading early drafts and assisting me with the publication process.

Finally, words cannot express the depth of my love and gratitude to my children, Madeleine and Nicholas, and my mother, Darlene Petralia, who have been my greatest champions all along. They believed in me even when I wasn't sure I believed in myself, and for that along with so many other reasons, this book is dedicated to them.

Introduction

As William of Malmesbury tells it, on the morning of the Battle of Hastings in 1066, after a long night of prayer, the Norman army took communion and "struck up the song of Roland to fire them as they went into battle with the example of a heroic warrior, . . . calling on God's help."[1] It is generally acknowledged that the allusion to the great crusade of Charlemagne and the Twelve Peers was meant to represent William the Conqueror and his loyal followers, supporting the righteousness of the duke's cause in England.[2] Although William of Malmesbury was writing well after Charlemagne's lifetime and was a couple of generations removed from the Normans who had come to England with William the Conqueror, the story suggests that in the eleventh and twelfth centuries Charlemagne's legend remained a potent symbol for *translatio*, and for establishing authority both secular and religious. This practice was not original to the Normans, however, but had been in place since the reign of Charlemagne. "Evoking the figure of Charlemagne becomes not only a way of imagining and legitimating one's origins, but it is also a way of doing so in relation to the Other,"[3] as Robert Morrissey observes. Legendary name-dropping was a favored practice among medieval elites for centuries after his death, even among the pre-Conquest Normans, especially for purposes of validating their authority and sanctioning imperial expansion. In spite of this, the influence of Charlemagne among the Anglo-Normans in particular has not been examined to any great extent,[4] leaving a significant gap in our understanding of their ideals of kingship as well as their desires for legitimacy and imperial sovereignty.[5]

Economic factors in Anglo-Norman colonizing impulses, such as the need on the part of William the Conqueror and his heirs to acquire more and more land revenue to reward their followers and to win support,[6] do not account for the importance of the ideological influences that may have affected the way they went about it. As Ann Laura Stoler points out, "the assumption that colonial political agendas are self-evident precludes our examination of the cultural politics of the communities in which the colonizers lived,"[7] which can be an obstacle to our understanding of the politics of Norman expansion and cultural appropriation. A neglected area of scholarly studies about the Normans and their influence in England is the history of their own cultural politics, in particular the underlying importance of Charlemagne for the early Normans as an imperial model, and the effect that their emulation of his kingship might have had on post-Conquest England. By considering the Normans' debt to an idealized, even legendary, interpretation of Charlemagne's *imperium*, this perspective offers a complementary reading to the idea that they were predatory opportunists as they sought to expand their economic base.[8]

By Charlemagne's legend, I mean the aggregate of historical and literary ideals, which may even be self-contradictory at times, that developed about Charlemagne after his death and shaped medieval definitions of kingship and civilized behavior, such as courtly culture, imperialistic desires, and sacral kingship. This perspective is not unlike the idea of King Arthur's legend, which was also influenced by Charlemagne's, except for the fact that some of the material for Charlemagne's kingship, such as cartularies and writs, continued to exist after his death, providing an additional layer of verisimilitude to his more fictive exploits. When considering medieval writers' use of the legendary Charlemagne in historiography, it is important to remember the medieval premise that truth can encompass what modern readers would consider fiction, such that, in the words of Jeanette Beer, "Truth and facts were polarized, with preference for the former over the latter."[9] This tendency valorizes legendary material as an illustration of a kind of truth that does not necessarily have to be "factual"; thus, the Charlemagne who destroyed the Saracens at Saragossa in the *Chanson de Roland* could carry the same ideological weight as the Charlemagne who defeated the Saxons in the eighth century. Materials that include "fiction" are still significant for this study because of the agendas of the authors and audience expectations of these texts. Suzanne

Fleischman argues that "there was a concept of history which was distinct from fiction, and which was linked to a particular criterion of truth. But historical truth did not imply, as it does for us, the authenticity of facts and events. . . . History was what was willingly believed. Thus the epic legends, even when invented out of whole cloth, were accepted as historically true."[10] The same holds for the legend of Charlemagne specifically, as brilliantly demonstrated by Anne Latowsky, who shows that for many generations following Charlemagne's reign great currency was given to his imagined life, which was used in a multitude of ways to legitimate authority, including royal biography, *res gestae*, chronicles, universal histories, relic-authentication texts, imperial decrees, and hagiographies.[11]

The influence of Charlemagne's memory on other western European rulers, such as the Ottonians, Anglo-Saxons, and Capetians, began shortly after his death in 814; indeed, subsequent Carolingian kings would imitate his style of kingship through the performance of rituals, such as anointings, crown-wearings, hunting parties, and the giving of tribute,[12] and through building practices, such as Charles the Bald's evocation of his illustrious grandfather's memory in his claim to have copied Aachen's palace chapel at his palace in Compiègne.[13] These practices would remain important for later dynasties of western Europe, whose propagandists would go so far as to rewrite their royal histories to align them with Charlemagne's bloodline and portray them as his direct descendants,[14] or whose kings would seek out women of Carolingian descent to achieve the same result, as did Philip Augustus when he married Isabelle of Hainaut. Other rulers were keen to associate themselves with Charlemagne's authority through the appropriation of his physical remains, such as Otto III, who took his ancestor's relics from Aachen in 1000, or Frederick Barbarossa, who returned the remains to Aachen in 1165 as part of his program for Charlemagne's canonization. Even in Spain, where Charlemagne's influence is not typically considered to be as great as it was in France and Germany, Alfonso VI the Brave of León and Castile "styled his image in imitation of Charlemagne" to such an extent that Charlemagne became conflated with Alfonso in the development of the Roland legend in northern Spain of the 1090s.[15] In time, the topos of Charlemagne's kingship would also become "a privileged locus for questioning the nature and limits of power, including cases in which the king is in the wrong, in which the person who embodies sovereignty abuses it."[16] Thus, the versatility of his legend could be manipulated to serve a variety of socio-political needs, especially where issues of royal authority were concerned.

It should be noted here that the idea of "empire" throughout the Middle Ages was not a homogeneous one, and medieval propagandists employed several models of authority for conveying *translatio imperii*; for instance, Charlemagne's biographers followed the Merovingian practice of using Old Testament exemplars such as David and Solomon for defining good kingship.[17] The Roman emperor Constantine also served as an archetype for a Christian emperor, as evidenced by Gregory of Tours's imitation of his baptism for his description of the baptism of Clovis, the founder of the Merovingian dynasty. Although Charlemagne was nicknamed "David" during his reign, references to him as a "new Constantine" are a common feature of the tributes written in his honor.[18] The importance of Constantine's image to Anglo-Norman secular authority is problematic in several ways, however.[19] Although he appears in some Anglo-Norman historiography with a British pedigree, and his mother, Helena, enjoyed great popularity as a saint in England from the time of the Anglo-Saxons for her discovery of the True Cross, Constantine himself did not achieve great prominence in the writing of Anglo-Norman scholars and poets and would not be considered important as an imperial model until well after the Middle Ages.[20] Indeed, in the first half of the twelfth century, William of Malmesbury mentions his origins as a British king, an idea which is taken up shortly thereafter by Henry of Huntingdon and others, who nevertheless lose interest in Constantine's history after he leaves Britain.[21] Another reason for this is Geoffrey of Monmouth's conflation of two historical persons named Constantine into a king of questionable morality who was only briefly in Britain and later alienated his subjects by crushing a native rebellion against the Romans.[22] As a result, not all writers considered the figure of Constantine as attractive a source for *translatio imperii* as other historical kings; moreover, his authority was further complicated by the church's exploitation of his memory, through hagiography such as the *Vita Silvestri* and the legend of the Donation of Constantine, which bestowed the temporal rule of the empire upon the pope, for purposes of promoting its own power—a power of which secular rulers were justifiably leery. John Cowdrey especially notes that Constantine, "as an ideal secular ruler who knew his place before God and the clergy,"[23] was a primary source for upholding the pope's temporal as well as spiritual power. Thus, perhaps because Constantine was more historically remote than other legendary personages and associations with the Roman emperor came with potential strings attached, Charlemagne was viewed by many later writers as a more suitable imperial model for Anglo-Norman kings who were striving to establish their legitimacy.

The Continuity of the Conquest, therefore, is meant to complement previous studies of these questions for a fuller understanding of the development of the ideologies of kingship and identity formation in medieval Europe. I explore the Carolingian aspects of Norman influence in England after the Conquest and demonstrate that the Normans' literature of kingship envisioned government as a form of imperial rule modeled in many ways on the legendary glories of Charlemagne and his reign, which endures to this day as a celebrated example of political and intellectual rebirth that reversed the cultural decline of the Dark Ages following the fall of Rome in the West. To do this, I attempt to discern the ways that Charlemagne's kingship may have affected the Normans in particular and informed certain aspects of their approach to rule independently of the Carolingian-inspired institutions that they inherited after the Conquest. As is well known, the Anglo-Saxons maintained a long-standing connection with Carolingian kings—for example, King Alfred's interest in the revival of learning, especially among the clergy, was influenced by Charlemagne's similar program—but the Anglo-Saxons' emulation focused more on the sacral aspects of Charlemagne's rule.[24] In contrast, the Normans concentrated on imperial expressions of power in their propaganda of kingship. At times, the portraits of kingship that they imagined in these expressions might diverge considerably from the behavior of real kings;[25] for their purposes, however, the fiction was just as relevant and useful as the reality and reveals more about contemporary values and practices than historical details of Charlemagne's kingship alone. By studying both factors, therefore, we can better appreciate how the Normans' manipulation of Charlemagne's idealized legend was adapted to new meanings, which would ultimately change the course of Western medieval history and literature following the Conquest.

The idea of Charlemagne's legend for the purposes of this study, therefore, is significant: it is important to remember that the Normans, such as William of Malmesbury in his account of the Battle of Hastings, called upon the memory of Charlemagne in order to sanction their political pursuits, even though specific details of his memory may not have had a solid footing in reality. In fact, Charlemagne's myth was constantly in flux, and, like all good lies, was often partially grounded in fact. Consequently, it is possible to examine the ways in which post-Conquest rhetoric drew upon the Carolingian past and the models it offered for propaganda, even as it claimed fidelity to its predecessor but differed sharply from it in actuality. Moreover, one could argue, as Gilduin Davy does, that the Normans deliberately used the power of the written word to promote their authority during the course of Normandy's development and their evolution from barbaric Viking to legitimate duke (as they would later do in England for the purposes of kingship), using a "neo-Carolingian archetype."[26] When royal power weakened during the course of the tenth century and the dukes began to claim more of it for themselves, the use of quasi-royal titles derived from Carolingian sources, such as *princeps*, *dux regni*, and *Dei gratia dux*, became an important tool for demonstrating legitimacy in official documents.[27] Furthermore, the promotion from duke to king must have been one of the appeals of conquest for William I, especially as it augmented his ability to exercise power in Normandy as well as in England;[28] he was certainly keen to publicize his royal authority there using rituals derived from Carolingian exemplars, such as the coronation *ordo* and *laudes regiae*. As Janet Nelson has shown, William was "aware of the propaganda-value of ritual, and that awareness was heightened by his situation as Conqueror of the English kingdom."[29] This recognition is further suggested, according to Nelson, by the *laudes regiae* of 1068, where we see the use of the imperial epithet *serenissimus*;[30] with this epithet, combined with regular crown-wearings, William was able to exploit the imperial image of these rituals to support his claim to divine appointment as king of England.[31]

For our understanding of the Norman approach to ruling, therefore, the variety of potential uses of the Charlemagne legend for legitimizing authority is more important to understanding the Normans' self-promotion than the documentary evidence alone can indicate. Instead, we must also turn to other, nondocumentary sources for support of the Norman interpretation and appropriation of Charlemagne's legend for purposes of realizing their political ambitions. Their methods all too often involved the creation of a fictional reality, which was no less real or effective for its audience because of its legendary qualities than because of its documentary "reality." We might even speak of an iconography of Carolingian kingship that requires analysis of such media as literature, art, and landscape; as a result, I employ a wide range of materials for my argument, encompassing literary fiction, historiography, and landscape studies, as well as documentary evidence and legal practices. The Normans' production of propaganda, like that of so many before them, can involve conscious imitation as well as a lack of awareness of their own purposes for invention; frequently, these writers tap into a contemporary idea or feeling without a conspicuous agenda, but, when considered in toto, these texts demonstrate patterns of thought and behavior beyond the obvious—the general temper not only of our authors or even their commissioners, but also of contemporary audiences and those audiences yet to come. The written word is not only "an exercise in rhetoric, elaborating purely literary and aesthetic effects . . . it is a version of the world, which is to say an interpretation, an ideological statement."[32] It is necessary, therefore, to look as fully as possible at the socio-cultural picture that Norman political ambitions paint for us in their texts through the manipulation of "history" and "legend" for their self-promotion on the medieval political stage.

Continuity and Carolingian Kingship: The Case of the Early Normans

The question of continuity in Normandy with regard to Carolingian traditions and rulership is fraught with controversy, due in part to the debate over the point at which the invading Vikings began to turn their focus away from their Scandinavian heritage and adopt the culture and mores of the Frankish world they inherited when they took control of the erstwhile duchy of Neustria. Scholars such as David Bates and Karl Ferdinand Werner have argued for a swift assimilation into Frankish society, in which the Scandinavian newcomers quickly sought to adopt the Carolingian institutions that the church had struggled to preserve in the days of chaos wrought by the Viking depredations; on the other end of the spectrum, Eleanor Searle and others after her model have claimed that the Scandinavian social structure of independent war-bands continued to exist in Normandy, along with their Viking identity, far longer than Bates and Werner have assumed, indeed well into the eleventh century.[33] One of the challenges to this discussion for both interpretations is the lack of a clear connection in documentary evidence from the late ninth into the mid-tenth century, which would demonstrate without a doubt what structures Rollo and his followers adopted in their new duchy. It is possible, however, to look elsewhere to study the persistence of Carolingian traditions in early Norman affairs.[34] As David Bates notes, "The long-term perspective more than justifies the general conclusion that the first settlers must have taken over many existing institutions, since, by the eleventh century, when documents become available, it is clear that rural estates had preserved essentially Carolingian features and that ducal government operated largely through mechanisms which were inspired by Carolingian notions of authority."[35] These views suggest that enough of the Carolingian approach to estate management and government survived (especially with regard to legal practices) to enable the new duchy to begin to function effectively soon after the establishment of Rollo as duke of Normandy. This perspective also advocates that the new Normans found it advantageous to cooperate with and even assimilate Frankish norms and customs in order to survive in their new environment and create the kind of political networks that would be necessary to protect and promote their interests.

Musset proposed that the preservation of Carolingian authority and institutions is due, in part, to the continuity of some episcopal hierarchies in the region,[36] and Felice Lifshitz has followed his argument by demonstrating how the bishops of Neustria governed the large majority of the towns and their administrative territories in the Carolingian style of the *pagi* around the end of the ninth century. As a result, according to her research, "no rupture occurred in Rouen around this time . . . with regard to Carolingian administrative practice."[37] Musset also argued that it was the preservation of Carolingian traditions, "les héritages carolingiens," that made life less difficult in Normandy than elsewhere during the upheaval of the tenth century.[38] In this interpretation, the continuance of Carolingian institutions in Norman government enabled the new duchy to stabilize surprisingly quickly, which fostered prosperity and expansion under subsequent generations of Norman dukes, as well as a more recognizable Carolingian style of government. The vexing question remains of determining exactly when this adoption occurred. On this point, however, the pendulum seems to be swinging back to the side of early continuity in studies such as those by Pierre Bauduin and Mark Hagger. Although Bauduin is somewhat cautious in his treatment of the argument for continuity, acknowledging the fluidity of territorial boundaries and aristocratic fidelity, which indicated a process of assimilation that was not uniform throughout the duchy, Hagger strongly claims to join "the debate about continuity or change in post-Carolingian Normandy very much on the side on continuity" by examining the preservation of legal terminology and usage.[39]

The Normans' integration into Frankish society would result in a slow evaporation of their Scandinavian attachments. Lucien Musset remarks, "these Carolingian remnants let themselves better integrate the feudal state that Normandy would become in the eleventh century, when Norse contributions would become victims of reactions of rejection."[40] The fading connections with the Scandinavian North throughout the tenth century can be observed, for example, in the decrease in the amount of Norman money in Scandinavian coin hoards.[41] In William Longsword's reign, the Rouen mint was revived in "a direct recreation of an institution of Carolingian government."

It produced money "in a typically Carolingian style," with only the names changed from those of Frankish kings to William's own.[42] Bates concludes, "From the very beginning the counts of Rouen made very definite efforts to rule in a Carolingian tradition."[43] Until 1204, in fact, the French kings had no jurisdiction in Normandy: they did not possess land, or patronize churches, abbeys, or dioceses; instead, "tous les droits utiles du souverain carolingien se retrouvent, du Xe au XIIe siècle, entre les mains des ducs" (all the pertinent rights of the Carolingian sovereign would be found, from the tenth to the twelfth century, in the hands of the dukes).[44] Scandinavian influences did not linger long among the Normans as the ninth century waned and they found themselves further embroiled in Frankish affairs. Other studies of architecture, literature, art, and patronage bear this out.[45] From as early as William Longsword's reign (927–42), moreover, religious architecture such as the abbey church of Saint-Pierre at Jumièges strove to emulate that of Carolingian buildings in scale, style, and structure.[46] Manuscripts produced at Jumièges and Fécamp during the course of the tenth century and into the eleventh were remarkable for their conformity to Carolingian classicism.[47] Many legal practices were also holdovers from earlier Carolingian usage.[48] Whether or not a significant rupture in the continuity of Carolingian authority and customs resulted from the Viking attacks in Neustria, most scholars agree that by the end of Richard I's tenure as duke in 996, the Normans had reinstated many of the prerogatives and trappings of their Carolingian inheritance.[49] *The Continuity of the Conquest*, therefore, is intended to enhance these studies by showing how the influence of Charlemagne's memory played into Norman identity and shaped their conceptualization of authority and ultimately their relationship to England and the English.

"An Obsession with the Continent": A Reconsideration of Insular Continuity

As the controversy surrounding the studies of Carolingian continuity in early Normandy suggests, the development of Anglo-Norman kingship as a consequence of the far-reaching influence of Carolingian culture demands further study to better understand its impact on later English society and culture. As R. W. Southern once observed, "Culturally the most obvious thing about England in the twelfth century is its dependence on France."[50] Thus, this study founds many of its insights on a reassessment of eleventh- and twelfth-century Anglo-Norman historiographers and writers for an increased awareness of the English experience after the Normans applied Continental mores and ideology to the Anglo-Saxon political and culture framework they inherited.[51] Today, scholars apply the term "hybridity" to this phenomenon in medieval societies.[52] Kathrin Audehm and Hans Rudolf Velten define hybridizations as "innovative and creative processes within in-between spaces, in which heterogeneous entities are linked and fused and, therefore, become indeterminate and ambivalent."[53] New identities often emerge in this "in-between" space, but it is necessary to renegotiate their composition repeatedly over time and with each new encounter. Certainly, the Anglo-Norman "obsession with the Continent"[54] could be said to have co-existed with an "obsession with the Anglo-Saxons": on the one hand, the perpetuation of the legend of Charlemagne and the Norman identification with him elevated their royal prestige in the rest of Europe, but their fascination with the Insular cultures and kings that existed before their arrival was equally strong. Indeed, were they to deny this connection, it would have certainly undermined their legitimacy and claims to sovereignty in England. The duality of this inheritance must be stressed: before the Conquest, Normans such as Dudo of Saint Quentin publicized their strong association with the idealized Carolingian past, and this legacy would endure in the Norman approach to kingship in England. The answer for the Anglo-Normans, therefore, was an elevation of their Anglo-Saxon inheritance to put them on an equal footing with Continental emperors, Charlemagne in particular. Studies regarding the socio-political continuity or rupture in England, therefore, must consider the influence that Charlemagne's kingship had on post-Conquest peoples and their anxieties about authority and identity.

The Anglo-Normans were eager to promote themselves in the European political world as a highly sophisticated and urbane imperial society and to establish their authority in England as well as on the Continental stage. For that reason, it is important to recognize the nature of the Anglo-Normans' Continental inheritance in the political and cultural environment that they redefined upon taking the throne of England. We do know that William was very practical and forthright in his administration of his new kingdom, as his establishment of the Domesday survey can attest, and one can hardly imagine that his approach to kingship was created out of whole cloth upon stepping on English soil. Some of the early charters and writs that remain express his desire for the continuity of English practices,[55] but this continuity was fundamentally married to elements of the Carolingian approach to kingship to create a hybrid entity that would ultimately absorb the ideals of both cultures; thus, the "Englishness" that would develop by the end of the fourteenth century would differ greatly from that of the tenth, while still retaining traces of its former identity.

The Norman ideology of sovereignty was one developed by William I's ducal predecessors and revolved around the Carolingian notion of a king's stewardship of the land and its people, of his responsibility for their betterment and salvation. However William may have envisioned a continuation of English custom in his reign, as he claimed in his early writs, the reality remained that he initially applied the veneer of Carolingian authority—borrowed from a pastiche of laws, administrative practices, and even legend—to several aspects of the governance of his duchy and later his kingdom, as did his Norman predecessors, which would ultimately have an impact on the Norman pursuit of *imperium* throughout Britain. Policies such as the introduction of the Forest Law and the Domesday survey, traditionally attributed to William I's rapacious greed by chroniclers and historiographers, and the development of elaborate, hybrid historical and legal texts, which created composite myths such as that of the *via regia*, take on new meaning when one examines the Carolingian legacy that informed Norman ideals of sovereignty and helped shape their practical approach to governing their new empire.[56] At the time of the Conquest, Norman law "was basically Frankish in origin and substance,"[57] and "all judicial authority in the duchy was the duke's or derived from him . . . [such that] there was a duke's justice in Normandy in a sense in which there was not a king's justice in England before 1066."[58] What evolved in the eleventh and twelfth centuries was a codification of these ideals, and thus the responsibility for stewardship became vested in the very person of the king.

Norman involvement and personal investment in Carolingian affairs began, of course, with the series of agreements after A.D. 911 between the Northmen (invading Scandinavians) and Charles the Simple and his successors.[59] This association would later become a cornerstone of Norman identity and be perpetuated in chronicles and other contemporary texts; indeed, the *Chanson de Roland* makes two allusions to England's having been part of Charlemagne's domains.[60] David Douglas also observes that "for such writers, it would seem, it was the loyalty of a Norman Duke to a successor of Charlemagne . . . that precipitated the most spectacular murder of the tenth century,"[61] that of William Longsword in 942. The duke would be shortly thereafter praised in a rhymed Latin dirge, where any questions about his Christianity and feudal virtues would be quickly laid to rest by his image as a "Christian champion and as a martyr for his loyalty to the Emperor,"[62] notions which would be perpetuated by successive historians such as Dudo of

Saint Quentin in the early eleventh century and Wace in the twelfth. Inherent in the association of Charlemagne's imperial role is the concept of sacral kingship, of his *gemina persona* as earthly king and the vicar of God, which was first mentioned by Cathwulf in a letter to Charlemagne and subsequently elaborated by influential writers such as Alcuin. The Normans "were most conspicuously active in promoting the notion of the priest-king" and the "divine sanctions of royalty."[63] Bates has argued that this was evident in the formulae of early Norman charters, for instance, which "show that princely power was exercised *Dei gratia*. Although the notion that this implies divine favour has been questioned on the grounds that it may simply be a reference to providence, the point remains that the princes are shown as considering themselves to have a place within the divine scheme."[64] Further after the Conquest, we see this in 1100 in the tractates of the York or Norman Anonymous, who was "one of the staunchest defenders of the spiritual essence of a Christlike kingship"[65] and in whose writing "the sacerdotal qualities of kingship were emphasized to an unprecedented degree."[66]

Perhaps Anglo-Norman writers found like minds in the Anglo-Saxon reformers of the tenth and early eleventh centuries, a period in which M. J. Silverman notes that "a Christ-centered theory of kingship" flourished that was derived from Carolingian and Ottonian models, notably in Edgar's coronation *ordo*, the Golden Charter for the New Minster at Winchester, and the writings of Æthelwold and his student, Ælfric.[67] It is apparent, in any event, that those Anglo-Saxon kings whose reigns were closely associated with the Carolingian court, such as Æthelstan, or strongly resembled the Carolingian ideals of sacral kingship, such as Alfred and Edgar (with some emendation, of course), seem to have resonated for the Anglo-Normans and figure prominently in the explosion of literary output in the twelfth century. The Anglo-Normans, it must be noted, reconstructed the history of their Anglo-Saxon forebears to better align them with Continental events and mores. Thus, in the early twelfth century, Symeon of Durham provided "unique" historical details in his writing and "was at pains to correlate what he knew of Frankish history with his information about the Anglo-Saxon past," possibly because he was of Norman origins himself.[68] In his entry concerning Eadberht, for example, which contains details that cannot be corroborated elsewhere, Symeon demonstrates a concern to show Anglo-Saxon kings on an equal footing with Carolingian kings. To do so, he emphasizes the respect that the Frankish rulers had for the good kingship of their Anglo-Saxon brethren: "[News of] Eadberht's excellent fame and virtuous works spread far and wide, and even reached the king of the Franks Pippin, who became his friend because of this and sent him many and varied royal gifts."[69] Another roughly contemporary example is from William of Malmesbury's *Gesta regum Anglorum* from 1125, in which he directly compares Æthelstan to Charlemagne by calling him "Magnus Adelstanus"[70] in an elegiac verse resembling Carolingian royal epitaphs.[71]

Sacral kingship was not the only Carolingian institution that appealed to the Normans before the Conquest, as John Le Patourel remarks; the variety of titles attributed to their rulers suggests that "their government had been scarcely less than royal. It can be argued that more rights and prerogatives derived ultimately from Carolingian royalty had survived or been revived in the hands of the dukes of Normandy than most other princes in Western Francia had managed to preserve."[72] Inherent in these "rights and prerogatives" is the establishment of justice in the person of the duke, and later the king. This development is twofold: first, we have examples of Charlemagne as judge and lawgiver in an echo of Old Testament kings. Sections of Alcuin's *Rhetoric* in particular, which Luitpold Wallach has identified as "a tractate on kingship or good government,"[73] represent "legal and juridical elements of Frankish procedures of law [that have] definite bearing on the functions of Charlemagne's kingship."[74] Historiographers would later apply this image to Anglo-Norman kings in reference to their "Solomon-like" kingship. During the twelfth century, Anglo-Norman kingship would further transform to incorporate a second, more secular dimension to the sacerdotal Carolingian ideal and be "transferred from the theological to the legal sphere"[75] in the role of the king as *iustitia* or *lex animata* that evolved in place of his former sacral status, as Ernst Kantorowicz has shown.[76] As "the very Idea of Justice,"[77] the king embodies the law and represents, in a very physical sense, the peace of the land he rules through the administration of justice.

For Anglo-Norman kings, there could be many practical applications of this new component to the Carolingian ideals, and some stemmed from their experiences with the early tenth-century Continental "peace movement," which began as an ecclesiastical response to the weakness of the Capetian dynasty. The proclamation of the "Truce of God" was intended first to proscribe fighting on days of religious significance, but was later extended to encourage "the idea that combat pleased God only in defense of Christendom" and gained momentum in conjunction with crusading fever. The idea was eventually appropriated by secular leaders and, as Thomas Head and Richard Landes note, "became part of the emerging constitutional order of governance and peacekeeping. By the mid-twelfth century in France, the Peace of God had become the king's Peace. In fact, truce days constituted the first moments at which, at least in theory and by legal definition, public authority held a monopoly on the legitimate use of violence."[78] The Norman dukes were especially precocious in this regard, however, as Howard Bloch emphasizes: "William I had enacted, as early as 1075, a 'Duke's Peace' limiting blood feuds and placing numerous restrictions upon the conduct of any but his own expeditions."[79] These restrictions were intended to severely hamper the nobles' pursuit of personal vengeance but also effectively enhanced the duke's/king's role in the dispensation of justice. When Henry I stated in his Coronation Charter, "I place strong peace on all my kingdom and order it to be held henceforth," John Hudson concludes that "he was deliberately invoking something more than general peacefulness, and something different from his protection specially given to individuals. Rather he was placing his power behind a strong peace closely associated with kingship."[80] It is this Carolingian ideal of *iustitia animata* envisioned for Norman kingship that would become a significant focus of the substantial legal and literary developments of the twelfth century.

Paul Hyams has observed that the "early medieval collections of *leges* are a distinct genre of legal writing, oriented towards a Carolingian kind of ideal written law."[81] Of later legal developments in Henry II's reign, Hyams claims that the "greatest Angevin achievement was to bring royal law within the sphere of noble interest,"[82] and this expanding awareness would echo in a variety of literary output. Some of the legal texts produced in the twelfth century reflect Anglo-Norman desire to preserve Anglo-Saxon history and culture, with the added authority of Carolingian precedent. The *Leges Henrici Primi* is a curious text, an early twelfth-century hodgepodge of English and Carolingian codes and even legal proverbs that purports to record laws during the time of Henry I. According to Patrick Wormald, the results of this combination are "bizarre," with over 10 percent of *Leges* incorporating clauses from sources with little or nothing to do with English law, including instead Frankish codes and Carolingian capitularies, and an entire chapter "lifted almost word for word from *Lex Ribuaria*," a Merovingian collection written five centuries earlier and still in use during the Carolingian period.[83] Wormald claims that "these clauses owed their presence to something other than a wish to describe English law as it currently functioned," because they "contributed to the work's coherence as an intellectual exposition."[84] I would argue that in light of the literary trend during the twelfth century toward revising history to suit Norman ideals and tastes, these inclusions are not surprising or "bizarre" but confirm an abiding interest in the Carolingian ideology and practice of kingship.

The *Leges Edwardi Confessoris*, for instance, compiled soon after 1136 for "a private collection not intended for any official purpose," demonstrates a "more purposeful bias" than the *Leges Henrici*.[85] Bruce O'Brien, in his recent edition of the *Leges Edwardi*, notes that the author, like that of *Leges Henrici*, transplants Carolingian passages into his text because he "sought more venerable or respectable literary vehicles to give his laws an authoritative birth."[86] As well as including lengthy discussions of *iusticia regis* and *pax regia*, the *Leges Edwardi* breaks off in the midst of a detailed discussion of *murdrum* fines to integrate a direct reference to the Carolingian ideal of sacral kingship in his explanation of the king as the vicar of God, represented by Charlemagne himself:

> The king, moreover, who is the vicar of the highest King, was established for this, that he rule and defend the kingdom and people of the Lord and, above all, the Holy Church from wrongdoers, and destroy and eradicate evildoers. If not, moreover, he loses the name of king, as Pope John testifies, to whom Pippin and his son Charles, not yet kings but princes under the foolish king of the Franks, wrote asking if those who were content with just the name of king ought to remain kings of the Franks? He responded: "Those ought to be called kings who vigilantly defend and rule the church of God and his people," echoing the royal psalmist's saying, "He who works with pride will not dwell in the midst of my house," etc.[87]

O'Brien cites Ado of Vienne's *Chronicon*, written in the third quarter of the ninth century, as the source for this paragraph, but its tone and sacral imagery also recall the writing of Alcuin from a generation or two earlier. Certainly, the author of the *Leges Edwardi* considered Charlemagne to be the ideal model for kingship, and his treatise demonstrates that the paradigm persisted well into the twelfth century.[88]

The few examples that I have mentioned thus far suggest that the sociopolitical legacy of *imperium* was complex and varied, requiring attention to the vast networks of influence and power that the Normans inherited when they took control of the duchy in the early tenth century. In *The Continuity of the Conquest*, therefore, I ask new questions about the interplay of historical events, historiography, and imaginative literature in order to illuminate the connections between the much-admired legendary Carolingian past and the conflicts that the Anglo-Normans faced as they took on the role of colonizers of England, Wales, Scotland, and Ireland. Because of this, to some extent I employ literary approaches such as postcolonial theory to achieve this end, but by and large I attempt to avoid distraction from the pertinent issues by relying on close-reading techniques to arrive at my conclusions, rather than the use of overcomplicated terminology. Thus, the next chapter, "Conversion Politics and the Ideology of Imperialism," examines the work of such writers as Dudo of Saint Quentin and Geoffroi Gaimar, who extol a more civilized approach to kingship, similar to that developed during Charlemagne's reign, in order to promote the idea of conversion politics for successful colonization. In these kinds of narrative, kings, rather than dominating subjects by the sword alone, entice them with the promise of economic or political gain and inclusion in a more civilized way of life by manipulating royal rituals to reinforce authority rather than bloodshed. The Anglo-Normans justified expansion into neighboring regions by focusing on the importance of converting other so-called barbaric territories to bring them within their ostensibly civilizing sphere of influence, projecting an image of themselves as the legitimate inheritors of a pan-British empire.

Chapter 2, "Making Their Mark: The Imperial Ideology of Topography," continues the exploration of Norman representations of civilized *imperium* by considering the importance of the symbolic landscape for projecting authority, underscored by the ideological reasons behind the Norman program of building castles and restoring roads across Britain. The Normans created an enduring image of their authority in stone, in imitation of Charlemagne's building program from the late eighth century for his palaces at Aachen and elsewhere, which established his new empire as a "second Rome" and his kingship as the unifying *via regia*. Charlemagne's intentions in appropriating the symbolic landscape, therefore, became a key mechanism for the projection of Norman power. The importance of the symbolic landscape for imperial ideology is further investigated with regard to the notorious New Forest in chapter 3, "Taming the Wild Beast: A New Look at the New Forest." This chapter considers the impact of Charlemagne and his imperial governance on the day-to-day routines of Norman kingship, which resulted in a sophisticated system of administration that reinforced a vertical social hierarchy, with the king at the top, and maintained strict control of the fiscal administration of the kingdom. The Carolingian legacy that can be found in capitularies and other legal texts shaped the Anglo-Norman kings' practical approach to governing, as is especially evident in their introduction of such prerogatives as the creation of the Domesday survey and especially the Forest Law. The forest, consequently, as a significant extension of royal authority in the eleventh and twelfth centuries, becomes a symbolic landscape for the exploration of literary tropes, as well as the exercise of royal power, and an ideal space for understanding conflicts resulting from abuses of royal authority that were rife in the twelfth century. The epilogue briefly considers the evolution of "Englishness" during the twelfth century by looking at some late treatments of Charlemagne's legend that point to an emerging pro-English sentiment in the wake of political and social unrest due to conflict with the French king. Here, I examine some early thirteenth-century texts that are critical of the legendary Charlemagne, as well as some that value him, as evidence of a renewed connection with an English past. A continued recognition of the sociopolitical advantages that can come from contact with the Carolingian mythical past remains in these texts, however: the symbols of Charlemagne's kingship are appropriated for the use of English kings, resulting in a connection that remains fused with images of his legendary authority. Thus, the resurgence of an idea of "Englishness" in the later Middle Ages must be viewed in its context as a consequence of the Anglo-Norman imagination and experience, as much as a reaction against it.

1 | Conversion Politics and the Ideology of Imperialism

By the end of the ninth century, Charlemagne's legend in western Europe as the world's most powerful emperor had solidified to such an extent that the Saxon Poet (Poeta Saxo), writing between 888 and 891, claimed that not only had Charlemagne conquered vast territories and peoples during his lifetime, but, as a result of his victories, the glory of his reign exceeded that of all previous emperors:

Among the leaders and kings of ancient times no one
had a more thoroughly illustrious reputation than
    Charlemagne.
With many leaders and over many years the Romans
Barely managed to bring the peoples of Italy under their sway:
single-handed, and in the space of a very short time, Char-
    lemagne conquered
and subdued the whole of Italy, and administered it as its lord.
Consider too all the peoples of Europe whom Charlemagne
    made
His subjects whose very names the Romans did not know.[1]

The Saxon Poet's rhetoric is reminiscent of the kind of panegyric that placed Charlemagne and his capital at Aachen above Rome in imperial authority, as I will discuss in chapter 2. Although his poem is not unusual in its praise of an *imperator* whose authority encompassed vast territories and subjugated multiple peoples—indeed, it imitates the language of many authors before him[2]—it is novel for its greater focus on Charlemagne's spiritual victories: for the Saxon Poet, Charlemagne's legend is not merely earthly but heavenly as well, because of the thousands of souls he saved through conversion to Christianity. These monumental achievements put him among the great biblical kings and emperors in the heavenly cohort:

Their earthly glory may perhaps have been equal to his
but now Charlemagne holds the highest honour in Heaven.
There he commands the respect paid to the courage of David,
in the company of Constantine and Theodosius;
there he rejoices on vanquishing the ancient enemy
and snatching many away from its snares.
There with Charlemagne thousands of spirits rejoice
on being saved by him through the grace of Christ.
Who can count how many souls he restored to the Lord
When he made Christians of the Saxon peoples?[3]

The importance of the conversion of the pagan conquered to Christianity to Charlemagne's legendary *imperium* is representative of an important development in Western medieval thinking about the nature of kingship, epitomizing the change in focus from military to spiritual leader. Later in Charlemagne's reign, however, conversion, used as a kind of "soft power,"[4] meant assimilation into Frankish society and adoption of Frankish mores as much as Christian ones, which was accomplished through rituals that reinforced his authority in addition to creating strong political bonds and encouraging acculturation. In this chapter, I will trace the increasing influence of this interpretation of conversion to the ideology of *imperium* as introduced and promoted by Charlemagne as a crucial function of kingship, in order to better understand its significance for the Normans as they sought to define their kingship in England. The Normans bolstered their claims as *imperatores* throughout Britain after the Conquest by using the Carolingian model of kingship and conquest, focusing on the "soft power" of socio-cultural rather than religious conversion and promoting Anglo-Norman society as more civilized than its predecessors in its dealings with British peoples.

This development of the king's role, though it began earlier in his father Pepin's reign, took root during Charlemagne's rule even before Pope Leo III crowned him as emperor in 800. Certainly, as an enemy Charlemagne was formidable, and his tactics were often quite brutal during the early years of his reign, as his treatment of the Saxons proved. It is not until just before his imperial coronation, however, that we see a transformation in the ideology of his court toward conquered peoples, of luring them not only to Christianity but also to Frankish society itself. Charlemagne accomplished this in several ways, but most importantly through the rituals of his *imperium*, including baptisms, royal feasts, and hunts.[5] These rituals were meant to impress the conquered peoples with the magnitude of his power, encourage their peaceful submission to his rule in order to benefit from his largesse, and "convert" them to follow his "more civilized" way of life. Thus, the Carolingians took the Gregorian ideal of nonmilitary conversion and made it realpolitik. As Norbert Elias has shown, imperialism and conversion have gone hand-in-hand in Western society since the Middle Ages.[6] Arnold Angenendt has further demonstrated that baptismal sponsorship was a significant aspect of imperial politics.[7] Thus, Carolingian notions of the civilizing process of imperialism shifted from Roman ideals, which focused largely on military conquest and the right to rule, to also embrace the obligation of conversion, not only to Christianity but, more importantly for later generations of kings, to an emerging courtly civilization. For the Anglo-Normans, this paradigm would ultimately advocate the importance of romance ideals like "fair love" and "good customs" for converting enemies; courtly rituals would reinforce the king's authority but also include the conquered in the civilized society of the king, a practice I call "conversion politics." Although it has long been recognized that the Normans vigorously promoted the legitimacy of their rule as the rightful successors to the Anglo-Saxon kings in their revisionist histories and literature, the quality of that authority requires further analysis: the Normans tended to project an image of their authority as a peaceful and civilizing one that established their empire through benevolent conversion of neighboring peoples to their courtly culture rather than conquering them by the sword alone.

The Politics of Allurement: Conversion and Charlemagne's Civilizing Impulse

The idea of "conversion politics" in Charlemagne's reign has received some important scholarly attention and must be considered in any study that strives to understand the influence of Carolingian kingship on subsequent generations. Although it may be an exaggeration to say that Charlemagne's approach to the conquest of pagan peoples was primarily for the purpose of

Christianizing them, as it was often portrayed in Carolingian historiography, it has been noted that he did consider it an important part of his duties.[8] The notion of conversion politics can be used to understand how dominant cultures create antipathy toward certain minority groups and marginalize them further, solidifying the control of the dominant culture while also controlling who has access to what material rewards and power structures. These practices were current in the early Middle Ages, during which forced conversions were a not uncommon practice. What is especially interesting about conversion politics during Charlemagne's reign, however, is the change it underwent to include a focus on "allurement," enticing a person to convert by charm or attraction rather than force, which Charlemagne achieved through the use of ritual and gift-giving. The concept of allurement, to be sure, potentially covers a lot of conversion bases, including the promise of economic or political gain for marginalized groups. The implications of conversion politics, and of allurement in particular, have unique relevance for understanding the development of conversion in Charlemagne's political tactics and, consequently, will also shed light on the Norman propaganda about their approach to *imperium* in Britain, which purportedly encompassed more than military conquest and brutal policies meant to exploit the conquered. During the course of his reign, Charlemagne began to rely more heavily on the attraction of the civilized trappings of *imperium*, such as the ritual of baptism and the benefits of sponsorship, for purposes of converting conquered pagans not only to Christianity but also to peaceful acceptance of his sovereignty. This paradigm resonated for courtly writers of the twelfth century as they sought to define the ideals of kingship for their own time: the Normans echoed this process to promote their ambitions for *imperium* throughout Britain by advocating clemency and "fair love" (*bel amur*) for rehabilitating Celtic peoples, whom they portrayed as barbaric, through what they considered to be the civilizing influence of Norman rule.

What some scholars have interpreted as Charlemagne's Augustinian, politico-religious approach to kingship stems in part from Einhard's statement in the *Vita Caroli* that Charlemagne's dinner entertainments were not complete without a reading, especially from his favorite book, Augustine's *De Civitate Dei*: "During his meal he would listen to a public reading or some other entertainment. Stories would be recited for him, or the doings of the ancients told again. He took great pleasure in the books of Saint Augustine and especially in those which are called *The City of God*."[9] The reality of his practices in his early years, however, calls Einhard's claims into question. One example, that of Charlemagne's treatment of the Saxons during the course of his reign, demonstrates this clearly. In 772, within a few years of his accession to the throne, Charlemagne turned his attention to conquering the pagan peoples to the east of his Frankish territories, the Saxons, in a campaign that initiated more than three decades of bloody insurrections and costly wars. One particularly gory episode occurred in 782, when Charlemagne decapitated some forty-five hundred Saxon prisoners at Verden in retaliation for a Frankish military disaster in which several young nobles were cut down by Saxon forces.[10] Even if the chronicler exaggerated the number of victims, such a report demonstrates that the event left a considerable impression on Saxons and Franks alike. At this time in his career, Charlemagne did not concern himself with displaying clemency toward the Saxons, and the nature of their conversion to Christianity at sword point did not seem to cause him much consternation.[11] This was no more than was expected of a king at this time, moreover; the contemporary prayer-poem *Prospice omnipotens deus* pleads, "Grant him, Omnipotent God, to be a most mighty protector of the fatherland, and a comforter of churches and holy monasteries with the greatest piety of royal munificence, and to be the mightiest of kings, triumphing over his enemies so as to crush rebels and heathen nations; and may he be very terrible to his enemies with the utmost strength of royal potency."[12] Charlemagne's victory over the Saxons by force of arms and his demands for tithes for the church from these conquered pagans were very much in keeping with the values articulated by the *Prospice*.

Slightly later, as evidenced by the *Capitulatio de partibus Saxoniae*, dated 782–85, Charlemagne was still concerned with practicing this model of kingship. The capitulary's descriptions of harsh punishments and extortionist tithes, tributes and fines, however, can be shocking to a modern audience that is accustomed to the more moderate legend of Charlemagne as a benevolent father-figure and wise, just ruler. For many infractions, especially those involving regression into "pagan" practices such as cremating the dead or simply refusing baptism, the perpetrator was to be put to death.[13] At this point in his reign, argues Matthias Becher, "Charlemagne used the Christian religion as a means of suppressing the local population"; he would eventually discover, however, that dealing with the Saxons in this way was not an entirely successful method of imperialism and would prove "more of a hindrance to long-lasting Christianization"[14] and, subsequently, to subjugating proud pagan peoples like the Saxons to his authority. Although Widukind, the leader of the Saxons, was baptized in 785 with Charlemagne standing as his godfather, the king's draconian dealings with the Saxons, as exemplified by the first Saxon capitulary, explain a great deal about their rebelliousness during the subsequent decades. It could be inferred from these texts that Charlemagne's main concerns at this point were not their inclusion in Frankish society through conquest and baptism, but the economic potential for himself and the church coffers of exploiting these newly Christian Saxons as well as the exertion of complete authority over their lives. Charlemagne's approach to subjugating the Saxons would change over time, in part due to Alcuin's influence in advocating clemency, but his tactics would expand to include more ritual-based methods that reinforced his authority by welcoming the defeated people not only to Christianity but also into Frankish society through the baptismal relationship that re-created the familial one of father and son.[15]

The change in Charlemagne's treatment of the Saxons in the late 790s in particular is frequently attributed to Alcuin's intervention on the behalf of recently converted pagans.[16] Alcuin's ideal of conversion becomes one of willing conversion because of the attraction of the virtues of Christian kingship, not as the result of a forced baptism. In the context of conversion, temperance and mercy toward enemies can be seen as necessary virtues of sacral kingship because of the necessity to practice restraint and clemency in the exercise of justice toward defeated peoples, especially pagans. In Alcuin's view, following this practice would better bring the pagans to Christianity and, subsequently, subdue them. This stance is especially evident in one of his letters to Charlemagne, also from 796, celebrating Charlemagne's defeat of the Avars as a direct result of his new restraint toward the Saxons:

> What glory will be yours on the day of eternal requital, most blessed king, when all those converted from the worship of idols to recognition of the true God by your righteous care will attend you as you stand, blessed in your lot, before the judgement-seat of our Lord Jesus Christ and your reward of eternal beatitude is made greater for the reason of them all! Behold the great devotion and benevolence with which you have toiled to soften the harshness of the unhappy people of the Saxons through the counsel of true health, that the name of Christ might be spread![17]

Alcuin further reminds Charlemagne that those newly converted must be won over by "gentler precepts" (mollioribus praeceptis), or, to use a similar idea, be converted by "allurement" rather than by force. The promise of earthly benefits of conversion is hardly a new one and was a frequent theme of saints' lives; it was no less useful for promoting Carolingian political agendas.

In Notker's anecdote of the baptism of pagan Danes during the reign of Louis the Pious, for example, increasing numbers of Danes come to be baptized each year as "devoted vassals" (devotissimi vassalli), not for the sake of Christ but for the "earthly advantages" (commoda terrena) that the emperor can bestow.[18] In the earliest known version of the *Vita Lebuini*, from the ninth century, the saint preaches to the pagan Saxons that, if they converted to Christianity, God would give them such benefits as they had never heard of before (tanta vobis bona praestabit, quanta numquam ante audiebatis).[19] It is noteworthy that Charlemagne's second capitulary for the Saxons from 797 is utterly changed in tone and content from his earlier capitulary. Any references to tithing are completely erased, and the opening statement is notable for treating the Saxons as equals in the creation of the capitulary, to which "all have with one accord agreed" (omnes unanimiter consenserunt).[20] Furthermore, all references to capital punishment are gone, and the king promises to defer to the decision of the Saxons regarding a malefactor whose crimes merit death according to the laws of the Saxons, even when that person takes refuge with the king. What is important for understanding the Carolingian view is that the role of *imperator* has evolved to incorporate the role of Christian missionary with that of military conqueror, but by sidestepping the brutal reality of conquest to focus on the idea of converting the barbarians peacefully through the rituals that reinforced the authority of Charlemagne's civilized, virtuous kingship.

Conversion Politics: Rituals of Submission and Unification

This "kinder, gentler" Charlemagne has been credited as the reason for the ultimate subjugation of all Saxon peoples by 804, as Einhard suggests, but recent scholars have attributed other demonstrations of imperial authority to the Saxons' submission, such as the pomp of feasts and rituals and the ostentatious display of power in architecture.[21] Even the practice of commanding a vassal's presence at court was a reminder of the king's authority, since he had the power to command; Stuart Airlie observes that the "fruits of empire, and the victims of conquest, travelled *to* the Franks" (emphasis added) and not the other way round.[22] The manipulation of these impressive visual displays of power is significant for our understanding of the perception of imperial kingship by the Normans, for whom the process of conversion also stresses acculturation, so it is helpful to briefly examine the Carolingian use of ritual, especially baptism, in order to illuminate Norman interpretations of it.

Feasts and processions at court, such as the ritual of the hunt, reinforced royal displays of power because they "manifested participation as well as hierarchy, reciprocity as well as patriarchal authority."[23] As I will demonstrate further in chapter 3, the hunt functions as a courtly ritual of patrimonial kingship designed to include members of the king's *familias* in the civilized behavior of the court while reinforcing the king's position at the top of the vertical social bonds his authority created. These hunts are often preceded by a sumptuous feast, honoring the submissive subjects present while conferring additional honor on the king who is the architect of the gathering. When Tassilo, the rebellious duke of Bavaria, submitted to the triumphant Charlemagne's authority at a feast in honor of the occasion in 787, the first lines of a poem by the "Hibernicus Exul" commemorating the event leave no doubt about the authority that the ritual conferred upon Charlemagne, even while he honored Tassilo at the feast with an exchange of gifts:[24]

[T]*he leading men of the world are seen to revere the king,*
carrying huge gifts of massive weight,
an enormous load of silver and of gleaming gold,
the holy ore thickly encrusted about the massed gems,
the vestments gleaming with purple and gold thread,
with a shining halter reining in the foaming horses
whose necks arch high under trappings of barbarian gold.[25]

The feast allowed for Tassilo to submit to Charlemagne in a publicly acceptable fashion and still retain the honor of the duchy, and it is clear from the poem that the true purpose of the feast was to demonstrate the new hierarchy. The treasures of barbarian kingdoms flow toward Charlemagne as a symbol of his overlordship, but the ritual of the feast, with its exchange of gifts, allows Charlemagne to demonstrate magnanimity by welcoming the now-subdued Tassilo into his *familia*.

The ritual of conversion, symbolized by baptism, operates in this way even more forcefully, embracing the newly born Christians within not only the faith but also the political world of the Carolingian court by re-creating the father-son bond through baptismal sponsorship.[26] Inclusion in these rituals also implies inclusion in the Frankish *gens*, as Janet Nelson has demonstrated, and the ennobling effect that unity with the civilized *imperium* entails,[27] and it would ultimately be this idea of conversion politics that would win over the Saxons to the idea of Charlemagne's authority. Although the conversion of the Saxon ruler Widukind to Christianity in 785 was itself an act of submission, the final capitulation of the Saxon people to Charlemagne's rule would be a longer process of cultural and political acculturation as well as religious conversion. According to Julia M. H. Smith, "the strong bonds of spiritual kinship created by baptism were exploited to cement alliances and further political ends," because "spiritual kinship was of the greatest importance at all social levels in the early Middle Ages, binding the Carolingians' subjects to each other in a web of overtly Christian symbolic ties."[28] The ritual of baptism reinforced this spiritual bond, such that "conversion and baptismal sponsorship were part of the rituals by which Carolingian imperial overlordship was asserted" through the impressive display of wealth and largesse, lavish feasting and extravagant gift-giving.[29] As Nelson observes, "gift events were episodes in ongoing cosmic relationships not just between people, but involving supernatural powers," in order to construct "new social bonds and political authority."[30] Furthermore, as an imitation of the practices common among Byzantine emperors, baptismal sponsorship reiterated the Carolingians' imperial status and their dual roles as *rex et sacerdos*.[31] When Pope Hadrian baptized his son Carloman in 781, Charlemagne took advantage of the ambiguity of the sponsorship tie and its terminology to place himself on par with the pope as *compater* of Carloman, emphasizing "equality over subjugation" in his own version of his new relationship to Hadrian.[32] By highlighting his similarity to the pope, Charlemagne undermines the importance of Rome in the conversion process and strengthens his position as *imperator* of a non-Rome-centered empire, a tactic that would become typical of the imperial ideology of his reign even though he had not been officially crowned as "emperor" at this time.[33] This approach is strikingly different from that of Anglo-Saxon kings and conversions that we see in Bede, such as that of Æthelberht, sponsored by Augustine of Canterbury in late sixth-century England, where sacral authority stems solely from the pope and his representatives and not from the conquering king.[34]

The feasts and gifts from the imperial sponsor further demonstrate the subjugation of the newly baptized. One of the most well-documented baptisms was that of the Danish king, Harald, in 826: Louis the Pious sponsored Harald, and his son Lothar sponsored Harald's son, thus cementing the alliance among the next generation as well. Harald and his son were presented with rich baptismal gifts before the ceremony and later fêted with a sumptuous banquet that included both the Franks and the Danes, underscoring their symbolic inclusion in the Carolingian empire, which was "made quite explicit when Harald commended himself to Louis and handed over himself and his kingdom into the emperor's service."[35] In a poem by Ermoldus Nigellus commemorating Harald's baptism, the Dane is urged to put aside the idols of his pagan gods and turn them into plowshares,[36] to symbolically put aside the barbarism of his pagan existence in favor of the more civilized life as a Christian. Harald's response to Louis's invitation to convert emphasizes the allure of the powerful Frankish society and the potential earthly benefits of Christianity, which tempts the pagan to accept: "It would please me to see the kingdom of the Franks and the faith of Caesar, his weapons and wealth, the glory of the Christians. . . . If your god is preferred in honor over ours, and gives us more gifts in response to our prayers, then reason will force us to give up our old gods. We should be pleased to obey Christ and cast away golden idols into the flames of the furnace."[37] When Harald arrives at Louis's court, Ermoldus goes to great lengths to describe the sumptuous feasting, hunt, and gifts of the royal baptism ritual and concludes with Harald kneeling to Louis to submit his "neck to the yoke of Christ" (colla jugo Christi).[38] Enriched in body and soul as a result of Louis's sponsorship, Harald mulls the benefits of association with the emperor, concluding that it would be to his great advantage to submit to Louis. He promises to recognize Louis as lord of the Danes in imperial language:

Soon after, he joined hands with the king and freely gave himself
And the kingdom with him, because it was right.
"Receive me, Caesar," he said, "neither myself nor my kingdom is conquered;
I place myself at your service of my own free will."
Caesar received that honorable man, hand in hand,
And yoked the kingdoms of the pious Danish to the French.[39]

The long process of Saxon conversion, which had developed significantly in the twenty or so years between Widukind's baptism in 785 and the Saxons' final capitulation in 804, set the stage for Louis the Pious's baptism of Harald. As Charlemagne's capitularies of 782/85 and 797 demonstrate, the manner of Saxon acculturation was as much a progression of Charlemagne's practice and ideology of kingship as it was a movement toward the Saxons' complete submission to his authority.

The Saxons' compliance with Charlemagne's rule, as he finally discovered, would require their undergoing a substantial ideological change of heart that was not merely spiritual. The political conversion of the Saxons, according to Henry Mayr-Harting, was a significant result of Charlemagne's imperial coronation: it was no accident that Pope Leo III met with the king in 799 at Paderborn just prior to the ceremony in Rome, and the meeting therefore "expressed Charlemagne's mastery of the Saxons, to an audience of Saxons."[40] Because the Saxons had a resilient pride in their own ethnic history that rejected submission to a royal authority, they "would not tolerate kingship" and balked at the very idea of Charlemagne's overlordship.[41] Certainly, this posed a considerable hurdle for Charlemagne, one that could not be overcome simply through physical threats and military dominance such as were seen in the capitulary of 782/85, a problem to which the Saxons' numerous uprisings during the following two decades can attest. Mayr-Harting concludes that Charlemagne's imperial coronation functioned "less to facilitate the acquisition and exercise of power, than to canonize power already achieved, and to canonize it first and foremost in the eyes of its holders."[42] Because this event accelerated the very process of imperial domination of the Saxons for which he was arguing, it can be inferred that the coronation ritual itself also participated in the process of "conversion politics," which ultimately won over the Saxons. Even though submitting to an emperor rather than a king allowed the Saxons to "save face," as Mayr-Harting argues,[43] it was further augmented by the allure of being associated with a powerful empire rather than being another defeated territory of Charlemagne's kingdom, as the meeting at Paderborn between Charlemagne and Pope Leo III would have demonstrated to the attendant Saxon lords. As a result, Charlemagne's policy change regarding the Saxons in the late 790s, encouraged by Alcuin and confirmed by the creation of the second capitulary, to which the Saxons contributed, ultimately mitigated the humiliation of military defeat for the Saxons and eased their acceptance of his *imperium*. Thus, in the 820s, Hrabanus Maurus would say that the Saxons had become Charlemagne's subjects through arms, but he converted them, as their superior, in the manner of lords (*ritus dominorum*) and with fatherly love, by asking the rhetorical question "Who does not know this plague under which the world dwells, before the Saxons, the Franks have been in Christ's faith and religion, those whom they have subdued afterwards to power of his arms, and made higher by the rite of lords, or rather more with paternal affection, withdrawing from the worship of idols, they turned to faith in Christ?"[44] Neatly blurring three decades' worth of bloody conflict with the phrase "those whom they have subdued by force of arms" (quos ipsi . . . subegerunt armis), Hrabanus's sharp focus is instead on the Saxons' promotion through the sacred ritual of lordship and Charlemagne's gentler role as spiritual father, such that, two generations later, the Saxon Poet would praise Charlemagne as a king above all others. It is this idea of conversion through "love" that would resonate in the literature of subsequent generations and become an integral part of the Normans' own ideology of kingship, both before and after the Conquest, and would even play a part in their identity formation, functioning as a link to the Carolingian kings. For these writers, such as Dudo of Saint Quentin, submission rituals were an important aspect of conversion politics, as a way of establishing and maintaining power relationships that would confirm their right to rule and allow them to downplay the violence of conquest.

The Pygmalion Effect: Dudo of Saint Quentin and the Rituals of Empire

The Normans themselves, of course, were relatively recent converts to Christianity and Carolingian imperialism, and their conversion was an important part of their identity and collective memory as Franks. In Airlie's analysis of Charlemagne's rituals of submission in his subjugation of Tassilo, mentioned earlier, he notes that negotiations of surrender and settlement affirmed Charlemagne's power through a public display of his authority, even while these rituals also allowed the subject to save face.[45] The public enactment of power is a significant factor of these ritual displays, wherein resolution and accord are not merely symbolized by the act but actually achieved through it, as well as the erasure of the subject's previous identity and reconstruction of a new identity as a subordinate, albeit an honored one.[46] Moreover, through the giving and receiving of gifts in a ritualized Christian context, the subordinate is "reintegrated into a properly ordered world."[47] This concept is especially important for the early Normans in the context of conversion politics, in which the identity of the erstwhile Vikings is redefined as Norman through the ritual of baptism, as demonstrated in Dudo of Saint Quentin's Virgilian history of the Norman dukes, *De moribus et actis primorum Normanniae ducum*. Written in the early eleventh century at the behest of Richard I and his son,[48] a full century after the Treaty of Saint-Clair-sur-Epte established the Viking territory in former Neustria, Dudo's version of the creation of Normandy emphasizes the integration of the Vikings into the orderly Frankish Carolingian culture and society through the baptism of Rollo, the very worthy ancestor of the Norman dukes. Geoffrey Koziol argues that Dudo's history is "entirely organized around the theme of supplication,"[49] which Koziol considers to reflect the crucial expression of political authority, and that "Dudo was fairly obsessed with ritual."[50] For Dudo's purposes, I contend that the ritual of supplication is embodied in the ritual of baptism, and, as such, it forms a link between the development of "conversion politics" of Charlemagne's reign and its influence upon the Normans and their practices as dukes and kings. Through Rollo's abandonment of his pagan existence for a life of power and wealth that results from his baptism, Dudo makes plain the connection between the ritual and the benefits it can bestow in an imperial context: reconciled to a Carolingian king on earth by marriage and to God in heaven through baptism, Rollo can now fulfill his divinely ordained destiny as *imperator*.[51]

Dudo strives to straddle the line between celebrating the autonomy and strength of Norman dukes and emphasizing the Normans' identification with Carolingian emperors and Capetian kings.[52] Indeed, his development of duke Richard I as a peacemaking *dux et sacerdos*, who baptizes some invading hordes of Danish pagans after preaching to them, draws upon the Carolingian ideology of sacerdotal kingship that made Charlemagne's reign unique among early medieval *imperatores*. Samantha Kahn Herrick argues that the similarity of Richard's combined martial and evangelizing role to that depicted in several contemporary saints' lives "suggests that the new [Norman] rulers enjoyed power tinged with apostolic holiness."[53] The kingly depictions of the Norman dukes in *De moribus*, which R. W. Southern has called "prophetic," emphasizes the fact that "by the early eleventh century the Normans were on the point of becoming the most influential Christian nation in Europe."[54] Dudo's rhetoric certainly reflects the self-aggrandizement of his patrons, Richard I and Richard II, dukes of Normandy: not long before 1006, when King Robert visited Richard II at Fécamp, Richard was using the titles *dux* and *patricius*.[55] In Dudo's Virgilian interpretation of the creation of a Norman "empire" with Trojan origins, the Normans are provided with a classicized lineage on par with their Frankish neighbors and a justification for their inheritance of Carolingian *imperium*.[56]

I disagree here with Emily Albu's assessment that Dudo was being ironic in his praise of the great Norman ancestor, Rollo, by creating a Trojan ancestor for the Vikings in the character of Antenor, the treacherous Trojan who released the Greeks from the horse so that they could destroy the city of Troy.[57] As Albu also mentions, Virgil himself is ambiguous about the character of Antenor,[58] and thus I would argue that Dudo uses the duality of the figure of Antenor to demonstrate how some Dacians (a name Dudo applied to the Danes) can be evil and perfidious, whereas the figure of Rollo can redeem this stain through the worthiness exhibited by his idealized character and especially the purifying effect of baptism. The practice of princely rituals among counts as well as kings was on the rise between the 990s and the early 1030s,[59] and as a result baptismal ritual and its political implications are strong themes of *De moribus*: Dudo uses these ideas not only to verify the sanctity of the Norman leaders, of course, but also to depict them as *imperatores* in the Carolingian mold. For the first baptism of his work, therefore, which is entered under false pretenses, Dudo invents the perfidious character of Hasting to highlight the worthiness of Rollo and his companions later in the history.

The first group of pagan Dacians encountered in the story harry the countryside of Francia, laying waste to the land and enslaving its people. Thinking themselves great conquerors, the Danes follow the advice of "the most infamous of all" of their following,[60] Alstignus ("Hasting" in English), and decide to sail to Rome and "force it to submit to [their] dominion."[61] Unaware of their navigational error, they land not at Rome, but at a fair city called "Luna." Thinking it the great city of Rome, however, they observe that they cannot take the city by force, and Alstignus concocts a deceitful plan: he sends an envoy to the count and bishop of the city to beg for a truce and to baptize him, saying that he is too ill to journey further. The leaders of the city are driven as much by greed as by holiness, and, immediately after agreeing to the pagans' proposal, offer to sell them whatever they need and look forward to receiving gifts from the supplicant. The "sacred mystery of baptism," therefore, is corrupted by the avarice of both sides, a fact that renders the baptism a curse instead of a benison: "The villain receives baptism, to the destruction of his own soul."[62] This false baptism, additionally, further undermines the legitimacy of the imperial desire of the pagans, who are undeserving of such an honor because of their evil duplicity and lack of understanding of true *imperium*. The pagans slaughter and enslave all the Christians of Luna and, thinking they have subdued Rome, rejoice and congratulate themselves on having conquered the empire.[63] But, like his baptism, Alstignus's empire is revealed to be an illusion. Returning to Francia in fury when he discovers this fact, the king offers Alstignus a four-year truce in order to save his people, who cannot prevail against this terror. Dudo describes this peace as a blessing for the afflicted Franks, but also a time of healing and moral rectification.[64] According to Dudo, God has sent the pagan affliction to prepare the land and its people so that they may be ready for their coming salvation,[65] that is, the advent of Rollo. Rollo's arrival and baptism, therefore, are key moments in Dudo's work, establishing the Viking leader's worthiness for rule while also confirming the authority of the Carolingian emperor, Charles the Simple, to whom the pagans submit.

Unlike Alstignus and his followers, Rollo does not go to Francia for the sole purpose of rapine and murder, but rather as the final destination of an epic journey after being unjustly exiled from his own lands in Dacia. Dudo describes Rollo in his youth in glowing terms, as "vigorous in arms, skilled in war, most handsome in body, and most steadfast in courage."[66] Although a pagan, Rollo has all the qualities of a future Christian duke in epic fashion; even his journey is guided by divine intervention when a voice speaks to him in a dream and instructs him to go to the English. When Rollo recounts this dream to a wise man who also happens to be a Christian, the man interprets the dream as foretelling Rollo's baptism and "everlasting glory" (perhennis gloriae) in heaven.[67] A second dream-vision, more detailed than the first, predicts his future as a great leader: finding himself on the summit of a mountain near a spring of flowing, sweet water, he washes in the spring and is cured of various contagions that plague him. At this moment, he sees a great gathering of birds around the base of the mountain: "Many thousands of birds of different kinds and various colours, but with red left wings, extending in such numbers and so far and so wide that he could not catch sight of where they ended."[68] These assorted birds seek the spring and wash themselves in it as Rollo has, and then proceed to build nests and live harmoniously together, yielding to Rollo's command. This dream is interpreted as yet another prophecy of Rollo's baptism, only this time it also prefigures his rebirth as an *imperator*. Another unnamed Christian tells Rollo that the birds signify the men of many provinces who will join him with shields on their arms and bow in fidelity to him. As a result, they will rebuild the walls of ancient devastated cities, and "men of different kingdoms will kneel down to serve you."[69] In this divine vision, Dudo makes the relationship between baptism and *imperium* clear: eternal salvation becomes secondary to the promise of power and glory in Francia as the ruler of many kingdoms. Furthermore, this new empire will be rebuilt from the old as a symbol of *translatio imperii*, an especially significant idea for its emphasis on the restoration of imperial cities, which was such an important expression of Charlemagne's declaration of authority, as I will discuss further in chapter 3.

Dudo additionally stresses the "allurement" element of conversion politics for Rollo and his companions: although Rollo's salvation is assured by his conversion, as Dudo emphasizes more than once in his poems,[70] the attraction of conversion to Christianity is depicted throughout his history in terms of material wealth and political advantage. When Charles sends Archbishop Franco of Rouen to Rollo to discuss the possibility of a truce, including conversion and marriage to the king's daughter, Franco exhorts Rollo to accept baptism due to the variety of earthly benefits it would bring because he "will be able to know peace, now and in future, and to remain in this land as a man of great wealth."[71] When Rollo calls his Danes for a conference to discuss Charles's offer, they echo Franco's sentiment by reminding him of the dream-vision, as well as pointing out the richness of the land that he would inherit and its independence from Francia.[72] In the advice of the Northmen, the new territory is described as a wild *locus amoenus* that should be tamed for Rollo's nascent empire, as foretold in the divine message of his vision. Once again, according to Dudo, the attraction of conversion for the pagans lay not in salvation, but in the political and economic advantage that such a spiritual alliance would purchase.

Dudo also uses the baptismal ritual to establish a positive relationship between the Northman and the progenitor of the Capetian king: in his version of events, Rollo's godfather is not Charles but Duke Robert of the Franks, the great-grandfather of the Capetian king Robert II.[73] Duke Robert sends a messenger to Rollo expressing his approval of the arrangements made between the king and the pagan and offers to sponsor him in baptism, because "even the duke himself kneels to you in his mind."[74] In so doing, Dudo establishes the godparent relationship with the house currently on the throne in France as one of mutual respect and obligation through the baptismal ritual, such that the two rulers will be united by an inseparable bond.[75] Rollo responds favorably to the duke's offer, claiming, "Let this man be to me as a father with fatherly love; I will be a son to him, with the love of sons. Let him aid me, if need be, as a father aids a son; I, him, as a son aids a father. Let him rejoice in my prosperity, and sorrow in my adversity. What is in my possession will be his by right, and what is mine by right shall be his possession."[76] Immediately upon concluding the week of baptismal ritual, Rollo is joined in marriage to the king's daughter, and thus Dudo cements the Northman's bond to two ruling families, one through baptism and the other through marriage.[77] Now

Rollo is in a position to create his empire, which he wastes no time about after his baptism, by taming the land and reestablishing civilization in the territory:

> He placed all the nations which desired to remain within his land under his protection. He divided that land among his followers by measure, and rebuilt everything that had long been deserted, and restored it by restocking it with his own warriors and with peoples from abroad. He imposed everlasting privileges and laws on the people, authorised and decreed by the will of chief men, and he compelled them to dwell together in peace. He raised up churches that had been demolished to the ground, he rebuilt temples that had been ruined by visitations of the heathen, and he made new and extended walls and defences of the cities.[78]

In the juxtaposition of baptismal and marriage rituals with the creation of his empire, Rollo participates in the kind of conversion politics that began in Charlemagne's reign. As Rollo embraces the life of power and wealth that results from his baptism, in conjunction with the alliances that are established as a result, Dudo creates the imperial dynasty that will find its fullest achievement in the poem in subsequent generations.

The Carolingian role of *rex et sacerdos* is ultimately fulfilled in the person of Rollo's grandson, Richard I.[79] Dudo's description of Richard resonates with the fanciful imagery of Carolingian and Ottonian emperors' flowing white beards and hawk-like eyes, which was becoming common after Charlemagne's death: "Most lovely to look upon, bristling with brilliant white hair, brilliant in eyebrows and in the pupil of the eye, resplendent of nostril and cheek, honoured for a thick, long beard, lofty of stature, practised in speech, virtuous in mind and body, wide-ranging in goodness, most sagacious in intellect, defended by the grace of God—he was the one salvation for all."[80] Dudo's language is also reminiscent of the memorable depiction of Charlemagne in the *Chanson de Roland*, where his beard is frequently referred to.[81] He goes on to praise Richard's leadership and exercise of justice within his *regnum*,[82] but it is obvious from this sampling that he was anxious to portray the duke in the most glowing of terms, which were, for a writer using hagiography and Virgilian models in emulation of a Carolingian style of imperial praise, those also used for Charlemagne and his successors. Richard's greatest accomplishment in Dudo's history, as *dux et sacerdos* like Charlemagne before him, was the baptism of invading pagan hordes and the peace it achieved for the Franks. This baptism, however, was accomplished only after a colossal test of wills and an all-night sermon with the pagans. Richard had attempted to secure a truce with the Dacians for more than two weeks in a great "peacemaking contest" that astounded the attendant Frankish prelates and magnates, but without success until he appeals to the earthly benefits that they can receive with the blessing of baptism.

Nelson has shown that gifts could be coercive as "signs of the donor's overwhelming power,"[83] which, for Richard's pagan audience, would be indicative of God's power and divine favor that they might also enjoy. When the talks with the Dacians fail, Richard volunteers to gather together the pagan elders privately and offer them great gifts and lands that will overwhelm them.[84] This scene stands in contrast to the leaders of the unfortunate city of Luna, who are blinded by the *getting* of gifts in their dealings with pagan invaders: Richard's humble generosity is meant to contrast with this earlier disaster borne of greed and selfishness, and also to remind Dudo's audience of the great rituals of submission to the Carolingian kings, such as that of Tassilo, duke of Bavaria. Of course, the greatest gift that Richard offers the pagans through accepting baptism is that of eternal life, but Dudo simultaneously emphasizes the great prosperity that the pagans can enjoy in the kingdom of Francia. He goes on at length recounting the religious lecture that the duke delivers through the night to his captive pagan audience. One can well imagine that after a long night of Richard's sermonizing, the pagans were begging for baptism, especially after the duke promised they would be generously rewarded for their submission:

> If your wish is to follow our advice, first I will have you baptised in the name of the Father, and of the Son, and of the Holy Ghost; then, to be instructed by the bishops more fully, through their copious preaching of the purest faith; then, to be enriched with the most generous gifts, and the most extensive grants of lands, on which you will be able to live, and not perish for evermore; for, if you have not renounced the happiness of the most unspoilt faith, which I am looking for, you will enjoy solace in the present life, and the prize of an everlasting future reward.[85]

Once again, Dudo highlights the "allurement" of baptism, which is equally the promise of earthly riches and of everlasting life, especially considering how the juxtaposition of baptism, wealth, learning, and eternal life dominates the duke's offer to the pagans.

Dudo also specifies how Richard illustrates the beatitudes because of his exemplary life, especially his use of conversion politics. Richard wins friends and converts enemies and pagans not by means of force but through his gifts and friendship:

> Blessed are the meek, for they shall inherit the earth. How gentle, how meek, how kind, how most benign he was: whoso reads the abbreviated story of his life will be able to gain some knowledge of his gentleness! The man restrained count Theobald, sometimes by pleading, sometimes by force of arms. This man defeated king Lothair by humility. This man coerced the Danes by the gentleness of his words and gifts. This man appealed to the Franks and other peoples with the humblest words and gestures, and received them into his friendship. This man protected the inhabitants of Normandy with the utmost zeal. This man looked after the members of his household like the devoted father of a family. He was kindly in all his undertakings; gentle words resounded in all his deeds and works. For he deserved to possess the land of the living in that he protected the land of his corporeal existence with mild benevolence.[86]

The change in approach to acquisition, from one of military conquest to Christlike meekness and humility, is an important one to note here: authority is not obtained through the force of arms, which has in fact failed repeatedly in Dudo's version of Norman history, but rather through Richard's fatherly role, demonstrated by his humility and generous words and gifts, in words reminiscent of Hrabanus Maurus's praise of Charlemagne discussed earlier. According to Nelson, the Frankish realm can be considered "a patrimonial regime in which power legitimised as divinely ordained was exercised as the ruler's personal authority like a father's over his household."[87] This idea played out as well in the Carolingian ideal of a ruler as a *rex et sacerdos*, as one who converts enemies not through military conquest but through the allure of imperial sovereignty, generosity, and benevolence, which had an unmistakable impact on the Norman imagination and its ideals of kingship, both for Dudo of Saint Quentin and his successors. The greatest display of power in this paradigm is a ruler who *could* crush an enemy, but chooses to exhibit mercy instead. For the later Normans, who were not dealing with "heathen nations" in the same way as Charlemagne was in the eighth century, the practice of conversion politics is instead translated to that of "converting" barbarous nations in the sense of civilizing them economically, socially, and culturally, not religiously,[88] due in part to the influence of twelfth-century courtly culture upon their interpretation of Carolingian ideals of kingship.

Converting the British Barbarian: "Sitting at High Table" at the Anglo-Norman Court

Both the literature and history of twelfth-century England suggest that Anglo-Norman imperialist efforts in Britain were not necessarily limited to military expansion and domination. The ideal of expanding God's empire, both in heaven and on earth, through the allure of social refinement and political gain appears in various propagandistic models of conversion politics in twelfth-century narratives. These illustrate the growing importance of things like "good customs" (bones costumes) and "fair love" (bel amur)[89] for consolidating dominion within British territories, and exemplify certain aspects of ideal kingship for Anglo-Norman writers. The civilized ideals that the Normans ostensibly put into practice included the establishment of peace and unity through legal reform, urban growth, and, significant for my argument, a more "humane style of politics" that emphasized the exercise of clemency toward enemies.[90] This was supposedly because of the practice of ransoming prisoners and the chivalric unwillingness to kill or mutilate defeated enemies,[91] although this ideal may not have been reflected in real practice at all times.[92] From a literary standpoint, however, it represents a significant change in how the Anglo-Normans perceived themselves and the image that they projected in their writing. John Gillingham has remarked that many twelfth-century historians "looked back at the Anglo-Saxon period and saw it as less peaceful, less well-organized and less humane than their own times. They saw the history of their own country as a history of progress, of civilising progress."[93] What is more, the early Continental perception of English barbarism was transferred, in the imperial designs of Anglo-Norman England, to British peoples; thus, the influence of courtly behavior on the ideology of conversion politics of this time places an even greater emphasis on the attraction of their supposed civilized mores and the promise of political advantage than was seen in Charlemagne's reign.

It must be noted that this image was a part of the Anglo-Norman propaganda of kingship, which was often at odds with the reality of Anglo-Norman society and its so-called civilized behavior, as Paul Hyams has argued.[94] He states that the hallmarks of Anglo-Saxon feud culture can still be seen in the conflict-resolution practices of early Anglo-Norman society, which suggests that scholars like Gillingham and Matthew Strickland may have overstated the case for civilized behavior to some extent. The significant feature for their arguments is the behavior among the military aristocracy: Gillingham notes that the demise of slavery meant that ordinary soldiers, who could not afford to pay ransom, were more likely to be killed,[95] in contrast to behavior among noble peers. Strickland also comments, "while significant chivalric constraints operated in warfare among the Anglo-Normans themselves, they might often behave towards their Celtic opponents with utter ruthlessness, which might include the mutilation, execution or even enslaving of prisoners."[96] But the killing among the aristocracy was not as limited as they might suggest; Hyams has shown that the violent elements of feud culture were still very much alive in England in the twelfth century, but would eventually fade during the course of the century after the Conquest, such that "the twelfth-century materials carry ghostly hints of features familiar from the later common law."[97] Despite the very real violence of Anglo-Norman warrior culture, the Anglo-Normans showed a preference for presenting themselves as being more civilized than the British, which included showing clemency toward defeated enemies. It is in this way that they differed from pre-Conquest society, which recognized the legality of, and even cultural preference for, feud culture, which resisted a "Carolingian-style downward justice" in the person of the king.[98] What is important for this discussion is the Anglo-Norman perception and self-projection of an image of their culture as one which approached conflict in a more humane, civilized manner, particularly with regard to their treatment of British peoples.

An instructive model of the civilizing notion of conversion politics is demonstrated by the writing of William of Malmesbury. For his many influential works, including the secular history *Gesta regum Anglorum*, completed in 1125, William of Malmesbury is considered an English "patriot" by some scholars today, but he was also "profoundly convinced that the society of his own day, a newly Frenchified and Europeanized yet still identifiably English society, was significantly superior to the one which had existed before 1066."[99] The *Gesta regum Anglorum* is replete with anecdotes from the "civilized" society of the Continent, many of them entertainingly wicked, that would have appealed to his courtly Anglo-Norman audience.[100] William's praise of the French impact on the aristocratic society of Anglo-Norman England, especially at the expense of Celtic peoples, whom he denigrated as "barbarians" in comparison,[101] reflected current thinking in Anglo-Norman culture, history, and ideals of kingship. William's "ardent and fawning Francophilia," according to Rees Davies,[102] inspired generations of writers, especially his vision of "English history as a progress from barbarism to civilization"[103] that resulted from the permeation of French culture into English society. For the purposes of demonstrating how this was portrayed in the literature of the Anglo-Normans, especially in relation to the use of ritual (civilized, courtly behavior) to unify disparate peoples and integrate them into the ostensibly "properly ordered world" of Anglo-Norman society, we can compare their notions of civilized kingship to Carolingian conversion politics.[104] Gillingham, for example, argues for the importance William placed upon the related concepts behind the words *civilis*, meaning "urbane or refined," and *compositus*, suggesting "put together or set in order,"[105] which implies that those people who were thought to be in disorder needed to be converted from their barbarism to a more civilized way of life. Several generations after William composed his histories, this notion was fixed firmly in the minds of writers: as a case in point, Gerald of Wales contrasted England and Wales by calling England a *regio composita*, whereas Wales was a *regio barbara*.[106] Because of the emphasis placed on acculturation in Charlemagne's later practices, the comparison is an important one for understanding the development of the Anglo-Norman self-image as more benevolent and civil in its approach to imperial expansion than pre-Conquest peoples.

It must be remembered that William of Malmesbury's admiration of antiquity colored his definition of "barbarian," which did not encompass the religious component of a post-Greco-Roman worldview; rather, he characterized it in terms of a people's learning, material culture, and economic development, and in his opinion, the British people were woefully deficient and in great need of civilizing.[107] This idea would prove to be very influential on Anglo-Norman thinkers, such as the mid-twelfth-century author of the *Gesta Stephani*, who laments the Welsh people's barbarism but notes that the Normans were quick to civilize them once they established their sovereignty in England, claiming that when "the Normans conquered the English, this land [Wales] also they added to their dominion and fortified with numberless castles; they perseveringly civilized it after they had vigorously subdued its inhabitants; to encourage peace they imposed law and statutes on them; and they made the land so productive and abounding in all kinds of resources that you would have reckoned it in no wise inferior to the most fertile part of Britain."[108] We can see that Anglo-Norman conversion politics would eventually meet with great success, furthermore, because by the end of the thirteenth century the Saint Albans chronicler would report that "[t]he Welsh began to live with English manners; they accumulated treasure and henceforth were in great fear of losses [to their wealth]."[109] Perceiving the Welsh as having converted over time to a more "civilized," English way of life, the chronicler concludes that they appreciate the benefits that Anglo-Norman culture offered them, suggesting that it would contribute to their eventual submission to Anglo-Norman rule, despite the fact that there continued to be unrest in Wales for several generations to come.

Davies's main point is that other, nonmartial influences were instrumental to furthering Anglo-Norman expansion in Britain, such as the economic impact of migration into Wales and Ireland. The ideal of civilized behavior as a cultural distinction (and here I refer to "courtly" or chivalric behavior in particular) was as critical an Anglo-Norman export as castles or legal reforms, both of which, indeed, are part and parcel of the Anglo-Norman perception of what makes up a civilized, courtly society. As evidenced by the comments made by the Saint Albans chronicler at the end of the thirteenth century, it was also credited for their ultimate success in solidifying their dominion in outlying British lands. Davies himself even mentions this omission in modern historical scholarship: "The Anglo-Normans had style and wealth; their courts opened a window onto a world of chivalry and courtoisie which must have been attractive and intoxicating for many of the native Welsh, Irish and Scottish dynasties and magnates. Historians . . . have rarely given sufficient credit to the social appeal of the Anglo-Norman courts—of sitting at high table, as it were—in the process of domination."[110] Because Davies's work attempted to demonstrate the various nuanced ways that the Anglo-Normans would expand their authority throughout Britain, his comments do not take into account the fact that resistance to Anglo-Norman dominion would continue to be an issue, both militarily and in literature.[111] His argument, however, explains the way the Anglo-Normans perceived their political, religious, and social roles when pursuing their imperial ambitions and the impact that it had among certain circles, which contributed to the process of acculturation within Wales, Scotland, and Ireland. Anglo-Norman ideals of kingship, indeed medieval ideals more generally, derived considerably from Carolingian exemplars, which in turn influenced their actions toward and relationships, first within English lands and later with their Insular neighbors, having far-reaching effects on Anglo-Norman practices within Insular politics.

The emergence of an Anglo-Norman identity in the twelfth century, however, requires qualification: William of Malmesbury writes that the Normans adopted English manners in eating and drinking, but in other ways the English adopted Norman mores,[112] such that the country now flourished with urban development and "new devotion."[113] These secular, civilized mores, such as William I's abolishing of the slave trade, urban growth, and, according to Gillingham, a more "chivalrous" style of politics,[114] separate their behavior in the literature of the period from that of the Celtic barbarians, which William of Malmesbury defines in a more classical sense than that of the Christian view of barbarians as pagans. The three major themes of William of Malmesbury's work, as defined by Davies, are, first, "the making of the English into one people (*in unam gentem*); the second that of the political unification of England under a single king . . . ; the third, . . . that of a cultural and social improvement in manners and civility, learning and governance."[115] In light of William's definition of "civilization" and its twinned aspect of *compositus*, I would amend Davies's themes to encompass all of Britain, especially in light of Anglo-Norman ambitions for *imperium* in Britain that took shape very quickly after they had consolidated their authority in England: although William I is not generally known today for subduing his neighboring British territories in the same way that his descendants are, the author of the *Anglo-Saxon Chronicle* entry for 1087 certainly recognized this possibility when he wrote, "The land of the Britons [Wales] was in his power . . . and if he might have yet lived two years more, he would have won Ireland by his prudence, and without any weapons."[116] The chronicler here suggests that the seed of Anglo-Norman *imperium* throughout Britain had been planted by the time of William I's death, and the notion that it could be accomplished by means other than the force of arms is central to its ideology. This idea would become a hallmark of the way that the Anglo-Norman writers would frequently represent the ruling styles of their kings, such that Henry I's reign would become known as one of moderation in all things, including militaristic endeavors, and suggests that the idea of domination through the allurement of civilized society has become an ideal of kingship for the Normans.

Warren Hollister and Thomas Keefe argue that Henry I's reign was "not a continuation of eleventh-century imperialism but a rejection of it,"[117] largely because of his love of peace and dislike of war,[118] but this claim should be revisited in light of the reports from William of Malmesbury and his contemporaries. Commenting on William of Malmesbury's assertion that Henry preferred to do battle by council rather than the sword,[119] Hollister and Keefe assert that Henry "had no taste for expansion" and favored pursuing the peace and security that castle-building and marriage alliances would bring, concluding that "neither through conquest nor through marriages did Henry I endeavor to expand the boundaries of the Anglo-Norman state."[120] Several contemporary Welsh chroniclers, on the other hand, contradict this notion in their claims that he was "king of England and Wales and all the island beside," and "the man who had subdued under his authority all the island of Britain and its mighty ones."[121] Furthermore, the rest of William of Malmesbury's statement, "uincebat, si poterat, sanguine nullo; si aliter non poterat, pauco," indicates that Henry was not averse to spilling some blood if it was necessary in order to conquer an enemy. It may not have been his love of peace that compelled him to reject the expansionist aims of his Norman predecessors (and even Anglo-Saxon, if we take into account the Welsh campaigns of Harold Godwinson and various Marcher lords), but rather, as Davies argues, that Henry was "in the habit of getting his way without using brute force."[122] Rather than suggesting a lack of interest in territorial expansion, therefore, William of Malmesbury's point about Henry's preference for peaceful methods of achieving his ambitions should be taken to reflect popular views regarding civilized good kingship and not necessarily to indicate a lack of interest by Henry in expanding or consolidating Norman influence in neighboring lands, which plainly many contemporaries accepted as fact.

As a result, the court of Henry I would become known as a model for the establishment of power and influence in neighboring lands, enticing them with the kinds of benefits that association with a civilized court might offer: like Charlemagne's use of various kinds of ritual at his court (not only baptism but also feasting and the hunt), courtly spectacles and lavish feasts marked Henry I's reign as a method of impressing those peoples he would most like to dominate, in order that they might more readily accept his lordship. David I of Scotland is one of the most notable success stories of Henry I's conversion politics. Exiled from Scotland by his uncle, Donald III, after the death of his parents, David found refuge at the court of the English king and was indoctrinated into Norman modes of civilization through the many honors bestowed on him, such as sumptuous gifts and prominence of place among the great Anglo-Norman lords,[123] customs which we are told he subsequently introduced to his own people when he later became king of Scotland. William of Malmesbury also praises David especially for erasing his rusticity with Norman polish: "A young man of more courtly disposition than the rest, he had from boyhood been polished by familiar intercourse with the English, and rubbed off all the barbarian gaucherie of Scottish manners."[124] Henry I's support of David I's claim to the throne after the death of his older brother in

1124 virtually re-created Norman England in Scotland, and forged an alliance that would last beyond his death. Although these policies were not original to Henry I's court,[125] it must be stressed that David was an honored guest and not a hostage, which further emphasizes Henry's preference for conversion politics over military expansion: his reformation of David ultimately achieved the same results without the rancor that conquest could engender—a secular interpretation of the goals of conversion that Alcuin promoted during Charlemagne's kingship.

These kinds of practices would be further exploited at his grandson's court, as Henry II strove to regain the political momentum in British affairs that was lost during the long years of civil strife in Stephen's reign. Henry II impressed the Welsh prince of Powys by having him to dinner and went to great lengths to inspire his guest's awe of his wealth and sophistication. As Davies recounts, "Henry II went straight for the palates and *amour-propre* of the Irish chiefs: He commissioned them to construct a wickerwork palace at Dublin at Christmas 1171, invited the native princes there, fed them unheard-of dishes (which they dared not refuse), and left them gawping in amazement at 'the sumptuous and plentiful fare of the English table and the most elegant service by the royal domestics.'"[126] The giving of gifts often accompanied these ritual feasts, usually as an acknowledgment of the capitulation of the prince or king in question, such as the celebrations of Charlemagne's court for the submission of Tassilo. A series of early thirteenth-century letters to the treasurer of Ireland and the king's representatives, for example, begs for repayment of debts incurred by the writer's having "spent much money [on gifts] in drawing to the King's peace divers petty kings," including one "who styles himself King of all the Irish of Ireland."[127] As Charlemagne found with the Saxons, Avars, and Bavarians and the Normans would discover with the Scots, Welsh, and Irish, "social submission was often the acceptable face of political deference."[128] The idea of converting one's enemies in such a way proved to be considerably more appealing as a practical and long-lasting approach to subjugation than costly and destructive warfare, because of its potential for accelerating the acculturation process as well as imperial expansion.[129] As is suggested by William of Malmesbury's development of *civilis* throughout the history of the kings of England, part of the function of a true *imperator* is the peaceful unification of multiple nations under one ruler. For Charlemagne and the early Normans, this was accomplished by the diplomatic conversion of pagans and its accompanying material benefits. The Anglo-Norman writers were no less concerned with conversion politics, as has been shown, and from their perspective, the conversion of culturally "barbaric" peoples to their more civilized customs was a necessary function of kingship. The growing romance literary tradition of the twelfth century demonstrates this fact in its revision of the glorious past to better reflect their own imperial ambitions and concerns about peaceful unification.

Written in the 1130s, slightly after William of Malmesbury's work, Geoffroi Gaimar's vernacular chronicle, *L'Estoire des Engleis*, was innovative in both style and content, and A. R. Press claims that it "proposes, explicitly, a new concept of historiography and, to sustain that concept, a new vision of court life."[130] Written in octosyllabic couplets, it is the earliest surviving chronicle in French, and begins with a translation of the *Anglo-Saxon Chronicle* into Anglo-Norman French, which Gaimar then continues into the twelfth century. His purpose for writing, as stated in his epilogue, was to chronicle the history of the British and English from the time of Jason and the Golden Fleece, although all that remains of the original corpus is the second part, from the arrival of the Saxons under Hengist to Henry I. It survives in four manuscripts, all of which also contain Wace's *Brut*; two also contain Jordan Fantosme's *Chronicle* and *Prophecies of Merlin*,[131] thus forming a compendium version of Insular history from its earliest times to the death of William II. One of the most remarkable features of the *Estoire* is its tendency to "civilize" the Anglo-Saxons by updating their history to reflect twelfth-century values. Although William of Malmesbury depicted Anglo-Saxon history as a slow progress from barbarism to civility through the influence of French mores and government, Gaimar's work is a celebration of English secular history, with a focus on courtly and chivalric behavior—"Anglo-Saxon history as seen through the eyes of romance," according to Antonia Gransden.[132] This is especially true when Gaimar diverges from the *Anglo-Saxon Chronicle* beginning with Edgar's reign and imposes what Press calls a "courtly ideology" on Anglo-Saxon history, "offered more as an object of aspiration, even of wish-fulfillment, than as objective historical fact."[133] Of Gaimar's inconsistency with other accounts of Anglo-Saxon history, Press explains that his history is "the imaginative, artistic realization of an *ideal* rather than the material statement of factual *reality*, . . . offered more as an object of aspiration, even of wish-fulfillment, than as objective historical fact."[134] This ideal is consistent with the Anglo-Norman projected self-image as a courteous, chivalrous society, and includes the responsibilities that this role necessitates in a civilized society, such as the conversion of so-called barbarians described above.

One of Gaimar's notable revisions occurs in the episode of Alfred's conversion of the Danes, where Gaimar augments the account of the baptismal ritual to make it the focus of the account and stress the importance of conversion politics. According to the *Anglo-Saxon Chronicle* entry for 878, King Alfred was finally able to defeat the pagan Vikings who had plagued his reign, and several of those before him, after a battle and two-week siege. In comparison to the protracted depictions of the events and skirmishes leading up to this climactic episode, the chronicler's portrayal of this pivotal moment in Anglo-Saxon history is surprisingly brief and matter-of-fact. Without the benefit of hindsight, it seems, the pagans' conversion represents only one relatively minor incident in the greater story of Alfred's reign. The chronicler concisely describes the pagans' surrender, including the giving of hostages to guarantee their submission to baptism and departure from Alfred's kingdom:

> [There Alfred] fought against the whole raiding-army, and put it to flight, rode after it as far as the fortification, and stayed there 14 days; and then the raiding-army granted him prime hostages and great oaths that they would leave his kingdom, and also promised him that their king would receive baptism; and they fulfilled it thus. And 3 weeks later king Guthrum came to him, one of thirty of the most honourable men who were in the raiding-army, at Aller—and that is near Athelney—and there the king received him at baptism; and his chrism-loosing was at Wedmore; and he was 12 days with the king, and he greatly honoured him and his companions with riches.[135]

On the other hand, Gaimar's depiction of Alfred's defeat of the Danes, which included civilizing them through baptism, does more than signify their unification with the English people; it calls attention to the admiration for conversion politics within the Anglo-Norman self-image, which reflects the growing approval of chivalric behavior in political undertakings beyond England's borders.

Gaimar's expansion of the narrative of Alfred's conversion of the Danes is remarkable for its focus on and development of the baptismal ritual itself. As in the entry from the *Anglo-Saxon Chronicle*, Alfred defeats the Danes in battle in a matter of a few lines, but Gaimar describes at length how Alfred wins their allegiance such that they beg him for conversion. The pagans do not promise to leave, but instead not to make war on Alfred, suggesting that they plan to stay and assimilate with his people, as did Rollo and his followers in Dudo's history. Neither do the Danes simply agree to baptism; they beg Alfred for it, as well as making "other promises," which are not mentioned in the chronicle:

In fifteen days [Alfred] so daunted them,
These Danes that I tell you of,
That they had a parley, they agreed together,
And gave good hostages,
And swore, however many they were,
That they would never wage war on him
And still more they promised him,
And asked him for Christianity.[136]

Moreover, the revelries at the baptism are reminiscent of the "pandering to a vassal's sense of self-importance and boosting his morale [that] were among the essential arts of lordship"[137] and that marked Henry I's reign. The changes also represent a significant interest in portraying the moment as central to Alfred's reign, as the moment of unification between the two peoples through the ritual of baptism. In Gaimar's retelling, King Guthorm is baptized with more than just thirty of his soldiers: he comes with the "nearest of his kin" to the font, which also suggests a more permanent commitment to the pledges of peace that accompany the ritual. They also receive new Anglo-Saxon names to accompany their baptismal angels, creating a new identity for themselves as English vassals, intimating again a desire for assimilation within English society and culture, which represents a more thorough conversion than just that of the baptismal ritual itself.[138] As a result, Gaimar's Alfred is a civilizing king whose conversion of the pagan Danes represents the kind of integration into civilized society that the Normans experienced after Rollo's conversion in Dudo's history.

After Alfred, it is Edgar on whom Gaimar lavishes the most praise. In his portrayal, Edgar becomes the most civilized of kings, even by French standards. From Gaimar's opening remark that Edgar rules the land like an emperor,[139] it is clear that he is no ordinary king. Gaimar uses the unmistakable rhetoric of the Norman civilizing impulse, as described by William of Malmesbury some ten years before: Edgar improves the land and is a friend to the church;[140] as a reformer himself, he establishes good customs;[141] and he is admired by his potential political rivals for love of him and his noble leadership, not out of fear:

All his neighbors bowed to him,
By fair love and by concessions
He turned them completely to him.[142]

It is important to note here Gaimar's emphasis on Edgar's use of "fair love" and "concessions" to subdue potential enemies, because these are the same tactics espoused by the late Carolingians, in imitation of Charlemagne's practices in the latter part of his reign, and the early Normans, according to Dudo of Saint Quentin. Gaimar is refashioning the history of Edgar in a courtly mold, establishing him as an ideal king who embodies the qualities of a civilized ruler. The idea of establishing power and influence in neighboring lands through conversion politics, of convincing others to follow a more civilized mode of behavior, seems to echo certain aspects of Gaimar's experience from Henry I's "peaceloving" reign, but Edgar's reign is viewed through the lens of the nascent courtly tradition of the early twelfth century. It is universally agreed that this protoromance would have appealed to a twelfth-century courtly audience, making Anglo-Saxon ancestors even more attractive to the Normans for whom the history was written by endorsing the same ideals that were influencing Norman military culture. What is subtler and potentially more influential is the correlation between Edgar as courtly and chivalrous king and Edgar as emperor. Although Edgar, along with other Anglo-Saxon kings such as Alfred, had a reputation as a pan-English ruler in his own lifetime, never before had the connection between courtliness and imperialism been so clearly defined as it was by Gaimar. As so many of the major concerns and transformations of the twelfth century—such as acculturation, legal reform, and urban development—are echoed in the revisionist histories of Anglo-Norman writers, it seems likely that these historians were reflecting current movements and attitudes toward their British neighbors in Wales, Scotland, and Ireland, specifically those which extolled clemency toward one's enemies and encouraged conversion to one's authority through civilized, even courtly, rule, as Gaimar claims that Edgar practiced. The theme of allurement, of conversion through "fair love" and "good customs," is an important one for understanding Anglo-Norman imperialism and subsequent generations of Anglo-Norman literature.

Because not all of his work has survived, the full extent of Gaimar's influence is unknowable, but his impact, as one of the first vernacular historiographers, can certainly be seen in such works as the prose *Brut*.[143] Peter Damian-Grint notes that Gaimar's work also influenced other romance writers who composed shortly after.[144] Although his influence on Wace is disputed,[145] the connection between the two authors was apparent to medieval readers, considering that the four extant manuscripts of Gaimar's *Estoire* also contain Wace's *Roman de Brut*, and Wace clearly demonstrates the civilizing impulses that inspired his predecessor. Wace's many significant alterations and additions to Geoffrey of Monmouth's text in his *Roman de Brut*, written during the early flowering of the romance tradition in England in the mid-twelfth century, go beyond doing lip service to chivalric ideals and further emphasize the far-reaching changes in ideals of kingship and the Anglo-Norman self-image. Judith Weiss notes that "his work provides a bridge to the newer world of twelfth-century romance. The words *curteis, curteisie, curteisement* are attached to his characters as they were not in Geoffrey . . . and seem to indicate a range of praiseworthy attributes."[146] Although it is significant that the figure of Arthur in the twelfth century was considerably influenced by the legend of Charlemagne (in fact, Geoffrey of Monmouth had Charlemagne in mind when he developed the character of Arthur in the *Historia regum Britanniae*),[147] Wace's emphasis on the sophistication and *curteisie* of Arthur's court in particular also reminds the reader of the developing chivalric ideals that were reflected in the Anglo-Norman self-image and political maneuverings.[148]

Arthur promotes civility in his court through Wace's invention of the Round Table, a device that, at once, elevates each of the legendary king's barons and promotes harmony among them by seating all of them near the place of honor; additionally, "No one—whether Scot, Briton, Frenchman, Norman, Angevin, Fleming, Burgundian or Lorrainer—whoever he held his fief from, from the West as far as Muntgieu, was accounted courtly if he did not go to Arthur's court and stay with him and wear the livery, device and armour in the fashion of those who served at that court."[149] Moreover, the superlative moral quality of Arthur's civilized kingship affects the quality of the land and even improves those subjects who are not of noble birth; for nobles at the court, their association with Arthur motivates them to even greater degrees of chivalry and wholesomeness:

> Beyond all the surrounding realms, and beyond all those we now know, England was unparalleled for fine men, wealth, plenty, nobility, courtesy and honour. Even the poor peasants were more courtly and brave than knights in other realms, and so were the women too. . . . There was no knight, however nobly born, who could expect affection or have a courtly lady as his love, if he had not proved

himself three times in knightly combat. The knights were the more worthy for it, and performed better in the fray; the ladies, too, were the better and lived a chaster life.[150]

This civilizing ideal of *curteisie* and its vastly ennobling effect on those even remotely associated with Arthur's court is a revealing enhancement of Geoffrey of Monmouth's depiction of Arthur's Pentecost feast; in his version, Wace asserts repeatedly that the greatness of Arthur's reputation and his *curteisie* not only entice the best knights to his court, but additionally encourage the compliance of neighboring rulers by linking the ideas of *curteisie* and *imperium*.

Arthur's civilized court in the *Brut* becomes an imperial court by virtue of allurement, not military conquest. In Geoffrey's version, Arthur inspires imitation in the kings of other lands but moreover a self-interested concern lest Arthur turn his attention in their direction, an anxiety that prompts a flurry of refortification. Their plans backfire because a flattered Arthur proceeds to devise a campaign for worldwide domination. Wace's Arthur, however, like Gaimar's Edgar, exhibits such courtly behavior during a twelve-year period of peace that conflict is unheard of and his reputation exceeds that of Roman emperors.[151] In another echo of Edgar, who swayed his neighbors through fair love and good customs, Wace emphasizes Arthur's influence over rulers in outlying lands, who come from far-flung places like Spain and the Rhine for Arthur's crowning at the feast of Pentecost because he is the ideal civilized king of a civilized court; indeed, "There was not a single baron, from Spain to the Rhine near Germany, who did not attend the feast, provided he heard the summons. Some came because of Arthur, some because of his gifts, some to know his barons, some to see his wealth, some to hear his courtly speech, some out of love, some because they were commanded, some for honour, some for power."[152] The language here is reminiscent of not only earlier Anglo-Norman writers, such as Gaimar, but also the literature of the Carolingian courts during Charlemagne's redefinition of kingship and conquest. The four rulers of Scotland, North and South Wales, and Cornwall carry golden swords in procession before Arthur, which is their "office" (*mestiers*) as his subject-kings when Arthur holds court.[153] Like Charlemagne's treatment of the Saxons, Avars, and Bavarians, Alfred's treatment of the Danes in Gaimar, and Henry I's and II's lavish entertainments designed to impress and "convert" neighboring princes, it is Arthur's *curteisie* in Wace's text that commands the deference of these kings and their attendance at his feast.

In light of the subject matter that is presented in Gaimar and Wace, I will consider, briefly, the *Chanson de Roland* as an example of the kind of conversion politics that flourished in the twelfth century. The poet inscribes the older, violent idea of conversion by the sword, but maps a more courtly version to its conclusion as an idealized alternative to brute force. Malcolm Parkes, among others, dates the Oxford Digby 23 manuscript specifically between 1119 and 1149,[154] based on comparative paleography. Additionally, internal evidence placing it within the milieu of a pro-Angevin court of increasing importance to Insular politics makes it a potential candidate for understanding Anglo-Norman society and culture, much as *Beowulf* is studied for insight into the Anglo-Saxon society for which it was written even as its subject matter is far from being strictly "English."[155] It was clearly a popular tale in post-Conquest society, since the legend sprang up very quickly that the poem was performed at the start of the Battle of Hastings. William of Malmesbury recounts the episode in his history: "Then beginning the song of Roland, that the warlike example of that man might stimulate the soldiers, and calling on God for assistance, the battle commenced on both sides."[156] Although the *Roland* poet focuses largely on the central battle of the rearguard at Rencesvals, the idea of conversion bookends the *geste* and suggests that this theme holds importance for understanding Charlemagne's role in the story. The poem opens, like Dudo's history, with a false request for baptism by the perfidious Saracen king, Marsile, which is meant to contrast with the true baptism of Queen Bramimonde at the very end of the epic. It is difficult to imagine that the poem's focus on baptism, as we have it today in the Oxford manuscript, would have inspired an army to warlike valor as William of Malmesbury claims, so I would argue that the new theme represents an addition to the core story of Roland's heroism. The fascination with baptism in the opening of the poem and the odd shift of gears in the last thirty or so *laisses* away from the epic description of battles in favor of subjects more suitable to romance, including those of Christian kingship and of converting one's enemies "by fair love," recalls the conversion politics seen throughout Anglo-Norman society.

The *Chanson de Roland* begins with a brief history explaining Charlemagne's presence in Spain before describing the Saracen king, Marsile, and his vulnerable position, helpless before the unyielding force of Charlemagne's approaching army. Almost immediately, a cunning pagan suggests that Marsile send gifts and hostages to Charlemagne and pretend to beg him for baptism, offering to become his vassal. The pagans are entirely in agreement with this ruse, and Marsile chooses ten men to deliver his message, allowing the poet to reiterate the theme of baptism once more:

[Marsile] summoned ten of his most wicked men:
. . . .
He said to his men: "My lords, you will go,
Carrying olive branches in your hands,
And on my behalf you will ask King Charlemagne
To show me mercy in his God's name.
Tell him that before this month passes
I shall follow him with a thousand of my most trusted men,
That I shall become a convert to Christianity,
And that I shall become his vassal in love and in good faith."[157]

The poet then turns to Charlemagne, who has just captured the city of Cordres and destroyed it, converting the population at swordpoint, such that "not a single pagan remains in the city / who has not been slain or become a Christian."[158] Marsile's nobles arrive and greet Charlemagne "with love and goodwill,"[159] relaying the Saracen king's message and requesting baptism in the baths at Charlemagne's great palace at Aachen.[160] The events that will lead to the tragedy of Roland's death at Rencesvals are now set in motion. After the great battle, a mortally wounded Marsile rides to Saragossa and sends to the emir, Baligant, for aid against the revenge that Charlemagne will surely take now. Baligant brings all of his forces to the aid of the Saracens in Spain, and Queen Bramimonde renounces the pagan gods as useless for having failed her husband in battle,[161] which makes her a potential candidate for conversion. At this point, the emir and the emperor are brought together and the second epic battle of the *geste* begins.

As the two kings meet face-to-face on the battlefield, Baligant having been depicted as a noble, kingly opposite to the magnificent Charles, they offer each other mercy, suggesting historical wise kings who temper victory with clemency. Baligant offers to forgive Charles the offenses of invading his lands and killing his son, but Charles answers his offer by proposing a battlefield conversion to Christianity:

The Emir said: "Think it over, Charles,
You'd be well advised to beg my forgiveness!
You have slain my son, of that I am certain,

You very unjustly challenge my right to this country.
Become my vassal and I shall give it back to you as a fief.
Come serve me from here to the Orient."
Charles replies: "This strikes me as a very contemptible notion,
I must bestow neither peace nor friendship on any pagan.
Accept the religion that God reveals to us,
Namely, Christianity, then I shall love you forthwith;
Then serve and believe in the almighty King!"[162]

Charlemagne is offering Baligant more than simply a new faith: he is also offering him a place in his empire and the opportunity to take part in a more civilized way of life in the Christian empire, not unlike Charlemagne's experiences with the Saxons and Bavarians. Baligant refuses his offer, of course, and Charles is left with no choice but to kill him and defeat the Saracens, thus proving the justness of his claim. Upon taking Saragossa, Charles initiates the conversions of pagans, but delays that of the queen for the purpose of converting her by love rather than force:

More than a hundred thousand are baptized
True Christians, with the exception of the Queen [Bramimonde]:
She will be led captive to sweet France,
The King wants her to be converted by love.[163]

This echo of Carolingian ideologies of conquest continues as the poet demonstrates how mercy is reserved for deserving individuals such as Bramimonde, who is being converted to Christianity "by love" and not by the sword. As part of the conclusion to the poem, Charlemagne calls his bishops and announces that Bramimonde has listened to sermons and thus has been taught properly of the faith, and has asked for baptism, not unlike the Dacians after hearing Duke Richard II sermonize in Dudo's earlier narrative:

There is a noble prisoner in my house.
She has heard so many sermons and exempla
That she wishes to believe in God, she has asked to be converted to Christianity.
Baptize her so that God may save her soul.[164]

She is subsequently baptized by godmothers, ladies of noble birth at the king's residence in Aix (Aachen).[165] Now accepted into Charlemagne's court through the ritual of baptism, she is furthermore described as the queen of Spain and given a new, more Frankish name, suggesting that she remains in this position now in her new identity as Charlemagne's vassal, much like the context in which Tassilo remained as duke of Bavaria:

At the baths at Aix, the . . . are very large,
There they baptize the Queen of Spain,
They found for her the name of Juliana.
She is a Christian out of sheer conviction.[166]

In the following *laisse*, the *Chanson*'s last, Charlemagne finally lies down to rest, only to have Gabriel call him back into action to relieve yet another city besieged by infidels, at which the king weeps and pulls his beard, wishing not to go. Charlemagne's reluctance in the *Chanson*'s final lines is potentially startling when compared to the poem's detailed descriptions of gory battles and the glorious defeat of Saracen armies, but only if we do not consider it in the context of the twelfth century's changing mores, which dominate the theme of conversion that frames the poem. Thus, we can view the *Chanson de Roland* as representative of a culture that was redefining its values and definitions of good kingship in view of current ideals of civilized behavior, which advocated conversion of enemies through allurement as a viable option to the destruction of battle and the rancor that it engenders.

In one final example, these issues can be brought to bear upon the controversial question of the Anglo-Norman colonization of Ireland in the second half of the twelfth century and the content of *Laudabiliter*, the common name for a bull quoted by Giraldus Cambrensis, supposedly from Pope Adrian IV, that gave Henry II the right to intervene in Ireland. Davies, for instance, argues that Ireland "did not figure high on the agenda of the Angevin rulers of England" because "so much is suggested by the fact that Henry II did not act on the bull *Laudabiliter*."[167] A lack of military invasion does not necessarily constitute a lack of interest. Indeed, several sources record Henry's interest in an Irish venture in 1155, which was perhaps ultimately scuttled in order to deal with conflicts in France.[168] If one considers Henry II's education within this environment of "civilized" views of imperialism, a great deal is explained regarding his resumption of his grandfather's role and practices as a dominant power in Britain after the upheaval of civil war,[169] especially seen in the very public displays of homage by the leaders of Scotland and Wales. The author of *Laudabiliter*, as a symbol of Henry's involvement in Irish affairs in 1171–72, reflects the civilizing impulses of conversion politics seen elsewhere in his use of conversion rhetoric to justify imperial expansion into Ireland and downplay the threat of violence in bringing Ireland under Henry's subjugation. Indeed, the bull suggests that it is Henry's duty as a Christian king to bring the wayward Irish into the true faith by asserting his authority there and saving the people from their vices, in much the same way that Alcuin exhorts Charlemagne to convert the pagan Saxons.

Laudabiliter itself, as found in Giraldus Cambrensis's *Expugnatio Hibernica*, is a problematic text of contested legitimacy that seems to verify John of Salisbury's account from 1159 that Adrian IV had granted Ireland to Henry II, as was his right because of the Donation of Constantine, which gave the church jurisdiction over the island.[170] Anne J. Duggan has studied *Laudabiliter* extensively and concludes that, while probably not an entirely forged document, it was most likely falsified from an earlier document that condoned Henry's action in Ireland only if it was requested by the Irish church, princes, and people.[171] What we have from Giraldus, however, is a document that establishes Henry's right to rule after the fact, "contrived to turn Henry's intervention into a kind of crusade to civilize the Irish, for which the falsified *Laudabiliter* provided the justification."[172] The bull, which I quote at length, presents the church's encouragement of Henry II to rectify the Irish church in terms much like a conversion of barbarous pagans:

> In right praiseworthy fashion, and to good purpose, your Majesty is considering how to spread abroad the glorious name of Christ on earth, and thus store up for yourself in heaven the reward of eternal bliss, while striving, as a true Catholic prince should, to enlarge the boundaries of the church, to reveal the truth of the Christian faith to peoples still untaught and barbarous, and to root out the weeds of vice from the Lord's field. . . . You have indeed indicated to us, most well-beloved son in Christ, that you wish to enter this island of Ireland, to make that people obedient to the laws, and to root out there the weeds of vices. . . . We therefore support your pious and praiseworthy intention with the favour which it deserves and, granting our benevolent consent to your petition, we regard it as pleasing and acceptable to us that you should enter that island for the purpose of enlarging the boundaries of the church, checking the descent into wickedness, correcting morals and implanting virtues, and encouraging the growth of the faith of Christ; that you pursue

policies directed towards the honour of God and the well-being of that land, and that the people of that land receive you honourably and respect you as their lord.... Therefore if you wish to bring into successful conclusion the design which you have thus conceived, take particular care to instruct the people in right behaviour.[173]

The echoes here of Alcuin's letter to Charlemagne celebrating his defeat of the Avars in 796 are uncanny and represent a recycling of the ideology of conquest espoused by the Carolingian court: the emphasis on military conquest is almost completely eliminated by the focus on converting barbarous peoples and instructing them in the virtues of civilized behavior, in the name of converting them to "the truth of the Christian faith" (the Irish were already Christian, of course, but they had resisted the authority of the church in Rome).[174]

As mentioned earlier, Giraldus Cambrensis was aware of the commonly held opinion that the British nations were barbaric in contrast to the more urbanized civilization of England, and he was keenly interested in promoting this notion in his work. Furthermore, his purpose in writing this version of events in the *Expugnatio* was "to demonstrate the prophetic nature of Norman dominion both in Ireland and in Wales," and his text's original title was *Vaticinalis historia* (Prophetic history) because it recounts several prophecies of Merlin predicting the rightful rule of the Normans.[175] Whatever its position as a legitimate historical document, *Laudabiliter* in particular remains a testament to prevailing attitudes on the necessity for conversion politics in British lands, which were perceived as being badly in need of civilizing. Marie Therese Flanagan advances a compelling argument for Irish support of Angevin claims to the throne that clarifies Diarmait Mac Murchada's plea for support from Henry II in 1166; that Henry II could not respond himself to this petition is explained in part by his Continental woes at the time.[176] Were it not for the dilemma caused by his irksome vassal, Richard de Clare ("Strongbow"), in accepting overlordship of Leinster in 1171, combined perhaps with the need to divert attention away from the furor caused by Thomas Becket's death, it is difficult to tell when Henry II would have been able to launch a campaign into Ireland. Like his grandfather before him, however, Henry II acted quickly when the opportunity presented itself, and preferred to contend by council rather than the sword: through long and difficult negotiations with Strongbow he was able to gain a foothold in Ireland for an overlordship in more than theory.[177] The question over *Laudabiliter*'s authenticity supports the idea that Henry sought an alternative to military conquest in an effort to portray the campaign as something other than a military venture: even a forged document suggests not that he sought to avoid bloodshed (he brought sufficient troops with him to support his claim), but that he desired to couch his claim to *imperium* in terms of conversion politics. Whatever convinced him, however, Strongbow died as Henry's agent in Ireland in 1176 after having proven his loyalty to the king during the rebellion of Young Henry,[178] and the Anglo-Norman kings had an established presence in Ireland through which to pursue their goal of *imperium*.

The literature and historical events of the twelfth century demonstrate that Anglo-Norman imperialism in Britain is not necessarily a clear-cut phenomenon of military expansion and tyrannical domination. They also reflect, in large part, the growing influence of the chivalric romance tradition, as well as an evolving view of kingship based on the Carolingian development of conversion politics, which sought to win the allegiance of peoples through the allurement of political or financial gain and inclusion in a more civilized way of life. Several "peaceloving" Norman kings advocated alternative methods of increasing Norman power and authority in neighboring lands, and, within the context of the imperial ideology of conquest, the effect of Carolingian ideals of sacral kingship on the military culture of the period cannot be overestimated. The virtue of Christian compassion, augmented by the Augustinist view, which supports expanding God's empire through conversion, results in various models of conversion politics in twelfth-century narratives that illustrate the growing importance of "good customs" and "fair love" for bolstering Norman authority within British territories. As evidenced through revisionist histories such as Gaimar's, the hybrid identity of Anglo-Normans, in the establishment of their legitimacy as inheritors of an Anglo-Saxon pan-British empire, may have justified expansion into neighboring regions. But the rhetoric of this expansion called for a change from what were portrayed as bloodier, more violent pre-Conquest practices, reflecting the changing Anglo-Norman self-image, in which they saw themselves as responsible for civilizing the Celtic barbarians by bringing the light of Norman mores to these benighted lands, like Charlemagne, through conversion *or* the sword.

2 | Making Their Mark
The Imperial Ideology of Topography

In May of 877, Charles the Bald issued a detailed charter for the palace chapel at Compiègne. In it, he appeals to the memory of Charlemagne and his great power center at Aachen for the purpose of transferring the glories and authority of his grandfather's reign onto his own kingship. He emphasizes that "[b]ecause our grandfather, to whom divine providence granted the monarchy of this whole empire, established a chapel in honour of the Virgin in the palace at Aachen . . . we therefore, wanting to imitate the pattern set by him and other kings and emperors, namely our predecessors, since that part of the realm has not yet come to us by way of share in its division, we have built and completed within the territory under our sway, in the palace of Compiègne, a new monastery, to which we have given the name 'royal.'"[1] In this important document, Charles is determined to establish himself as the rightful heir to Charlemagne's empire, even though he does not possess it in reality, by explicitly recalling Aachen and its "dynastic associations"[2] and suggestively aligning himself with his grandfather's authority through his comparable building program at Compiègne. A similar sentiment would be expressed in the first half of the twelfth century, when William of Malmesbury claimed that Robert Losinga, the Norman bishop of Hereford, rebuilt the cathedral there in 1080 "in rounded form, modelled, so far as he could, on [Charlemagne's] basilica at Aachen."[3]

In the centuries after his death, Charlemagne's persona took on a foundational value for interpretations of kingship that few models can surpass, but there remains a large gap in our understanding of the impact of his kingship on the physical landscape, which is seen in later imitations of his building program. This is especially true with regard to the ideological possibilities of the *via regia* (royal road) for developing a model for kingship and of castles for projecting an imperial image onto the landscape itself that would remain as a physical reminder of authority. Although several scholars have demonstrated that Charlemagne, seeking to appropriate the Roman and Byzantine emperors' image of imperial power for his own reign, emulated their building styles in the construction of his later palaces, most famously at Aachen,[4] few have explored how the Anglo-Normans utilized this approach as a tangible manifestation of *imperium* throughout the British territories. The goals and ideals of Anglo-Norman dominion, represented physically by the topography of England, are legitimized by the echoing symbol of Charlemagne's imperial leadership. In order to support their appropriation of the Anglo-Saxon landscape, both symbolic and real, the Anglo-Normans exploited the authority conveyed by related material culture to create an enduring image of themselves as emperor-kings with Britain as the center of their empire. They achieved this by keeping a Carolingian ideal in mind while also being keenly aware of the potency of the imperial past for use as propaganda for the present.

There exist throughout the world "landscape depictions which may be powerfully evocative because they are understood as being a particular kind of place rather than a precise building or locality,"[5] as societies created and manipulated the symbolic meaning of topography in order to reinforce cultural ideals. In his authoritative work on the interaction between culture and landscape, D. W. Meinig has shown that ultimately these "symbolic landscapes" become "part of the shared set of ideas and memories and feelings which bind a people together."[6] Building with stone in medieval Europe is especially loaded with cultural memory because of its durability and association with the imperial Roman past. Charles McClendon argues that the "very concept of building in stone or brick and mortar was Roman in origin and a structure built with such materials was deemed a potent symbol of 'Romanness' or *romanitas*."[7] The rich possibilities for symbolism in stone, of course, are not limited to the Roman past; prehistoric Insular stone monuments, for example, "drew part of their power and significance through appropriating and making reference to landmarks that already had an embedded cultural significance."[8] But it is exactly this authoritative weight, which the stone represents, that lends *romanitas* its psychological effectiveness. In the context of the symbolic landscape, the power of the past is integrated into monument construction such that the "ritually and symbolically effective placing of monuments in the landscape became of vital significance in the creation, reproduction and articulation of authority ... [and the] past was actively appropriated so as to naturalize and legitimize the present."[9] As a result, the use of stone or spolia can suggest a wide range of possibilities for expressing *translatio*. In his study of the significance of Roman authority for early Anglo-Saxon Christians, for example, Nicholas Howe observes that "the human progress toward the holy" can be demarcated by a Roman arch, probably plundered in its entirety from a Roman building and later installed in a church,[10] which created an enduring image of power that appropriated the imperial landscape of Britain that remained after the fall of the Roman Empire. In a similar fashion, the expansionist desires of the Normans in Britain are dependent on, and symbolized by, the integration of tangible symbols of Anglo-Saxon and Roman authority into post-Conquest claims of legitimacy, especially those that would provide an enduring visual reminder of Anglo-Norman power.

Imperial Unification and Sacral Kingship: Henry of Huntingdon's *Via regia*

Both on the Continent and in Britain, the roads that the Romans built across their empire not only provided a practical and easy means of transport and communication but also united even the most far-flung territories with the center. Physically representing radiations of Roman power etched across the landscape itself, they became part of the legacy of imperial authority. As Robert Harbison has observed, the idea that "all roads lead to Rome" could make a great impression on the people who were subject to Rome's authority, because it indicates that "the center has absolutely been ordained by human will, that all journeys have been plotted at the start, that the quality of clockwork has been imparted to human affairs. Roman roads were laid perfectly straight in an outlying place like Britain not because it was easy to do it that way but to show that even this wild did not defeat the Roman mind."[11] Like the barbarian landscape, the indigenous populations were ultimately overcome by Roman imperial ambitions; subsequently, the constant reminder of Roman presence in the form of the roads would have "set the relation between the colonizer and the colonized in a literally hierarchical material form."[12] The imposition of Roman will upon the very landscape of what would become Britannia implies a kind of inevitability of Roman rule, and the roads' connection to those on the Continent suggests that the linkage of the island to the imperial center in Rome replaced native identities with a Roman one as much as did the change in the name of the island itself to a Latin one. Laid out without consideration for extant foundations, and thus "slighting pre-existing boundaries, political groupings and patterns of kinship and symbolizing the domination of Rome,"[13] the roads further erased the boundaries and influence of individual power centers and emphasized the inadequacy of native tribes to rule their lands. The very creation of the roads symbolically confirmed the superiority of Roman imperial order, civilization, and culture to anything that may have been present beforehand, and the idea of the roads, like the Roman Empire itself, had a lasting psychological impact upon the peoples of Britain, as it did upon their Continental contemporaries.

The roads in Europe would ultimately become indistinguishable from the idea of royal power, and indeed would come to represent that power, enhanced by Old Testament precedent, especially with regard to the peace brought about by the strength of wise, just kings such as David and Solomon. This notion derives from such examples as God's command to the Hebrews to stand "in the highways and see, and ask for the old paths, where is the good way; and walk therein, and ye shall find rest for your souls" (Jeremiah 6:16), and his promise that "a highway shall be there [in the desert and the wilderness], and a way, and it shall be called the Way of Holiness. The unclean shall not pass over it, but it shall be for those; the wayfaring men, though fools, shall not err therein" (Isaiah 35:8). God also promises to send teachers to guide his people as they travel this highway, and "though the Lord give you the bread of adversity and the water of affliction, yet shall not thy teachers be removed into a corner any more, but thine eyes shall see thy teachers. And thine ears shall hear a word behind thee, saying, 'This is the way; walk ye in it,' when ye turn to the right hand and when ye turn to the left" (Isaiah 30:20–21).

Although these teachers can take many forms, most important for my purposes is that the role of teacher becomes integral to kingship, specifically in the king's function as mouthpiece of God and guardian of his commandments. The king thus becomes the primary savior of his people through his morality and adherence to God's law. We see the relationship between the highway (*via*) and morality clearly defined, furthermore, through the lives of David and Solomon and their intimate relationship with God. We are told explicitly that the king must follow the correct road to salvation, not only for himself but above all for his people. On his deathbed, David instructs

Solomon in the sacral role of the king, reminding him of God's promise to David that guarantees the security of his people as long as the king maintains God's laws (1 Kings 2:3-4). Many of Alcuin's letters contain wording reminiscent of this biblical passage. As Luitpold Wallach observes, "When speaking of the *via regia* Alcuin does not make a distinction between ethics and law," and moreover, "Alcuin identifies the *via regia* with *via iustitiae*."[14] In this way the king becomes not only the embodiment of the law but also the symbol of the moral health of his people, such that any sin that the king commits can result in divine retribution upon the people as a whole.

On the other hand, God rewards with great success the good king who undertakes this task with humility. When Solomon prays to God for wisdom and discernment so that he might better fulfill his role as judge, God is pleased with his request and blesses him with wisdom and much more (1 Kings 3:10-14). His father David, of course, is a prime example of the rewards that God will provide the just king, especially with regard to his success in a lifetime of battles and his defeat of the Philistines (2 Samuel 23). Consequently, the biblical idea of the *via regia* is also imbued with nuances of divinely sanctioned imperial expansion as the Israelites solidify their presence in the Holy Land as God's chosen people. We see, for example, the peregrinations of Moses and the Israelites in the desert as they request safe passage for their journey through the lands of King Sihon of the Amorites (Numbers 21:21-35). They promise him to "go along the king's highway" (*via regia gradiemus*) and not stray from the king's designated road. Medieval theologians understood this episode as exemplifying "unwavering religious faithfulness and moral restraint,"[15] and the *via regia* would become directly responsible for the fecundity of the land, peace among its people, and victory in battle (Isaiah 48:16). Accounts such as these demonstrate the divine support that the righteous king can expect and suggest why later generations of Christian rulers might focus on Old Testament precedent for guidance rather than on the gentler message of Christ's model of kingship. The success of David, for example, in uniting the Kingdom of Israel under his authority, and his role as the keeper of God's laws, were particularly appealing to several medieval kings.[16] Certainly, Charlemagne's reign was frequently likened to that of David as well as those of Moses and Solomon: Alcuin, who dealt "with questions of government as moral issues,"[17] addressed him as "King David" in letters at least as early as 796.[18] The benefits of sacral kingship that permeate the accounts of David's life, therefore, would become essential components of kingship in the Middle Ages. Especially attractive for a medieval king with imperial ambitions like

Charlemagne, as he strove to solidify his expanding empire through both military and divine means, was God's promise in the "Covenant of David" that he would "establish the throne of his [David's] kingdom forever" (2 Samuel 7:13) and its consequences for the unification of the kingdom of Israel.

As J. M. Wallace-Hadrill notes of the Carolingian period, "The *via regia*, the king's way, was also God's way, as the ninth century saw it."[19] For Carolingian *specula principum* such as Alcuin's *Rhetoric* and Smaragdus of St. Mihiel's *Via regia*, therefore, the *via regia* became an important motif intended to provide instruction on the exercise of kingship, as represented by the practices of Charlemagne himself, in order to restore peace and unify a disparate empire. It is important to briefly note here the development of the *via regia* as a symbol of the king's justice, especially for understanding how the Anglo-Normans might have manipulated it to justify their ambition to expand their authority throughout Britain. Although both England and the Continent derived their legal concepts about the highway from Roman legal ideals, Roman laws about roads were primarily about their care and upkeep. The Roman road was not so much a royal highway, as it would become for later generations, as merely a *via publica* (public road).[20] Lucien Musset notes that evidence of the significant changes in the perception of roads in the Middle Ages can be seen in their names, as the abstract term "public road" came to be replaced by the titles of the specific individual who had jurisdiction over the highway (i.e., the "king's [or duke's] highway"). This is because, according to Musset, the responsibility for justice on certain roads became of primary concern, rather than land ownership, and was one of the expressions of royal power that the holders of sovereign authority claimed the most clearly.[21]

In the earliest medieval law codes, therefore, we begin to see "deterrents designed to guarantee the safety of the traveller."[22] Although the laws in Anglo-Saxon England and on the Continent both are concerned with the safety of the traveler along the king's highway,[23] those of England treat the highway as a public road, "a zone under a special peace, where strangers could travel without fear of being branded a thief and where everyone could travel temporarily immune from the dangers of feuds."[24] Thus, the Anglo-Saxon law of the highway "suggests that the highway was intended to fulfill the king's Biblical duty to protect strangers by protecting those travelling between the king's towns and markets."[25] Most significantly, the strongest reference to a law of the *via regia* that is supposedly from the pre-Conquest period is actually within the *Leges Henrici Primi*, an early twelfth-century compilation of Anglo-Saxon and Continental laws; the fact remains that, although pre-Conquest law codes contain references to highways, they do not explicitly define the concept and "without the teleological framework offered by the *Leges* . . . the references to the highway in Anglo-Saxon law codes are so terse as to be almost meaningless."[26] As a result, any understanding of Anglo-Saxon references to the *via regia* is the product of reading backwards from the post-Conquest law codes, in spite of the impossibility of determining how much the references might be "corrupted" by Norman influences. Admittedly, Carolingian legal references to the *via regia* are thin on the ground and do not become a commonplace in Normandy until the twelfth century,[27] when they are becoming more frequently used in England as well, but we do see the use of the idea of the *via regia* in important Carolingian treatises on kingship, which also had an impact on how subsequent generations viewed it.

Throughout the work of several of the writers of Charlemagne's court, his kingship emerges as a paradigm of stewardship, not only in a practical sense in his governance of the land itself, but also in a moral sense in his responsibility for the salvation of his people. Examples of the *via regia* as a moral guide in the biblical sense abound in patristic writing: in *De Civitate Dei* 10, Augustine writes of the *via regalis*, the royal road, as an ethical model that represents "the only route to the kingdom of heaven."[28] But, as Wallach notes, "During the Carolingian age the expression [of the *via regia*] gained general recognition as a political idea,"[29] partly because of medieval theologians' approach to exegesis, which Mayke de Jong has shown was frequently directed toward interpreting the books of the Old Testament and the moral lessons that they provide as models for kingship.[30] Alcuin composed his *Rhetoric*, for example, which is essentially a treatise on kingship or good government,[31] with the idea of the *via regia* in mind: he closely associated it with the ruler's exemplary mores as a guide for his subjects. In a letter to Charlemagne, Alcuin reminds the king of the unifying quality of the idea of the *via regia*,[32] which would also become an important concern for later Anglo-Norman kings grappling with the unification of English and Norman peoples. Smaragdus of St. Mihiel's own *speculum principi*, an exegetical instruction book on sacral kingship appropriately entitled *Via regia*, was most likely composed for Louis the Pious when he was king of Aquitaine before Charlemagne's death in 814. As Paul Kershaw wryly observes, "Smaragdus brought, even by Carolingian standards, a sensibility steeped in scripture to mapping a king's path."[33] The second chapter of his treatise is dedicated to "observing the commandments of the Lord," and, in an echo of God's promises to the Israelites and their kings, discussed earlier, he retools God's injunction for Louis the Pious by claiming that for those who "carefully and diligently keep His commandments . . . , the Father and the Son and the Holy Ghost will come to thee . . . , [and] thy peace will be happily increased, and thy joy as a river forever be fulfilled."[34] For these writers, then, the *via regia* is the symbol of good kingship and, at least as importantly, the earthly benefits it can bring to a chosen people.

As it was for the Carolingians, the relationship between good kingship and the *via regia* was a concrete and practical concern in the minds of Anglo-Normans, and subsequently the royal road came to symbolize their ideal of peace throughout the country, maintained by a strong king's laws, as seen in Henry of Huntingdon's myth of the Four Highways. In such a way, the king himself becomes directly associated in a physical sense with the laws of the *via regia* and its implications for peace and unity in all of Britain. Cooper suggests that, for the Anglo-Normans, "there was a new understanding of the highway as an object belonging to the king and thus an asset that he might exploit," and on "a more universal level, in the twelfth century, legal collections begin to include the spurious idea that the king had only four particular highways under his jurisdiction."[35] I would suggest that the Anglo-Normans saw the *via regia* not only as a material asset to exploit but also as an ideological one. What is most significant about the Anglo-Norman emphasis on defining the laws of the *via regia* is that the highway's relationship to the king's authority becomes more prominent, especially as the concept of the King's Four Highways develops as a visual symbol of that power and its propagation as an instrument for solidifying and increasing Anglo-Norman authority.

The association between the king's highway and his authority is essential to understanding why the *via regia* becomes a compelling image for certain Anglo-Norman writers who are concerned with issues of Norman kingship, not only in terms of the legitimacy of their rule in England but also in regard to their justification for expanding their empire to include the rest of Britain. The "symbolic landscapes" in the context of the *via regia* for the Anglo-Normans represented an imperial civilization and its unifying strength, order, and stability, as exemplified by the Romans, who built the roads, and especially Charlemagne, whose reign emphasized the function of the king as the image of God's justice on earth. Thus, Anglo-Norman expansion and unity are dependent on, and symbolized by, the network of Roman roads uniting the island with its web of interconnecting arteries, and its lifeblood flows from the strength of the king and his law.[36] This notion can be clearly seen in Henry of Huntingdon's invention of a history for the King's Four Highways in the *Historia Anglorum*, which provides a royal parentage for the *via regia* of Britain and dramatizes the highways' creation, emphasizing the strength of the king's laws, which unite the entire island, including Wales and Scotland, in peaceful coexistence. Written and verbal representations of a constructed landscape can be essential for our understanding of that landscape, "not as 'illustrations,' images standing outside it, but as constituent images of its meaning or meanings."[37] For Henry of Huntingdon, whose historical concerns centered on the progress of *regnum*, the reminders of imperial rule that the Roman roads represented became at once an emblem of the legitimacy of Anglo-Norman sovereignty and an enduring symbol of the kingship that was responsible for the protection of the land and its people. Henry of Huntingdon wrote the *Historia Anglorum*, which exists in six versions in more than forty manuscripts and numerous fragments,[38] in the second quarter of the twelfth century, at a time when the Anglo-Normans were becoming increasingly concerned with the laws of the *via regia*, as seen not only in the law codes but also in histories and literary works.[39] The *Historia Anglorum* is remarkable for several reasons, including Henry's treatment of Britain's wondrous landscape, where he emphasizes commercial overabundance, material wealth and beauty, and especially the roads spanning the island, uniting the various *gentes* under the protective aegis of the king.

In the *Historia Anglorum*, the *locus amoenus* of the British landscape, inherited from Bede's descriptions,[40] one of Henry's main sources, becomes an Eden tamed and enhanced by imperial civilization, where nature and society exist in harmony with God's grace. As John Howe argues, "It seems to have been generally accepted that human improvements could enhance natural paradises," indeed, that they "could and should be transformed."[41] This view corresponds with classical and Christian ideas regarding the king's stewardship over the land, as part of man's mission on earth to improve it, "serving as a partner of God in overseeing the earth."[42] Twelfth-century writers certainly had plenty of criticism to heap upon those people who they thought violated this sacred trust. The author of the *Gesta Stephani*, for example, laments the Welsh people's barbarous waste of God's natural bounty in not improving the land by peacefully building towns and cultivating fields, but rather living like animals and cultivating treachery: "Now Wales is a country of woodland and pasture, . . . abounding in deer and fish, milk and herds; but it breeds men of an animal type, naturally swift-footed, accustomed to war, volatile in always breaking their word as in changing their abodes."[43] The Normans were quick to remedy the lawless and egregious disrespect of God's gifts, however, because when "the Normans conquered the English, this land [Wales] they also added to their dominion and fortified with numberless castles; they perseveringly civilized it after they had vigorously subdued its inhabitants; to encourage peace they imposed law and statutes on them; and they made the land so productive and abounding in all kinds of resources that you would have reckoned it in no wise inferior to the most fertile part of Britain."[44] Here in the *Gesta*, the relationship between peaceful stewardship of the land and imperial dominion is made perfectly clear, as it is in the *Historia Anglorum*. Expanding upon Bede's ideas, Henry of Huntingdon changes the focus of Britain as a pastoral *locus amoenus*, shifting the description away from the landscape and the island's natural wealth to the urban civilization of his great land in a lengthy account of Britain's twenty-nine magnificent cities. He eschews completely Bede's celebration of Ireland's paradisiacal wealth and glory (which "in breadth, and for wholesomeness and serenity of climate, greatly surpasses Britain")[45] in favor of continuing his theme of *regnum*. In detailing the relentless progress of English kings and their control over the land, he makes the connection between Anglo-Norman civilizing progress and the land even more clear.

Henry quickly returns to his amplification of the theme of the civilized *locus amoenus*, the divine harmony of the urban setting with its natural environment, by claiming that the "cities mentioned above are sited in delightful positions and glitter on the banks of fruitful and very beautiful rivers."[46] These "glittering" jewels of man's handiwork adorn the natural beauty of God's creation, which, in Henry's text, serves to convey the material wealth that flows into the land to enrich its inhabitants, who cut the most sophisticated, well-dressed figures in foreign countries.[47] Thus, the auspicious combination of Britain's natural wealth with Norman rule produces a civilization that ultimately outshines its Continental exemplar. The relationship between imperialism and civilization is emphasized most significantly, however, by Henry's invention of the myth of the Four Highways that past rulers have created across the island to establish peace:[48]

> Britain was so dear to its inhabitants that they constructed four highways in it, from one end to the other, built by royal authority, so that no one would dare attack an enemy on them. The first is from east to west, and is called the Icknield Way. The second runs from south to north, and is called Ermine Street. The third goes across from Dover to Chester, that is from the southeast to the northwest,

and is called Watling Street. The fourth, longer than the others, begins in Caithness and ends in Totnes, that is from the beginning of Cornwall to the end of Scotland. This road, which is called the Fosse Way, takes a diagonal route from southwest to northeast, and passes through Lincoln. These are the four principal highways of England, which are very broad as well as splendid, protected by the edicts of kings and by venerable law codes.[49]

There are several noteworthy things suggested by this development, where Henry digresses radically from Bede. The first, of course, is the invention of the myth of the Four Highways itself, which Alan Cooper suggests "was one small part of a movement that sought, a full lifetime after the Norman Conquest, to uncover England's pre-Norman past"[50] in its contemplation of the imperial legacies of "the succession of the most powerful kings who have existed" (de serie regum potentissimorum qui per orbem terrarum hucusque fuerunt).[51] However, Henry's history does not evoke a nostalgic longing for the recent Anglo-Saxon past, as might be suggested by Cooper's statement, but rather places Henry I squarely at the head of a long line of strong rulers who quelled social disorder and conflict. Because Henry of Huntingdon is focused on the progress of *regnum*, the civilized advancements that he praises have been wrought by the Norman kings, not Anglo-Saxons. Although Robert Allen Rouse traces the post-Conquest *via regia* motif to Bede's account of King Edwin, claiming that it functions as "an important social concern within English and wider Germanic culture,"[52] Rouse fails to consider the Carolingian ideological exploration of the *via regia*, especially its possibilities for exploiting the imperial dimensions of Charlemagne's sacral kingship to justify Norman expansion throughout Britain.

In addition to reinforcing the Anglo-Norman position in the grand scheme of European history, Henry's elaborate identification of the Four Highways with the king's legal authority and the roads' physical spanning not only of those lands we consider to be "England," but also the British lands of Wales and Scotland, visually underscores the Norman and Angevin kings' ambitions to overlordship of the entire island, since the Four Highways stretch from top to bottom and from side to side, including the territories of Wales and Scotland in their purview. His development of the monarchy as a main theme of the *Historia Anglorum* climaxes with the rule of "the glorious and invincible" (Gloriosi et inuictissimi) King Henry I, whom Henry calls "the conqueror and ruler of kings" (Regum uictor et dominator).[53] Henry of

Huntingdon's rendering of English history highlights the Anglo-Norman inheritance from imperial Europe, symbolized not by the natural glory and wealth of the island, as stressed by Bede, but by its civilized culture, seen, for example, in the building of royal roads, which was brought by the Romans and augmented by Norman mores and government. The idea of Norman rule as *imperium* would be further emphasized by Henry's explicit reference to Charlemagne's legacy: he quotes Psalm 76:11 (77:10) when introducing Charlemagne's accession to the throne in 769 and describes it as "a change [by] the right hand of the Most High" (Incepit fieri mutatio dextere excelsi),[54] evoking the sacral charge of his kingship in an imperial context. The psalm follows the statement "haec mutatio dexterae Excelsi" by recalling God's past miracles to redeem his chosen people and lead them to the promised land; Henry, therefore, evokes the memory of Moses and the deliverance of the Israelites in order to suggest that Charlemagne's imperial rule has brought salvation to his people. It is important to note that Henry uses this phrase on another occasion in reference to William the Conqueror after the Battle of Hastings; I will return to this point below. He thus directly compares the Norman duke to Charlemagne, drawing a clear parallel between the two rulers and justifying Norman sovereignty in England and ultimately all of Britain as a deliverance from bondage.

That Henry of Huntingdon might have called upon Charlemagne's legendary memory in this context should not surprise us. Indeed, it is clear from Henry of Huntingdon's use of Psalm 76:11 that he considered the Normans Charlemagne's legitimate successors in coming to power by "the right hand of the Most High" as he did. This imperial impulse was partly the result of an Anglo-Norman obsession with the Continent from the eleventh century,[55] which would have a profound impact on their political culture and developing identity. Even as late as 1165, a time when many scholars claim that Angevin kings were identifying with Arthur to legitimize overlordship in neighboring British lands,[56] Henry II was working with Holy Roman Emperor Frederick Barbarossa to have Charlemagne canonized as both king and confessor. Each ruler had a similar motive in mind: "to strengthen the authority of the reigning successor of the new saint."[57] In 1175, Jordan Fantosme's *Chronique de la guerre entre les Anglois et les Ecosssais* hails Henry II as "the best king that ever lived"[58] and explicitly equates him to Charlemagne: Henry "is the most honourable and the most victorious king who ever was anywhere on earth since the time of Moses, save only Charlemagne, whose might was immense through the deeds of the twelve peers amongst whom were Oliver and

Roland."[59] Furthermore, the conclusion of Fantosme's *Chronique* makes the correlation even clearer by describing Henry II rushing to Rouen's aid after the Scots are vanquished,[60] in an echo of Gabriel's command to Charlemagne to relieve the siege of Imphe at the close of the *Chanson de Roland*. What is especially curious about Fantosme's praise is the fact that he eschews the names that one might expect to see in a poem about great kings since the time of Moses, such as David and Solomon, and skips right to Charlemagne. In so doing, he singles them out for approbation in a way that underscores their role as *Christian* kings, in keeping with the Carolingian development of sacral kingship, and their responsibility to lead their people in the *via regia*.

The idea of "empire" available to the Normans was clearly not a homogeneous one, however, especially after Charlemagne's reign significantly revised its own imperial model. Accordingly, the importance of the *via regia* to the Anglo-Normans in this context as a visual reminder of a pre-Norman imperial past cannot be overestimated. While the Anglo-Saxons, Matthew Innes notes, were required to treat the Danelaw provinces north of Watling Street "with the greatest of care" to avoid clashes along this political and ethnic boundary,[61] under the Normans there existed a deliberate blurring or blending of ethnicity and regional identity, which can be traced to the Carolingian ideal of *imperium*, under which the neighboring peoples were conquered, converted, and integrated, expanding the boundaries of Charlemagne's authority. Although the roads "endured as evidence for the fading transience of all that was human-made within the scope of Christian history,"[62] they also commemorated the spread of imperial power and civilization. The Normans' appropriation and expansion of the idea of the *via regia* to include an imperial interpretation participates, therefore, in the tradition of *translatio*, which derived from a Continental foundation, as well as a biblical one, as exemplified by the life of David. In his evocation of the ideology of the *via regia* in creating the myth of the King's Four Highways, Henry of Huntingdon is simultaneously a champion of *translatio imperii* and deeply concerned with the heavenly kingdom and the achievement of immortality through a Christian kingship, as evident in his advice in a letter to Henry I: "Consequently you may evidently learn whether, with your usual great exertion of mind, you should cherish and preserve this kingdom, which you possess by hereditary right, or rather, and far more admirably, you should summon up and concentrate your strength on seeking and gaining another kingdom" (i.e., the kingdom of heaven).[63] This sentiment is reminiscent of the writers of Charlemagne's court, who strongly associate Charlemagne's imperial role with his persona as earthly king and the vicar of God; this was first mentioned by Cathwulf in a letter to Charlemagne and subsequently elaborated by Alcuin and others.[64]

The link between the Anglo-Normans and imperial Europe is reiterated in Henry of Huntingdon's discussion of the British peoples' common origins in the Trojan Dardanus, the illustrious ancestor of Bruto, who settled the rich island and founded a great dynasty.[65] Although Trojan origins were frequently invented in the Middle Ages to create an ancestry that would connect one's people with Rome, for Henry, the glory of the association with the Roman Empire would ultimately be outstripped by the supremacy of Charlemagne, as evidenced by his use of Psalm 76:11, mentioned earlier regarding Charlemagne's accession to the throne of the Franks. The only other time Henry uses the phrase "there began to be a change [by] the right hand of the Most High"[66] is in his description of William's stunning victory at the Battle of Hastings, divinely foretold by a comet. Consequently, it becomes an allusion to Charlemagne's imperial sovereignty: "William, taking possession of this great victory, was received peacefully by the Londoners, and was crowned at Westminster by Ealdred, archbishop of York. Thus occurred *a change [by] the right hand of the Most High*, which a huge comet had presaged at the beginning of the same year."[67] Many modern scholars of Norman history and literature tend to ignore this overt comparison between the two rulers in favor of Henry's depiction of the Normans as one of the five plagues sent by God, the first being the Romans, which they see as evidence of his condemnation of the Normans and their authority over England.[68] It is important to look at the rest of the picture, however: Henry later claims that the Romans "ruled splendidly by right of conquest,"[69] and that the Normans "by right of kingship granted to the conquered their life, liberty, and ancient laws"[70] because they "were justified according to the law of peoples, in both claiming and gaining possession of England."[71] The Normans came to power "at God's command, so that evil would befall the ungodly"; furthermore, "he had decided to exterminate [the English people] for their compelling crimes, just as the Britons were humbled when their sins accused them."[72] Thus, in Henry's account, some of the "plagues" sent by God are not to be viewed as a pestilence, but rather as a healthful purgative, like bloodletting as a cure for disease.[73] In his unusual interpretation of *translatio imperii*, Henry maintains that it is necessary for God to send worthy rulers, who rule by the civilized means of law, to claim the rich land once its existing inhabitants prove themselves undeserving of the bounty of their island paradise. For Henry and the Anglo-Norman kings, furthermore, this empire is justifiable because of the legacy of Charlemagne and his rule brought about by "the right hand of the Most High," which they, and they alone, have inherited. In their sacral capacity, according to Henry of Huntingdon, the Norman kings were able to restore justice in England, especially along the *viae regiae*, which had become the King's Four Highways.

The nature of this kingship is a complicated one, however, weaving royal law and sacral authority with the image of the king as *imperator*. The Normans took quite literally the concept of the *via regia*, which was developed into a model of kingship by the Carolingians. Thus, the *via regia* is at once the royal road, the public space that the king protects with his strong laws, and the symbol of his power. In promoting this idea in the law codes, histories, and other literary works, they also advanced their ambitions to empire-building in Britain: the map that Henry draws in his myth of the Four Highways, which span the length and breadth of the island of Britannia, clearly reveals the Anglo-Normans' tenacious aspirations to overlordship of all the British lands. This would become more than a myth for subsequent generations of Anglo-Norman kings; it would inspire them to make it a certainty, further writing their claims on the symbolic topography of the land itself, not only with roads, but with castles.

Charlemagne's Imperial Memory and the Symbolic Landscape: Geoffrey of Monmouth's Castles

Like the Roman roads that stretched across Britain and played an integral part in the Normans' symbolic visualization of *imperium*, the ruins of Roman villas that dotted the landscape—and the authority of the *romanitas* that they represented—would also be exploited as the Normans established and expanded their empire. One aspect of Anglo-Norman kingship that has fascinated both medieval and modern students of history is the impressive program of castle-building and urban development that William I initiated upon taking the throne of England. In the first quarter of the twelfth century, for example, Orderic Vitalis attributed part of William's success in promoting peace in England after the Conquest to his ambitious program of castle-building: "To meet the danger the king rode to all the remote parts of his kingdom and fortified strategic sites against enemy attacks. For the fortifications called castles by the Normans were scarcely known in the English provinces, and so the English—in spite of their courage and love of fighting—could put up only a weak resistance to their enemies."[74] This image of castles as symbols of oppressive military occupation, as Robert Liddiard notes, "still dominates popular and scholarly opinion; indeed, it is difficult to underestimate the extent to which the idea that the Norman Conquest was a ruthless military take-over is deeply ingrained within English historiography."[75] The castles themselves, however, reveal a different ideology at work in William I's ambitious building program: a desire for legitimacy and imperial continuity. This objective is evident in both the sites and the choice of building materials, especially in the early phases of development in the eleventh century. Moreover, the architecture itself is reminiscent of Carolingian exemplars in such a way as to reveal the Normans' desire to promote their legitimacy in both an Insular and a Continental context. In building their castles, the Normans reused Anglo-Saxon lordly sites, known as *burhs*, as well as Roman spolia in imitation of Carolingian building practices to underscore their legitimacy and intimate continuity with Anglo-Saxon authority and to project an image of imperial power. Thus, the castle in England would ultimately serve Anglo-Norman writers such as Geoffrey of Monmouth as a symbolic landscape for the promotion of a Norman "new Troy," an imperial ideal that plays upon the imagery of a "new Rome" that was exploited by the Carolingians for Charlemagne's capital at Aachen.

Although the Anglo-Saxons lived "in a landscape punctuated by the remains of a Roman stone world that was falling into ruin," early Anglo-Saxons "had little use for the architectural remains of Roman rule."[76] As a result, their contact with and emulation of Rome would exist within a postconversion Christian context. Because they preferred rural sites to urban centers and villas and had limited experience in building in brick and stone, Roy Liuzza notes that "these Roman buildings were taken as the mysterious work of giants, *enta geweorc*, and their builders de-historicized from the Romanized Britons whom the Anglo-Saxons had dispossessed into the inhabitants of a generic heroic age."[77] This perspective would change for later Anglo-Saxons as they appropriated the Roman materials to imbue their own structures with the authority of Rome, but their building in stone would be largely limited to religious architecture. The vast majority of structures that were built after the withdrawal of Roman troops were of organic materials such as timber and cob; it was not until the arrival of missionaries from Rome in the late sixth, seventh, and eighth centuries that the art of building in stone was reintroduced.[78] Anglo-Saxon churchmen frequently used Roman ruins in religious architecture to emphasize imperial continuity and earthly mutability, because the ruins were "loaded with memory."[79] In a similar way but in a secular context, the Normans utilized a hybrid style of architecture not only to underscore their authority in England and their right to rule, but to clearly demonstrate that their creation of a "new Rome" at London superseded the antiquity and glory of the Roman Empire.

The desire on the Continent, however, to appropriate imperial authority by building on preexisting lordly sites and imitating imperial Roman practices can be traced to the first generations after the fall of Rome. The civilized appeal of the trappings of Roman *imperium* lingered long after its collapse and would continue to be exploited in a variety of contexts, both secular and Christian. In the early centuries after the fall of the Roman Empire in the West, the title of *imperator* came to be used by any ruler of multiple dependent kingdoms, especially one who came into power through military conquest.[80] Subsequent rulers, therefore, strove to align themselves ideologically with Rome and its power, in imitation of an empire to which they hoped to appear as equal in prestige, especially through the employment of images of Roman rule, such as portraits on coins, seals, dress, insignia of office, and flattering epithets. When Pope Leo III crowned Charlemagne emperor in 800, the ceremony in Rome added a whole new dimension to the early medieval idea of *imperium* by enhancing the title's prestige as an appointed office "redolent of Roman Antiquity"[81] and creating a ritual from this illustrious past to secure his position in the present, as well as the position of the pope who anointed him.

Similarly, during the early sixth century, Theodoric strove to restore the Roman Empire and its culture to its former greatness, however much his rule may have been a fusion of Roman and Gothic styles in reality. He is quoted by Cassiodorus as saying, "Our kingship is an imitation of yours, modeled on your good design, a copy of the only Empire. By as much as we follow you, so much we precede all other peoples."[82] Part of his efforts included building and restoring the cities of Rome and Ravenna, his capital; the church of S. Apollinare Nuovo in Ravenna, to mention one example that would have an influence on later architectural styles (including that of Charlemagne's palace at Aachen), was "originally built as his palace church . . . [and] follows the outlines of buildings fifty years earlier."[83] Theodoric's desire to demonstrate Roman imperial continuity was also echoed in the early art and architecture of Frankish Gaul, where Childeric's tomb portrait (c. 482) shows him in Roman military dress with a lance balanced on one shoulder, which "clearly imitates the armor and spear-bearing gesture of fourth- and fifth-century imperial coins of which several were found" in the tomb.[84] It is noteworthy that his son,

Clovis, inherited Childeric's appreciation for imperial symbolism: as the first Orthodox Christian ruler of the Franks, to whom Gregory of Tours referred as a "new Constantine" at his baptism, he founded a burial church dedicated to the holy apostles "in clear imitation of the first Christian emperor."[85] Thus, for the Franks, emulation of Roman imperial rhetoric and architecture intensified as they rose in power in the West and envisioned themselves as inheritors of Rome's glory; as they unified more and more regions and peoples under their aegis, they projected a vision of themselves as *imperators* and conquerors in Rome's image.

Of all the Frankish kings, Charlemagne in particular promoted the notion of his rule as a resurrection of Roman imperialism with a Frankish emphasis, as evident in the frequent appearance of the epithet *novus Constantinus*, first used by Pope Hadrian I as early as 778.[86] The progression of his building program, from Paderborn to Ingelheim to Aachen, reflects "the evolution of Charlemagne from Germanic king to Roman ruler."[87] Like the Norman castles in England centuries later, the Carolingian palace was utilized as a fundamental instrument of royal rule, and therefore it was essential that it present an unassailable image of authority. Because of this, Paderborn, architecturally a fusion of Germanic and Roman styles, was built over the remains of a Saxon settlement; in spite of Saxon rebellions that destroyed it on two separate occasions, Charlemagne persisted and rebuilt the palace on its earlier foundations, each time making only minor alterations to the original plan.[88] Not only was Charlemagne projecting a daunting image of his authority as a king who always triumphs over his foes, but his perseverance in maintaining that impression also sent a clear message to his enemies that his imperial power would not be easily overcome. This implication is further emphasized by his palace at Ingelheim, where Charlemagne used as his model a major imperial monument in the region, the forum in Cologne. The Saxon Poet claimed that the marble columns of the palace were brought from Rome and Ravenna, and the frescoes within, as described by Ermoldus Nigellus, place Charlemagne and earlier Frankish kings among the great rulers of Rome, thus presenting Charlemagne's kingship as directly descending from the authority of the emperors of antiquity. Clearly, the imperial program that would become a reality in the beginning of the ninth century was already being shaped well before Charlemagne's imperial coronation in Rome.

Architecturally speaking, this idea is gloriously demonstrated by Charlemagne's capital palace at Aachen, built just before the end of the eighth century: meant to rival Rome and Constantinople, the structure was not only built on a former Roman site but emulated Roman architecture through its copying of various structures in Ravenna, Rome, and Constantinople,[89] the use of Roman spolia, and its strict conformity to the layout of Roman towns.[90] The use of spolia was not just a practical concern, however; Constantine's purpose, as he claimed, was to adorn his palace with precious marble and to build "with the maximum possible labor and expense."[91] To accomplish this end, Charlemagne specifically imported materials from Ravenna and Rome, even though there were Roman ruins closer to Aachen from which he could have taken them.[92] It can be difficult at times to discern the purposes for reuse of materials, from the practical to the ideological, but it is not always necessary, as the two ideas are not mutually exclusive. As Tim Eaton, Abigail Wheatley, and others have shown, the practical and economic reasons for recycling Roman materials and imitating Roman building practices do not eliminate the possibility of interpreting the reuse from a symbolic or ideological standpoint. Indeed, in several cases, the care and expense of transporting spolia, even when other materials are locally available, and imitating Roman building techniques invite interpretation as an expression of *translatio imperii*. On their own, these practices might not always reveal the intentions of the builders, but if they are taken in conjunction with other sources, a compelling argument for the deliberate appropriation of past authority can be made.[93] It must be remembered, however, that according to influential thinkers like Alcuin,[94] Charlemagne's authority did not bow to Rome's. The layout of the palace in relation to the chapel, therefore, underscores his intentions: the chapel was built along an east-west axis, of course, but his main audience hall was set on a parallel axis to the church, with its main apse in the west, not the east,[95] thus sending the unmistakable message that the sun may rise on the church, but it sets on Charlemagne and his imperial authority.

Charlemagne's imperial program, therefore, would contain an important difference from earlier medieval emulation of the glory of Roman antiquity: the writers of his court claimed that not only did his sovereignty over a vast *imperium* equal that of Rome, it would ultimately exceed it in power and sophistication. In their eyes, Rome's star had descended and Charlemagne's was quickly on the rise; Alcuin describes the Rome of his day in one of his poems as the erstwhile "capital and wonder of the world, golden Rome," of which "only a barbarous ruin now remains."[96] Charlemagne's palace and chapel at Aachen, as mentioned earlier, were constructed in the 790s on the site of Roman ruins and hailed as a "second Rome" in the Virgilian epic *Karolus Magnus et Leo Papa*, a panegyric written to commemorate the legendary meeting at Paderborn between the king and Pope Leo III just prior to Charlemagne's being declared emperor:

King Charles, head of the world, love and adornment of his people,
venerable summit of Europe, very best father, hero,
Emperor, and also sovereign of a city where a second Rome
flowers anew, rising to great heights with its massive walls,
the lofty cupolas on its walls touching the stars.[97]

Here, Charlemagne's power extends not only over the world but also into heaven itself. Thus, the poet challenges the very standing of the pope as Holy Father and intercessor for mankind to God and places Charlemagne in a superior position to the bishop of Rome,[98] a notion reflected in the palace's position in relation to the chapel at Aachen. Additionally, the poem describes Charlemagne as "a second but mightier Aeneas,"[99] and its account of his construction at Aachen, the symbol of his greater *imperium*, echoes Virgil's narrative of Aeneas's building of Carthage.[100] The poem as a whole, moreover, "does not simply imitate its model; it consciously attempts to outdo it" in its effort to demonstrate that Charlemagne is superior to Rome's legendary founder,[101] just as the poet claims Charlemagne is superior in learning and eloquence to Cato, Mark, Homer, and all the "masters of old."[102] Similar language to that of *Karolus Magnus et Leo Papa* is used to describe Aachen and its king in another contemporary work, the *Egloga* of Moduin of Autun, a poet of Charlemagne's court:

My Palaemon [Charlemagne] looks out from the lofty citadel of the new Rome
and sees all the kingdoms forged into an empire through his victories.
Our times are transformed into the civilisation of Antiquity.
Golden Rome is reborn and restored anew to the world![103]

Moduin's poem is a debate between an old man, "Senex," and a young one, "Puer," used to couch political praise of Charlemagne in the style of Virgil and Calpurnius. Senex consistently slights the enthusiastic and often unsophisticated panegyric of Puer, but Puer has the last—successful—word in the poem, underscoring in the narrative the poem's theme of the superiority of the new Carolingian imperial civilization to that of the old as he cries, "Yield, old man, vanquished at last by the weapons of a boy!"[104] The fact that biographical critics of the poem have not been able to find a historical candidate for Senex further suggests that Puer, identified as Moduin himself, is debating with "the classical past" as an iconic figure.

What is important to recognize in these two remarkably similar passages is their focus on the *re*-creation of Rome, not at the site of the pope's city but in its idealized successor, the palace of Charlemagne's making on the foundation of Roman ruins in Aachen: in doing so, the two poets appropriate the glory of "Golden Rome" for Charlemagne by highlighting the transfer of power and influence from the former empire to its new successor, and they also diminish significantly the importance of the pope and his Rome in the process. Although Charlemagne and the Normans both appropriated the civilized aura of Roman antiquity in creating their sacred landscapes, they were mindful of the distinction between Rome, the empire of classical antiquity, and Rome, the contemporary political territory coming into its own as a Western Christian center separate from the Eastern one of Byzantium, and they strove to remain clear of its entangling political complexity while making the most of the legitimacy such an association transferred to themselves.[105] When Charlemagne invested "his new-found title [of emperor] with the rhetorical mantle of historical authentication" by placing the motto of "the renewal of the Roman Empire" on his seal in the spring of 801,[106] he instituted a program to advance the new image of *imperator* that made the most of his connection with Rome while still maintaining his autonomy as ruler. After his visit in the winter of 800–801, he never saw Rome again. In exploiting the benefits of *imperium* while maintaining a non-Rome-centered empire, Charlemagne instituted a form of kingship that would be emulated all over Europe for generations to come: as Julia M. H. Smith notes, for example, Alfred of Wessex "found useful precedent in Carolingian ideologies of royal authority,"[107] and the *ordo* for Edgar's coronation ceremony at Bath in 973 relied heavily on the images of sacral kingship from Carolingian and Ottonian exemplars.[108] It was the Normans, however, who imitated his program of imperial propaganda most closely in England, as seen in their emphasis on creating topographies of power derived from Charlemagne's ideal of "historical authentication" that appropriated the authority of Rome in order to demonstrate further how they surpassed it. Echoing Charlemagne's ideology of *imperium*, which proclaimed Aachen a "new Rome," defining his sovereignty as greater than that of the Romans and their civilized achievements, they deliberately exploited their hybrid legacy, combining the image of the symbolic landscape of England with that of the former greatness of the Roman Empire, suggesting that the kingdom would become even greater under their own powerful rule.

When the Normans first arrived in England, the idea of the castle there was still a new one, and any mention of pre-Conquest *castels* was largely associated with Edward the Confessor's Norman followers and treated as a "foreign" importation.[109] William I and his nobles were the first to use stone regularly in a secular context in England, echoing the practice on the Continent, where Carolingian architecture, especially the great halls built of stone at Charlemagne's capital at Aachen and elsewhere, was increasingly being copied.[110] In so doing, they exercised power in spatial dimensions, especially in the symbolic landscape, which would become a foundational symbol of *translatio* as the Normans infused themselves into Insular society and history. Thus, the symbolic landscape of the castle, especially those structures that utilized preexisting sites of Roman and Anglo-Saxon power as well as Roman spolia in emulation of Charlemagne's building program, represented a hybrid approach to achieving imperial civilization and its unifying strength, order, and stability.

The first stage of castle-building after the Conquest was the foundation of royal castles. The vast majority of these early castles were built in the centers of local government; twenty-four of the thirty-six castles known to have been built by William I were associated in some way with existing urban centers,[111] and twenty of these were built within or against the defenses of the town.[112] These sites were chosen not for convenience or to control the roads at key intersections, as might be supposed, but "to dominate and control urban population and . . . to overawe the citizens"; of course, "most eventually became centres for public administration,"[113] much as the Carolingian palaces themselves did. O. H. Creighton argues that "we should not overlook the immense psychological impact of castle-building in Saxon power bases,"[114] since several of the early royal castles were built on sites, both rural and urban, that had political and cultural significance for their predecessors. These sites were primarily Anglo-Saxon lordly seats and fortifications known as *burhs*, which could indicate urban works raised by West Saxon kings or rural residences of the pre-Conquest thegnly aristocracy.[115] The urban *burhs* were large communal enclosures that had locally considerable concentrations of population with substantial economic and governmental roles. The rural aristocratic *burhs* or residences seem to have served little military purpose and may have been ceremonial, for display purposes.

There is increasing evidence showing that a number of William's castles were placed over existing high-status structures to project his new royal authority. The Domesday Book states that at Wallingford one noble "holds the land where the housecarls lived," which indicates, in Robert Liddiard's view, that the castle was raised over a pre-Conquest high-status structure.[116] An important example of Norman practices in comparison to Anglo-Saxon is evident at the site at Cheddar, frequently regarded as a great Anglo-Saxon royal palace. Initially a religious community with a double minster of men and women, it was built on a site of possible Roman significance, evidenced by the presence of a villa adjoining the church itself and other Roman materials found nearby.[117] The crown annexed Cheddar's surrounding estates over a period of a few decades until we see, in the mid-tenth century, an assembly at the hall there referred to as being held *in palatio regis in Ceodre*.[118] John Blair concludes that "the buildings excavated at Cheddar are best seen as the physical signs of royal life encroaching in upon the fringes of monastic life, and eventually swallowing it up."[119] What is further significant about Cheddar, however, is that it is referred to in Domesday as an ancient holding of the king, and the Anglo-Saxon West Hall was subsequently replaced by a post-Conquest East Hall and a later thirteenth-century stone hall. This kind of progression, of a Romano-British site being overlaid by a prominent Saxon *burh*, which is later supplanted by post-Conquest stone towers and halls, is repeated at other sites such as at Goltho,[120] demonstrating a very definite pattern of systematic reuse of Anglo-Saxon lordly sites for the assertion of Norman power.

The continuity of form between these early castles and urban *burhs* did not last long after the initial period of Norman settlement, however:[121] elements of the Anglo-Saxon *burh-geat* structure were integrated into early Norman castle entrance towers[122] and even later incorporated into the stone keep or *donjon*, which was introduced from the Continent, such as at Richmond, in order to symbolically display Norman sovereignty.[123] In spite of its cliff-edge position, Richmond Castle historically had little military involvement; tucked into a bend in the River Swale and situated away from communications routes, it was instead "an essential part of establishing, maintaining, and enhancing economic and territorial control."[124] And much of this control is inherent in the aura of lordly power that the castle itself projects as a result of its appropriation and emulation of the image of previous powerful rulers. When William I began one of the earliest and most ambitious secular building projects at Colchester in 1076,[125] therefore, he chose the building site and materials with the greatest of care: not only was Colchester possibly "the core of a late Saxon *villa regalis* (royal manor) within which the royal castle was raised for symbolic and political reasons," but the castle was raised on the site of a former Roman temple dedicated to the emperor-god Claudius and built using stone plundered from the nearby Roman town of Caerwent. Moreover, the castle keep itself has "clear architectural links to the great Carolingian palaces of northern France and was thus a conspicuous symbol of William's imperial ambitions."[126] By incorporating Roman masonry and using bands of colored stone in the construction, like those utilized by Romans themselves, the builders of Colchester Castle even went so far as to imitate Roman building practices, thereby emphasizing imperial continuity.[127] This same technique was used slightly earlier on the border of Wales at the castle of Chepstow, which differed significantly from the construction of Chepstow priory, where builders created the façade of the priory using freshly quarried sandstone blocks *à la mode Caennaise*, the latest architectural style on the Continent, even though Roman stone was available for the construction of the priory as well.[128] What is unique about Chepstow Castle, however, is the fact that the Roman stone was only used on the north, south, and west sides of the keep, those sides facing Wales, but not on the eastern face, directed toward England. This evocative and lasting statement indicates the Normans' early ambition to build empires throughout Britain, as symbolized by the building of castles as markers of lordly power perhaps even more than as effective military strongholds.

The multilayered symbolism of William's castles is most suggestively demonstrated, moreover, at Rougemont, the earliest example of an urban stone castle, in spite of its being one of the least impressive constructions in terms of defensive capability, compared to the motte-and-bailey castles, or size and grandeur, compared to, for example, Colchester Castle.[129] William's message in the creation of Rougemont, built at Exeter in 1068 after a failed rebellion spurred by taxation, is more elegant and subtle than those at Chepstow and Colchester, but would have nevertheless resonated deeply with the city's populace: the gatehouse was built in the manner of a pre-Conquest *burh-geat*, a display tower used not so much for defense as for a marker of rank, facing inwards toward the people of Exeter as an enduring monument to William's power and place as Edward the Confessor's successor. That William's message was not lost on subsequent generations is revealed by the author of the *Gesta Stephani* in the mid-twelfth century, who describes Exeter as being "fortified with towers of hewn limestone constructed by the emperors [Caesars]."[130] Like William's other early castles, Rougemont was constructed on Roman remains, here the Roman city of Isca Dumnoniorum, and two sides of the castle were built into the existing city walls, thus preserving and appropriating in the same moment the city's imperial and Anglo-Saxon history for his own legacy in stone. Robert Liddiard concludes, "Thus at Exeter we see a curious blend of continuity and change: a dramatic assertion of authority, but what might be termed, in Charles Coulson's phrase, 'peaceable power.'"[131] This hybrid ideology is further enhanced in the visual impact of Rougemont's resemblance to the west face of Charlemagne's palace at Aachen,[132] which was itself a part of Charlemagne's own vigorous program of imperialist propaganda, which embraced a combination of styles to better enhance his authority.

Rather than appropriating the authority of the Roman Empire by incorporating it into contemporary Christian philosophies, as did the Anglo-Saxons, the Normans followed Charlemagne's custom of non-Rome-centered *imperium* by first absorbing Roman civilization and power and then professing to exceed the Romans in imperial accomplishments. The result was an ideological shift in the literature of England after the Conquest. Perhaps because Rome's cultural and political significance by the year 1000 was, for the most part, religious in nature,[133] the Anglo-Normans looked to Charlemagne as a model *imperator*, focusing on his image as the emperor of a "second Rome," symbolized by his palace at Aachen.[134] For the twelfth-century Anglo-Normans writing of their sacred landscape, Charlemagne's authority rivaled that of the Romans: as previously noted, William of Malmesbury claimed that in 1080 Robert Losinga, the Norman bishop of Hereford, consciously imitated Charlemagne's cathedral at Aachen when he rebuilt the cathedral that had been destroyed by the Welsh.[135] As W. Eugene Kleinbauer notes, the cathedral bears little resemblance to Aachen in reality, but the modern idea of an architectural copy indicating actual physical reproduction did not apply in the Middle Ages.[136] Thus, statements like William's reflect "the widespread fame of Charlemagne's exciting monument and testify to its politico-religious significance";[137] though Hereford Cathedral's resemblance to Aachen may be symbolic, William I's castle of Rougemont at Exeter resembles it in reality.

The appropriation of Carolingian imperial history to reinforce Anglo-Norman legitimacy and project an image of power and influence can be found throughout the literature of the twelfth century. The writers of Charlemagne's court and the following generations changed the tone of imperial rhetoric from admiring imitation, as exemplified by the claims of Theodoric mentioned earlier, to demonstrate a new world order that does not simply mimic the glory of Rome, but surpasses it.[138] Notker the Stammerer, writing in the late ninth century for Charles the Fat, expands upon this sentiment in his *vita*, *De Carolo Magno*. Stressing that Charlemagne's *imperium* rests on cultural as well as ethical achievements,[139] Notker opens his work by praising the great ruler as a divinely appointed emperor sent to replace the Romans, whom God has destroyed: "He who ordains the fate of kingdoms and the march of the centuries, the all-powerful Disposer of Events, having destroyed one extraordinary image, that of the Romans, which had, it was true, feet of iron, or even feet of clay, then raised up, among the Franks, the golden head of a second image, equally remarkable, in the person of the illustrious Charlemagne."[140] Notker also asserts that the capital at Aachen, which "Charlemagne, Emperor and Caesar Augustus, caused to be constructed on a magnificent scale,"[141] is "finer than the ancient buildings of the Romans."[142] According to Simon MacLean, Notker creates "a concept of *renovatio imperii* which pitched its claim neither as purely Christian nor a Roman empire: the Frankish empire of Charlemagne was universal, and stood at the pinnacle of world and sacred history."[143]

We see these same ideas echoed by William of Poitiers, who was particularly sensitive to the relevant ideologies that would bolster the post-Conquest Normans' search for imperial legitimacy due to his rare understanding of both medieval and classical *imperium*. His experiences, both as a knight in his youth and as one of William's chaplains, and his extensive familiarity with classical authors permeate his eulogy of William I in the *Gesta Guillelmi*.[144] For William of Poitiers, Duke William surpasses the glory of the Roman Caesars in valor and martial prowess. Furthermore, he demonstrates that the duke's qualities of leadership, which surpassed the greatest of emperors, destined him to be the salvation of the English and to restore their glory.[145] William's protracted comparison of Julius Caesar's difficult subjugation of Britain to William I's easy victory inverts the topos of Roman historiography regarding the unresisting surrender of foreign kings to the Romans,[146] and it diminishes Julius Caesar's image as an *imperator*. While detailing how the duke is superior in every way to the Roman emperor, William pointedly asks, "What then did [Caesar] accomplish that deserves the praise to be given to the man of whom we are writing?"[147] The answer, of course, is that Julius Caesar's great accomplishments were far overshadowed by those of Duke William, who is therefore clearly more deserving of praise such as he received in the *Gesta* and of the empire that he claimed; likewise, his empire will reflect his superiority and usher in a new imperial age that will be celebrated for generations to come. It can be inferred from William's panegyric that the Normans absorbed the Carolingian rhetoric of *renovatio imperii* into their own imperial ideology; thus, in the history of the Normans' own "empire," the Carolingian stamp is unmistakable in their exploitation of the idea of a new or second Rome.

This idea is given an interesting twist by Geoffrey of Monmouth slightly later in the twelfth century. Because of its reputation as the "history" that introduced the legend of King Arthur as a British king, his influential work *Historia regum Britanniae* is not normally a text to which one might immediately turn to examine the Normans' Carolingian imperial legacy, and yet Gordon Hall Gerould once claimed that "Geoffrey formed Arthur in the image of Charlemagne."[148] Even Roger Sherman Loomis, in his blustery response to Gerould's essay, rather grudgingly admits that "[i]t is most likely that Geoffrey was *partially* inspired by the purpose of furnishing the Norman kings with a predecessor as exalted as Charlemagne" (emphasis in original) and that "Geoffrey was not unmindful of the parallel which his Arthur presented in a vague fashion to Charlemagne."[149] This is not to say that Arthur supplanted Charlemagne in prestige at this time, since his importance as an illustrious ancestor would not proliferate until a couple of generations later, but that his prominence as a leader who can conquer even the Roman emperor reaffirmed the dual legacy of Anglo-Norman legitimacy as they began to align themselves with these two powerful rulers. Geoffrey's Arthur represents the kind of hybrid *translatio imperii* that the writers of Charlemagne's court were mindful of: the promotion of an illustrious ancestral heritage that would reinforce and endorse the authority of the current regime, whether in Wales or England, or even in Rome.

Geoffrey of Monmouth's history is a crossbred concoction itself, emulating the great Insular historiographers such as Bede and Gildas while also incorporating Celtic legend, classical epic, and wholesale fabrication. In imitation of Charlemagne's greatness, for example, Geoffrey has many kings bow down before Geoffrey's Arthur "either in fealty or fear,"[150] and records the Twelve Peers of France among Arthur's vassals.[151] Considering the popularity of works like the *Chanson de Roland*, the earliest written version of which was produced at Oxford around the time that Geoffrey was writing in the 1130s,[152] there can be little doubt that Charlemagne provided an imperial benchmark against which other rulers, mythological or historical, might be measured. But it is important to recognize in this context that Geoffrey's Arthur is projected onto a Continental stage, and his near-conquering of Rome underscores the imperial anxiety that pervaded Anglo-Norman culture in the first half of the twelfth century. The rumor of Norman imperialist desire certainly informed the general opinion of the Normans on the Continent during William I's reign; Lambert of Hersfeld reports in his *Annales* entry for 1074 that Hanno, archbishop of Cologne, encouraged William I to take possession of the royal seat at Aachen.[153] Geoffroi Gaimar, writing his revisionist Insular history at about the same time as Geoffrey, implies that William Rufus had set his sights on controlling all of France, and Rome as well, to "reclaim his ancient rights to the country, which Belinus and Brennius before him had enjoyed there."[154] Belinus and Brennius were the legendary kings of Britain who conquered Rome, according to Geoffrey.[155] Clearly, the imperial ideology of Charlemagne is still very much in the atmosphere of post-Conquest political culture; in the spirit of the Carolingian revitalization of *imperium*, however, Geoffrey of Monmouth's *Historia regum Britanniae*, rather than simply reproducing Rome in an Insular context, neatly sidesteps Rome as an imperial ancestor by inventing a parallel, rival empire in Britain to the one created by Aeneas in Rome, a "second Troy" established instead in London.

Geoffrey's myth of origins recalls the Carolingians' own investment in the idea of their own Trojan origins,[156] which paralleled but did not necessarily spring from Aeneas's experience in Rome: in the mid-seventh century, Fredegar, in a bold move that evaded the question of Roman political ancestry and established the Franks as Roman cousins of sorts, traced the origins of the Carolingians back to the Trojans as descendants of Priam.[157] Nearly a century later, an unrelated account of Frankish origins in the *Liber Historiae Francorum* also goes back to Priam, but includes Antenor in the myth.[158] Slightly later, in the *Vita Arnulfi*, Paul the Deacon strays from his narrative of Arnulf's life to mention that the name of one of the saint's sons, Anchisus, is derived from Anchises, the father of Aeneas, because the Franks are descended from the Trojans.[159] What is distinctive about Paul's account is his saint's subsequent prophecy that Anchisus's progeny (Pepin, Charles Martel, and so on to Charlemagne) would be so blessed that the kingship of the Franks would be transferred to them. As Rosamond McKitterick argues, Paul's connection of the Carolingian house with the Trojans also provides an opportunity to reunite the "two branches of the Trojan diaspora" by "describing Charlemagne as the conqueror of Italy and ruler of Rome."[160] Thus, Carolingian historiographers created an alternate history where Charlemagne is able to appropriate imperial glory without owing his achievement entirely to Rome, an idea that would resonate with the Anglo-Normans as well.

Geoffrey of Monmouth's Carolingian legacy is most forcefully evident in the imagery of Brutus's divinely inspired dream at the oracle of Diana, in which the goddess exhorts him with Roman imperial rhetoric to found a new empire with his company of Trojan refugees:

Brutus, to the west, beyond the kingdoms of Gaul,
lies an island of the ocean, surrounded by the sea;
an island of the ocean, where giants once lived,
but now it is deserted and waiting for your people.
Sail to it; it will be your home for ever.
It will furnish your children with another Troy.
From your descendants will arise kings, who
Will be masters of the whole world.[161]

Brutus, after having "at last set eyes upon his kingdom," decides to build his imperial city upon the river Thames, which he calls not "new Rome" but "new Troy."[162] In Francis Ingledew's view, Geoffrey's history relocates the Anglo-Saxon genealogical model, which proceeds from Noah through Woden, to France by "grounding his history in a classical source and imitating the already long-held Frankish belief in their Trojan origins,"[163] much like Dudo of Saint Quentin, who displaced the Scandinavian material of the Normans. Using the Carolingian imperial archetype, Geoffrey's alternative portrayal of the genesis of a British *imperium* allows for "another" Troy (*altere Troia*) in a pristine land and opens a new space for an empire that existed long before that of Rome, which is ultimately doomed to fail. In doing so, Geoffrey's "new Troy" is superior to that of Rome from its inception. An imperial city is not complete without grandiose architecture, like Charlemagne's Aachen, and in most manuscripts it is Brutus himself who so loves his city that he "circles it with walls" and "strengthens it with high towers."[164] Generations later, after Brennius and Belinus defeat Rome and Belinus returns to Britain, the new co-*imperator* makes in Trinovantum "a wonderful gate beside the Thames," which will be called Billingsgate by future generations, and above it he builds "a huge tower,"[165] which has been generally associated with the White Tower of London.[166] There is a remarkable similarity between Colchester and the White Tower in London, built at the same time, and their likeness to the apsidal projection of Charlemagne's palace chapel at Aachen further emphasizes the imperial ideology behind their construction.[167]

It is perhaps a great irony that the White Tower, built in the 1070s at the order of William I as an imperial symbol to support his presence in the city and promote his sovereignty,[168] would be given an ancient and illustrious imperial heritage to rival the greatest cities on the Continent, but Geoffrey's Trojan foundation legend imbues the tower with an authenticity that bypasses Rome's authority through an association with an imperial antiquity that predates Rome's. Subsequently, the narrative macrostructure of the *Historia* is shaped largely by the power struggle between these two rival empires, while its microstructure focuses on the transfer of authority between individual kings. The usual assumption about Diana's prophecy to Brutus is that the descendant who will subdue the world refers to Arthur, largely as a result of a misunderstanding of Geoffrey's statement at Arthur's death regarding his being carried off to Avalon, combined with a hopeful interpretation of the *Historia*'s various prophecies that are generally considered to foretell Arthur's return. It must be observed, however, that Geoffrey never explicitly predicts Arthur's return: we are only told that the dying king is carried off to Avalon to have his "mortal wounds" treated,[169] and generations later an angel tells Cadualadrus, the last native king of Britain, to abandon his plans to regain his throne because "God did not want the Britons to rule over the island of Britain any longer." The angelic voice qualifies this prediction with the caveat "until the time came which Merlin had foretold to Arthur,"[170] a prediction that appears to be spurious once the reader realizes that such a prophecy does not exist in Geoffrey's *Historia*, nor even in the *Prophetiae Merlini* that are specifically about Arthur.

Merlin's prophecies are central to both the physical structure of the text itself and our understanding of it, functioning as the linchpin between the narratives of the rise and the fall of the Britons; Michael Faletra notes that they are "deliberately obscurantist" in order to offer "the promise of Briton resurgence only to stifle it."[171] Arthur never completes his conquest of Rome, in spite of progressing all the way to its gates, because of Modred's treachery, which causes him to return to Britain and fail in his quest for empire; additionally, it is quite clear at the end of the *Historia* that the Britons, as a people, have degenerated to such an extent that they no longer deserve to have control over the island: "Being overrun now with barbarism, they were no longer called Britons, but *Gualenses*, Welshmen; a name derived either from Gualo their leader, or Guales their queen, or from their barbarism."[172] Geoffrey makes plain here that the Welsh are no longer true Britons because they have devolved into a barbaric Other, which renders their claim to lordship of Britain a questionable one at best. This privilege, however, will be taken up by subsequent inhabitants of the island empire who are more deserving of the mantle of power. Geoffrey's apocalyptic narrative regarding the Britons turns its attention abruptly to the positive qualities of their conquerors, the Saxons, and thus *imperium* is justifiably transferred to the new peoples of the island, because the "Saxons acted more wisely, living in peace and harmony, tilling the fields and rebuilding the cities and towns; thus, with British overlordship overthrown, they came to rule all Loegria, led by Athelstan, who was the first of them to wear its crown. The Welsh, unworthy successors to the noble Britons, never recovered mastery over the whole island."[173] We know, however, that the Saxons will also ultimately be defeated by William and his Norman followers, so the understanding then is that the king who will subdue the earth has yet to come. As a myth of origins and a justification of *imperium*, Geoffrey's narrative pattern throughout the *Historia* of the power struggle between Britain, as the "new Troy," and Rome urges us to look not only westward, to Wales, but also eastward, to the Roman Empire. These final paragraphs, combined with Diana's prophecy and the idea that was in the air within decades of the Conquest regarding Norman desire for sovereignty throughout France and even Rome and beyond, suggest that the colonization of Wales was perceived as practically a *fait accompli* because of the Welsh people's degenerate nature and God's will that the Britons not reign in Britain any longer. The bigger concern for the Normans, therefore, was solidifying control of England in order to expand their Continental empire. In a chronicle obsessed with naming and renaming in the progression of *imperium*, the fact that the Britons in Britain are no longer known as such, but are called Welsh, "barbarians," is also important: the angel additionally tells Cadualadrus that "through his blessing the British people would one day recover the island, when the prescribed time came, but that this would not happen before the British removed Cadualadrus' relics from Rome and brought them to Britain."[174] The implication here is that the true Britons would be those who brought "Cadualadrus' relics" home from Rome, but it is not explicitly stated that this would be the Welsh, or Arthur either, for that matter, leaving the answer to the puzzle in doubt for future generations of unnamed "Britons" to resolve. Taken in its context along with such examples as the Carolingian poetry extolling Charlemagne's "new Rome" at Aachen and the construction of castles such as Chepstow and Exeter, therefore, Geoffrey's imperial history for the White Tower of London reflects previous generations' efforts to establish legitimacy by transcending the glory and accomplishments of Rome.

Geoffrey of Monmouth's revision of the tower's history attempted to appeal to the civic pride of the English, erasing any tensions surrounding its purpose and eliminating it as a potential target of discord and unrest, by transforming William I's imperial symbol into their greatest monument and inviting them to embrace the imperial legends that were being promoted after the Conquest. The transformation of the tower into a symbol of imperial unification, however unlikely it may have been in reality, was similar to the twelfth-century evolution of the myth of the King's Four Highways. This idea, which developed from Carolingian treatises on kingship and the preexisting ruins of the Roman roads, was not unlike the ideology that the Normans utilized in their strategy for castle-building in politically volatile territories. This should not surprise us, as early Anglo-Norman kingship was often fraught with difficulty: the kings were continually striving to establish their legitimacy, unify the different peoples of their realms, and consolidate their empire, in the European political world overall as well as in Britain. The physical reminders of Roman imperialism, such as forts, walls, baths, villas, and roads, dotted the landscape of England and served to emphasize the passing nature of earthly *regnum*, but were also appropriated by the Normans to justify their ambition and expansion in the tradition of *translatio imperii*, as others had done before them. A Rome-centered empire did not appeal to the Anglo-Norman kings, however; instead, they looked to the imperial model offered by the unparalleled career of Charlemagne and the Carolingian manipulation of the tradition of *renovatio imperii* to create a new or second Rome at Aachen. Here they found a wealth of material to adapt to their needs, and they made certain to emulate this legendary king in their histories, laws, and practices, adding the patina of a Carolingian style of sacral kingship to the legitimacy of their rule.

3 | Taming the Wild Beast
A New Look at the New Forest

In the two decades between his assumption of the throne of England and the compilation of the Domesday Book in 1086, William I brought several tracts of land, some wooded and some not, under the purview of royal control and established the notorious Forest Law, which existed outside the common law to protect the king's interests.[1] In response to the Forest Law and the New Forest in Hampshire in particular (referenced for the first time in the Domesday Book as *Nova Foresta*), contemporary accounts from the *Anglo-Saxon Chronicle* and later historians such as John of Worcester and Orderic Vitalis decry the king's actions as presumptuous and arrogant. The *Peterborough Chronicle* in particular gives with one hand and takes with the other, using William's creation of the forests as damning evidence for an accusation of cruelty and greed in the midst of a homiletic eulogy praising him for bringing strong peace to the land:[2]

He was fallen into avarice,
and he loved greediness above all.
He set up great game-preserves, and he laid down laws for
    them,
that whosoever killed hart or hind
he was to be blinded.
He forbade [hunting] the harts, so also the boars;
he loved the stags so very much,
as if he were their father;

also he decreed for the hares that they might go free.
His powerful men lamented it, and the wretched men complained of it
but he was so severe that he did not care about the enmity of all of them;
but they must wholly follow the king's will
if they wanted to live or have land—
land or property or his good favour.
Alas, woe, that any man should be so proud,
raise up and reckon himself over all men.[3]

In other ways, however, William was known to be "mild to the good men who loved God" (He wæs milde þam godum mannum þe God lufedon), who were presumably monks like those who were writing the chronicle.[4] The conflict between the two representations of William, one as a lawgiver and a peacemaker and another as a king whose pride and greed caused him to abuse royal privilege, perhaps reveals a great deal about the church's feelings about disenfranchisement in the area of forest rights. It has been argued that the "Rime of King William" (as this end-rhyme poem has been called by some scholars) was the source of twelfth-century antiforest polemics and steeped in the legal rhetoric that informed forest law itself.[5] The *Anglo-Saxon Chronicle*'s ambivalence about William's kingship, especially with regard to the conflict between what was perceived as good law (e.g., protection against theft and injury) and how forest laws deviated from this ideal, indicates that a new examination of England's forests is necessary. Such a study must not only consider the myriad effects of afforestation and the imposition of a new system of law on the English, but also investigate the Normans' purpose in establishing the *foresta*, which they experienced as a function of strong kingship, drawing on what they considered to be Carolingian administrative and legal practices.

By understanding the process by which the forest was essentially politicized and made a theater of royal power rather than a zone where governance ended, we can better understand how Anglo-Norman writers, such as Geoffroi Gaimar and Marie de France, used an idea of the forest derived from Carolingian ideals to negotiate the possibilities and limitations of royal behavior in twelfth-century England. However William may have envisioned a continuation of English custom in his reign, as some of his early writs and charters claim, the reality remained that in many respects he shaped the governance of his duchy and later aspects of his kingdom in emulation of the more recent of his Norman ducal predecessors, which involved the perpetuation of royal power at the expense, frequently, of that of the secular and even religious aristocracy.[6] The changing status of the king rendered the forest a political sphere of activity, and therefore a courtly one, and the social and political tensions engendered by the increasingly strict forest administration over the course of the twelfth century brought the political meaning of the forest to the fore. These changes were not lost on the writers of the twelfth century, for although they were already aware of the classical significance of the forest as a locus of savage wildness and erotic possibility, the forest emerges in the courtly literature instead as an extension of the royal court that combined the civilizing authority and order of the king with the ritualized violence of the hunt. The Carolingian dimension of the Anglo-Norman forest becomes especially clear, therefore, both historically and from a literary perspective, in the conflicts that arose during the course of the twelfth century as the forest came to symbolize the king's projection of his power upon the English landscape.

Keeping It in the *Familia*? Norman Forest Law and Its Carolingian Ancestry

Tracing the influence of Carolingian kingship on Norman ducal practices is not, unfortunately, a clear-cut exercise that reveals a definitive paper trail. Consequently, historians have been divided about the extent of continuity of Carolingian administrative systems in Neustria after the depredation caused by Viking raiders during the ninth century. Some late twentieth-century scholarship favored a view that saw a breakdown of Carolingian institutions and the establishment, during the first generation or two of settlers, of a looser style of government resembling Scandinavian practices, with each war leader protecting his own small territory in the region, with varying degrees of success.[7] Supporters of this view speculate that during William Longsword's tenure as duke of Normandy (c. 927–42), and more certainly that of Richard I (942–96), many Carolingian institutions were restored as ducal prerogatives, for both practical and ideological purposes. Indeed, Gilduin Davy demonstrates that the Normans promoted a "neo-Carolingian" archetype of ducal power that emphasized the similarities between the image of the duke and royal power as practiced by Charlemagne and his heirs.[8] In a charter dating from 990, Richard I's title is styled as "consul,"[9] a Roman title which gives him further prestige not only as a successor to Roman *imperium* but also Frankish: Anastasius bestowed the same title upon Clovis, the founder of the

Merovingian dynasty.[10] Ducal charters and privileges also reflect the style and structure of Carolingian diplomatic exemplars,[11] such that by the reign of Richard II, the idea of the *gens Karolinorum* had been regenerated in the *gens Ricardorum*.[12] Perhaps because of the rehabilitation of these Carolingian structures and images of power, the new duchy stabilized surprisingly quickly, which fostered prosperity and expansion under subsequent generations of Norman dukes. Consequently, the administration of the forest on the Continent was, like so many aspects of eleventh-century Frankish economic and legal systems,[13] inherited from the reign of Charlemagne and developed to suit local needs by the ruling aristocracy.

For the Carolingians, as François-Louis Ganshof demonstrates, hunting reserves (*forestis*) "could in fact embrace lands which had never, or no longer, formed part of the royal patrimony."[14] This reflects a critical difference between Carolingian and Anglo-Saxon practices; in the latter, the right of free capture, in which a hunter was allowed to chase down his wounded quarry without concern about property boundaries, was more common.[15] Bringing the forest within the jurisdiction of the imperial court makes the forest itself a potent symbol of the Carolingian courtly sphere, a political entity redolent of royal power that would become ultimately associated with the idea of kingship itself. Anyone who breached the *forestis* or hunting reserves would be severely punished; moreover, to ensure compliance with these edicts, "the emperor made their observance, and the duty of informing on those who contravened them, matters of fidelity."[16] We see this clearly in the *Capitulare missorum generale*, dated c. 802, where the punishment to be exacted for trangressions in the royal forest is vague, but Charlemagne is very clear on the point of the faithfulness of his subjects in regard to swearing to uphold the law in addition to obeying it, stating:

> So that in our forest no one would dare to steal our game, as I have many times forbidden to be done, now we again strictly forbid that anyone shall do so in the future, just as each man should desire to preserve the fidelity promised to us, so let him take care. But if any count or centenary or bassus or any one of our *ministeriales* steal our game, he shall be brought to our own presence to account for it in full. But if anyone of the remaining people shall have stolen our game, let him pay what is just in full, [and] let no man henceforth be released from this. If, however, anyone knows that this has been done by another, in order that he may preserve the fidelity which he

has promised to us and which he now has to promise, let him not dare to hide the fact.[17]

The notion of fidelity here, indicating not only that a subject would commit no offense against his sovereign but that he would protect his king by not turning a blind eye to the transgressions of other subjects, marks a significant change in the approach to oath-taking during Charlemagne's reign in making the protection of the king and his property an important responsibility for all of his subjects.[18] The extension of this accountability even to the protection of the king's game and other forest "property" further underscores the position of the *forestis* as an important context for the display of power and fidelity.

Forests also became an important source of royal economic power. Charlemagne further expanded on this slightly later in the *Capitulare de villis* (hereafter cited as CV), which dates from later in his reign (early ninth century) and remains an important remnant of Carolingian economic and legal policy. As a set of detailed instructions to his officials regarding the running of his estates and the annual recording of revenue, it is significant for our understanding of the day-to-day accounting of Carolingian wealth and daily life. For purposes of this discussion, the outline of forest management contained within the CV sheds light on our understanding of the uses of capitularies for legislation and suggests how the subsequent development of forest law was perceived as an acceptable aspect of estate management for Carolingian kings and later the Norman dukes. The CV makes clear from the start that its purpose is to guarantee the estates' profits for the king,[19] and thus it establishes a rudimentary form of legislation for estate management. Unlike the vague threats of the *Capitulare missorum generale*, it includes more specific punishments for infractions of its decrees, as it reminds the *missi*, "If one of the men in our service commits a crime of theft or other neglect against us, he will make amends; for the rest will be by law punished by flogging."[20] For those violators not in the service of the king, abuses are furthermore punishable by flogging or other measures as prescribed by law: "For a crime committed by a man other than our own, then strive to serve justice, conforming to the law to which they are subject; for a crime of one of our own men, as we have said, then they shall be whipped. On the other hand, the Franks who reside in our *fiscs* or in our estates, who have committed such a crime, then let them strive to make amends according to their law and whatever they give for their fine shall be put to our use."[21] The Forest Law of England would become a separate law in addition to common law, but the implication is clear here that capitularies such as Charlemagne's CV serve as illustrations of royal prerogative that brought every aspect of the *forestis* and its administration explicitly within the control of the king and the law.[22] As such, it functions as a forerunner to the forest administration that the Normans promoted in the duchy of Normandy in the tenth and eleventh centuries, and would introduce to England after 1066.

Although the CV addresses many aspects of estate management in addition to that of the forest, the foresters are listed second among the offices of the estate, after the deputies, and their prominence underscores their importance in the estate hierarchy and the significance of their office, the responsibilities of which also take precedence in the rest of the CV. One of its longer sections is devoted to the administration of forest alone and represents an early manifestation of the kind of forest administration that William would eventually introduce in England:

> So that our forests be well taken care of, where the place should be cleared woodland, they should do the clearing and not permit fields to increase from the woodland; and where woodland must be, not permit it to be cut down too much and greatly damaged. And they should guard well our wild game in the forests; likewise, they should provide falcons and sparrowhawks to our service; and they should diligently collect our rents there. And if the stewards were to have let their pigs go into our woodland to fatten, or our magnates or their men, they shall themselves first present their tithe to set a good example, such that in future the remaining men fully pay their tithe.[23]

Additionally, the CV records the minute details regarding the accounting of every aspect of the production from the estate and reiterates the census of the forest and its yield, including wood products and poached game.[24] Janet Nelson observes that these basic structures of the Carolingian state endured, in spite of the fragmentation of Charlemagne's empire in the ninth century, because of a "shift from an economy of plunder to an economy of profiteering" from revenues gained through granting ecclesiastical benefices and increasing income from royal lands "through more vigorous management,"[25] which included the utilization of the economic benefits of the *forestis* as well as the ideological reinforcement of royal authority imparted by the ritual of the hunt. Charlemagne's attention to the harvest of the forests as part of the income from the royal estate in the CV highlights its value in this new "economy of profiteering." Its huge potential for revenue was unreservedly exploited by future generations.[26] When William I first introduced the Forest Law to England after 1066, therefore, he was not simply initiating a tyrannical system for the exploitation of natural resources at the expense of the needs of indigenous peoples, as it is usually represented; his actions could instead be interpreted as an attempt to establish the forest as one aspect of his kingly authority whose revenues would support the crown.

As Charles Petit-Dutaillis and Georges Lefebvre argue, "Under Charles the Great and his immediate successors, the Forest was essentially a royal institution,"[27] and it "did not disappear with the Carolingians. In the tenth and eleventh centuries the dukes and counts among whom Gaul was divided evidently revived it to their own advantage in all districts where there was plenty of wood and game."[28] The *forestis* could also include settlements as well as cultivated land, with royal consent.[29] This institution differed significantly from that in pre-Conquest England, even if considerable material evidence exists in some Anglo-Saxon charters that demonstrates the importance of hunting and woodland usage.[30] Although the Anglo-Saxon kings and aristocrats enjoyed hunting, they did not have a formal system of forest management as did their counterparts on the Continent, in spite of a growing need for it.[31] Oliver Rackham notes, "The husbandry of deer begins right at the end of our [Anglo-Saxon] period, when there is a solitary reference in a will of 1045 at Ongar (Essex) to a *derhage*, 'deerhay,' which appears to be the medieval Ongar Great Park, the prototype of English parks."[32] In another late Anglo-Saxon example, Cnut forbade the hunt in all areas that were conserved by the royal ban,[33] but there is no detailed reference to the forest or a specific kind of management, as is seen in Carolingian and Anglo-Norman treatises. One might point to the *Constitutiones de Foresta*, a later legal text that was attributed to Cnut and outlines a variety of violations of royal hunting privileges, but, as Della Hooke observes, these references "are known to have been added to after the Norman Conquest and cannot therefore be taken to be reliable."[34] In spite of these instances of Anglo-Saxon interest in the institution of forest management, Rackham concludes, "Forests, wooded or not, are a post-Conquest development."[35]

On the Continent, on the other hand, the great royal *forestis* became a symbol of imperial authority from the reign of Charlemagne,[36] and activities within it (i.e., hunting) become a performance of the king's supremacy,[37] as evidenced by Carolingian writers like Einhard, whose work promoted the ritual of hunting as an expression of kingly power.[38] As Janet Nelson has argued, the hunt was crucial as a ritual of patrimonial kingship, "an exercise in, and a demonstration of, the virtues of collaboration" between king and vassal, which "manifested participation as well as hierarchy, reciprocity as well as patriarchal authority."[39] Often employed in conjunction with assemblies where major political crises were resolved, the *ritus venandi* exemplified Charlemagne's expression of imperial authority.[40] The epic poem *Karolus Magnus et Leo Papa*, from the first decade of the ninth century, illustrates this idea admirably in its heroic depiction of Charlemagne hunting a boar with members of his court, the court hierarchy mimicking the hierarchy of heaven.[41] The importance of the hunt to the maintenance of this hierarchy cannot be overstated. "At the Frankish court," Régine Hennebicque remarks, the hunt "is furthermore raised to the level of an institution."[42] This idea would have far-reaching implications for the king's image, moreover, because the hunt serves crucial, related functions: "to demonstrate royal superiority and power to the nobles," "[to provide] the victorious king an almost magical aura," and above all, "[to ensure] the king a material superiority indispensable to his political power."[43] Thus, it is no surprise that, when the administration of the *forestis* devolved to seigneurial control, the dukes of Normandy in particular were keen to establish for themselves the authority from the forest institutions created by the capitularies in emulation of the Carolingians.[44] When William I solidified control in England, therefore, he quickly brought the forests under royal control, a move intended to reinforce his authority and legitimacy.

William I's court, like Charlemagne's, eliminated the horizontal bonds of social power that had existed in Edward the Confessor's reign in favor of a vertical hierarchy with himself at the head, thereby consolidating not only political but also economic control of England. The abrupt process of afforestation in that practice, however, engendered the kind of antipathy evidenced by the "Rime of William" in the *Anglo-Saxon Chronicle* because it necessitated the curtailment of local control of the forest and its revenues for the benefit of the crown. Monastic clergy and laymen alike endured the effects of William's assertion of royal authority in the forests, which inconvenienced them in a number of ways: not only did it make it more difficult for them to procure skins for bookbinding, meats, timber, and other forest produce, but they also failed to benefit from the considerable revenues that could be had from fines, rents from pannage and pasturage, and the sale of privileges and exemptions.[45] Furthermore, the lists of pardons and fines in the pipe roll of 1130 from Henry I's reign show clergy as well as laymen, demonstrating that the clergy were not exempt from forest law.[46] Although the fines represented a considerable source of royal income, another significant resource was the money paid by barons to avoid judgment or to make assarts within the forest boundaries.[47] William I's introduction of the forest administration in the form of strict forest laws and the establishment of a forest legal system did more than simply allow the king to indulge his passion for the hunt, as he was accused of doing by the chronicler of the *ASC*, William of Malmesbury, and others; it provided considerable support for the royal household once the initial "economy of plunder" from the Conquest was exhausted, and furthermore confirmed royal authority.

As W. L. Warren observes, however, "The Forest was not, as has sometimes been supposed, a strictly private preserve of the Crown, from which other men and their rights were rigorously excluded."[48] Because of poaching by the men of Count Robert of Eu, for example, William I issued an unusually detailed charter safeguarding the hunting and forest rights of Battle Abbey,[49] which claimed extraordinary protection from its founder and exemptions from outside authority, as shall be demonstrated later. Henry I gifted local monasteries and bishops with a tithe of meat and hides whenever he hunted deer, and favored several abbeys with the right to make parks, maintain warrens, take wood for their own use without permission from the foresters, make assarts and cultivate forest land, and pasture their livestock.[50] In addition, the forest could be, and frequently was, manipulated as a political tool through the granting of exemptions and modifications of the law, which were frequent under Henry I.[51] When one considers that theft in general was considered an offense worthy of hanging, and taken in the context of Charlemagne's changes to the oath of fidelity in the *Capitulare missorum generale*,[52] suddenly the severity of punishments for transgressions against English forest laws becomes clearer: to steal the game from the *forestis* was to steal from the king himself, a great offense indeed that smacks of disloyalty. The accusations from the chroniclers of early Norman reigns that poachers of deer faced mutilation or even death, however, are not borne out by the evidence of the pipe rolls or records of pleas. H. G. Richardson and G. O. Sayles have shown that "abundant entries in the pipe rolls make it plain that the law can rarely have been enforced in all its rigour, though the menace of mutilation lay everlastingly in the background. Did we not know the [Assize of Woodstock of 1184], we should, on the evidence of the pipe rolls, regard the forest law and forest eyres primarily as a source of revenue in the twelfth century, and it is hard to escape the conclusion that within a very few years the motive of gain came to outweigh any other consideration."[53] Certainly, William Rufus came quickly to recognize the forest's potential for financial gain and expanded the afforestation of territory from that of his father's reign, which Henry I would later retract in his coronation charter.[54] William Rufus also accused fifty men of taking deer from one of his forests, an accusation which Eadmer later claimed was solely for the purpose of defrauding these remaining English nobility of their money.[55] Whether or not Eadmer's claims about William's perfidy are true, his words remain as eloquent testimony to the anxiety and resentment within monastic circles that could result from forest law and its administration.

What is additionally striking about the chroniclers' accounts is how quickly the king and his court became symbolically associated with the forest as a result of the controversy surrounding it. As I discussed in the case of the castles, certain landscapes become emblematic of a particular kind of place that has resonance among the populace, rather than being associated with any specific locality. This is also true of the New Forest, which promptly came to represent the tyranny of all the royal forests in England and the restrictive bureaucracy and laws associated with them. In its ideal sense, however, the forest came to be an extension of the king and his court through his ability to exert his authority over man and beast alike. The romance forest as a civilized, even courtly, *locus amoenus* differs significantly from the primitive physical world of eremitic hagiography or the classical depictions of the forest as a negative allegory for untamed emotion and lust, such as was evident in the love affair of Dido and Aeneas in the *Aeneid*.[56] In this interpretation, the king can impose his royal will on the wild landscape of the forest and tame it to serve his needs, and the ritual and spectacle of the royal hunt at the Carolingian court, similar in formality and purpose to royal processions, was also integral to this process. Likewise, as William Perry Marvin observes, "after the Conquest the Normans used their *forestae* and their hunting-progresses through the country as instruments of rule, to assert their presence everywhere and assert their lordship."[57] Consequently, the royal spectacle of the hunt in the literature of the twelfth century is redolent of the imperial pageantry of Carolingian courts. As Anne Rooney has shown, "the briefest evocation of the hunt is taken to suggest the whole realm of courtly activity and behaviour."[58] The association of the court and courtly activity with the presence of the king is profoundly paralleled by the development of the forest in England, especially as a symbolic space. Eventually, it is the very presence of the king in the forest that defines it as a "courtly space" that symbolizes royal authority and activity. Moreover, it is the presence of the king that defines the "court" itself, wherever it may be, because "it is an actual space, but it is also a group of individuals who accompany the monarch, an organism whose configurations are fluid, and which includes all those who are within this space, even if temporarily."[59] For the Normans the forest becomes, like their castles, a symbol of imperial authority as a result of the ritualization of the hunt and the imposition of courtly order upon the landscape of the forest; unfortunately, it would also create a long-standing grievance among the aristocracy of Anglo-Norman England that would be reflected in many accounts of Norman kingship.

In the Dreams of Snoring Monks: The King's Body in the New Forest

A greater understanding of the symbolic use of the forest in relation to medieval portrayals of Anglo-Norman kingship may cause modern scholars to rethink some aspects of the reign of William Rufus, one of the most notorious English kings for his abuses of royal privilege and disrespect for the church. Current perceptions of his kingship may be distorted by negative descriptions of his behavior from several twelfth-century historiographers,[60] who seem to relish narrating William Rufus's ignominious death as a cautionary tale about royal arrogance, particularly in the creation of the New Forest. Their examples of the debased body of the degenerate William Rufus after his death show, in their interpretations, that divine retribution is sometimes written on the king's body as a sign of his neglect of royal sacral responsibility. The concept of the body politic as a living organism was a fixture of medieval political theology, as Ernst Kantorowicz and others have shown,[61] so that the king's body could be employed as a metaphor for kingship itself and as such could serve multiple roles in historiography, exempla, or *specula principum*. Therefore, many medieval writers conceptualized punishment and salvation as physical manifestations of moral corruption or virtue, especially in relation to developing notions of ideal kingship. In Geoffroi Gaimar's courtly interpretation, however, William Rufus's death becomes a national tragedy, the heartrending loss of a great hero-king's potential, that longs for "what might have been" in terms of his empire-building. Geoffroi Gaimar tells a very different story than other churchmen. For him, William Rufus's death becomes a tragic tale in the tradition of romance literature about the death of a beloved and chivalric king at the hands of a traitor. Lamenting the heartrending loss of the king's potential and the empire-building he might have accomplished, Geoffroi's account resurrects the memory of William and of his kingship's glorious courtliness and high reputation. The widely divergent narratives of William's death signify how the forest became an extension of the body of the king and a symbolic space for exploring symbols of kingship and the tensions between the secular and religious authority that existed in the twelfth century.

William Rufus, son of William the Conqueror and second Norman king of England, was no great friend of the church, to say the least; his unpopularity among the clergy provoked a storm of invective after his death in the New Forest, much of it centering on salacious tales of divine retribution for his father's creation of the New Forest after taking the throne of England.[62] Orderic Vitalis relates a famous interpretation of the episode, claiming that on the morning of August 2, 1100, William Rufus received an ominous message from the abbot of Gloucester: it seems that the previous morning, a venerable monk had received a vision of a young virgin begging Jesus on his throne in heaven to strike out in vengeance against the wickedness of her earthly royal oppressor. The young virgin, it is said, represents the church, and King William's crimes against her include robberies, foul adulteries, and heinous crimes of all sorts. Jesus promises that her prayers will soon be answered. The abbot further warns William that a foreign monk's sermon from the day before had predicted the king's death more specifically in the form of divine vengeance from a swift arrow, because England's body is polluted by leprosy as a result of universal iniquity, and "from head to foot it is infected with the sickness of evil." Orderic recounts with disgust that William, in response to this dire warning of his impending doom, burst out laughing, scornfully dismissing the abbot's concerns as the mere "dreams of snoring monks" (somnia stertentium).[63]

Like Orderic, many ecclesiastics who relyaed these events saw William's subsequent death in the New Forest as symbolizing well-deserved divine retribution for his abuses of the church, especially in the area of forest law and the disenfranchisement of the church in its rights to the revenues of the forest. The contemporary account of John of Worcester is particularly critical of William I's actions, claiming that they directly accounted for a number of deaths, including those of another of his sons and an illegitimate grandson, and attributes these tragedies to William I's exploitation of the forest for his own pleasure:

> Then, on the second day of August . . . William the younger, king of England, while hunting in the New Forest, was struck by an arrow

> aimed carelessly by a certain Norman, Walter Tirell, and died. . . . Doubtless, as common report has it, this was verily the righteous vengeance of God. For in the days of old, that is, in the days of King Edward and other kings of England before him, that land flourished plentifully with countryfolk, with worshippers of God and with churches; but at the bidding of King William the elder, men were driven away, their houses thrown down, their churches destroyed, and the land kept as an abiding place for beasts of the chase: and thence, it is believed, was the cause of the mischance.[64]

Thus, the deaths of William Rufus and others have become inextricably linked with, indeed caused by, William I's tyranny over the forest. This negative symbolism would participate in the evolution of outlaw romances in generations to come.[65]

That the wholesale destruction of Anglo-Saxon civilization in this area of Hampshire never took place to the extent that John of Worcester describes it was no deterrent for Orderic Vitalis, who recycled the story some thirty-five years after William's death.[66] While telling the story of Robert Curthose's illegitimate son, Richard, Orderic pauses to relate the divine curse on the forest that caused his death:

> Now, reader, let me explain why the forest where this knight perished is called "new." That part of the country had been populous in earlier days, and was scattered with hamlets providing support for the settlers. Indeed a dense population thoroughly tilled the county of Hampshire, so that the southern district provided the city of Winchester with all kinds of country produce. But after William I conquered the realm of England, so great was his love of woods that he laid waste more than sixty parishes, forced the peasants to move to other places, and replaced the men with beasts of the forest so that he might hunt to his heart's content. There he lost two sons, Richard and William Rufus, and his grandson Richard as I have described; and visions appeared in many terrible forms to various men, by which the Lord plainly showed his anger that consecrated buildings had been given over to be a habitation for wild beasts.[67]

Orderic expands John's account to underscore William I's barbaric nature—symbolized by his excessive love of the hunt—which would cause him to destroy a civilized *locus amoenus*. By stating that the king caused the land to revert from a productive, God-fearing community to the wild wasteland of the forest, Orderic aggrandizes William's crime as described by John of Worcester. Both chroniclers are additionally critical of William's cavalier disregard of the dire warnings from various ecclesiasts of his own death. Orderic stresses moreover that William's dissolute life made him unworthy of salvation: "But the doctors and the prelates of the Church, considering his squalid life and dreadful death, ventured to pass judgement, declaring that he was virtually past redemption and unworthy of absolution by the Church, since as long as he lived they had never been able to turn him from his vices."[68] Both Williams are damned by one badly aimed arrow, and the son's ignominious death in the New Forest is no more than they both deserve. It is no surprise, therefore, that in the 1180s the chronicler of Battle Abbey goes a step further to assign the creation of the New Forest to William Rufus himself.[69] The chronicler's error suggests that by this time a popular image of a degenerate William Rufus is associated in the worst way with the perceived evils of the New Forest.

Geoffrei Gaimar's version of Rufus's life and death in the *Estoire des Engleis*, written around the same time as Orderic Vitalis's,[70] is all the more curious, therefore, for redeeming the notorious king by ending his history in spectacular fashion "with Rufus as a model of chivalrous kingship."[71] Written for a provincial Anglo-Norman baronage,[72] his *estoire* celebrates secular values over religious ones, which results in a significantly different interpretation of William Rufus's reign that emphasizes his courtly style of kingship for a noble audience. Throughout his portrayal, Gaimar's William represents the height of kingly accomplishment: having been crowned by both the English and the Normans,[73] he ruled them well and equally,[74] bringing peace to the land.[75] Moreover, his cavalier behavior is presented as strength of character rather than evidence of moral weakness. He is fearless in the face of danger from either man or nature, responding to dire warnings against such things as exceptionally treacherous sea crossings with an easy carelessness that reflects his rejoinders to the premonitions of his death in the other chronicles. As Gaimar tells us, "Against the wind he crossed the sea. The helmsman asked him if he wished to cross with a headwind and imperil himself on the sea. The king responded, 'Brother, silence! No one ever saw a king drown, nor will I be the first. Let your ships sail.'"[76] Although radically dissimilar, the different chroniclers' versions of William Rufus not only confirm his high-spirited character but also underscore the importance of considering the author's point of view in their depictions of this controversial king for a specific audience: whereas Orderic Vitalis's William is high-handed, Gaimar's is gallant and chivalrous. A wise, generous, and courtly king, he richly equips the numerous retainers of his household (seventeen hundred in all), who joined him solely for "his great nobility," whether or not there was a war. After William brings the territory of Maine within his control, Gaimar describes him in imperial terms, claiming that he was feared throughout France and could have taken Rome if he so desired.[77] At his victory feast upon his return to England, William Rufus stages a spectacle which is so splendid that people will talk about it forever: he knights several noblemen and thirty youths. It is the first literary depiction of a chivalric knighting.[78]

As a consequence of William's chivalrous kingship, in Gaimar's account his accidental death in the New Forest is depicted not as God's vengeance on a greedy, cruel king but as a great tragedy of romance, an emotional episode the pathos of which is on par with Roland's death in the *Chanson de Roland*. Before recounting the unfortunate story, Gaimar mentions William's forest administration and conflates it with his administration of justice, which is of the most righteous kind, because "when he had reigned some time and well established the peace, he dispensed true justice and right, such that no one lost anything through wrong-doing, nor was any free born man destitute or needy in his kingdom. Moreover, he sent his justices throughout the land, his foresters in his forests, so neither dog nor archer ever entered there."[79] The archers and dogs, Gaimar says, will be punished for trespassing in the forest, but solely for the purpose of keeping the forests for the king, implying in this context that the justice of the forest is as reasonable and desirable as that for men; moreover, this justice is balanced by the great bounty that the people enjoy as a result of William's kingship. There is certainly none of the invective against the cruelty of the Norman kings that exists elsewhere; instead, Gaimar concludes that "[t]his noble king, with great splendor, held his kingdom with honor."[80] In the following lines, the king decides to go hunting in the New Forest with his cherished friend Walter Tirel. Unlike the more sympathetic depictions of Tirel in the other chronicles, Gaimar's rendering of William's slayer is caustic: he calls the knight *fel*, one of the most despicable epithets for a character in a romance, and accuses him of plotting his evil intent against the king in his heart.[81]

In Gaimar's account of William's final moments, gone are the other chroniclers' condemnations of the king's life of vice, the sordid confusion of his brother and other magnates rushing off to prepare for war and protect their own interests, the humiliating image of his corpse covered in rags, carted off without ceremony by peasants.[82] Instead, we have the romantic image of a beloved monarch dying among his faithful barons, who mourn him deeply. His immortal soul is of chief concern, as William cries out for the final sacrament three times, in an echo of Roland crying out three times to God. His soul is preserved through the quick thinking of one of his hunters, who "took some herbs with all their flower and made the king eat a little; thus he thought to give communion to him. [The king] was with God, and ought to be. He had taken consecrated bread the previous Sunday: that should be a good guarantee for him."[83] His noble companions mourn him visibly, even violently, in a physical display of extreme grief: they "tore their hair and showed their sorrow without restraint. Never was there such grief demonstrated."[84] In his despair, Roger fitz Hamon asks one of his companions to kill him and repeatedly faints like a courtly lover, which is suggestive of Alde's reaction upon hearing of Roland's death: "So much he loved [the king] that he grieved greatly, and said often: 'Who will kill me? I would rather die than live longer.' Then he fainted and fell down. When he came to he wrung his hands. He became so weak and feeble that he almost fell again. He heard terrible mourning from all sides."[85] The universal grief felt by the king's companions and servants explicitly contradicts the disdainful accounts of other chroniclers, and Gaimar's redemption even goes so far as to return the king's body to his court in an honorable state. The companions construct a bier and cushion it with flowers and ferns and wrap the king's body in a new gray cloak, which just the day before had been worn by a young knight when Rufus dubbed him. Weeping and despondent, William's companions conduct their beloved king's body back to Winchester on a bier transported by two palfreys, in a symbolic parallel to the image of King Arthur's mortally wounded body being carried to Avalon.

In stark contrast to his contemporary Orderic Vitalis's claim that the despicable William Rufus was only mourned by "mercenary soldiers, lechers, and common harlots [who] lost their wages through the death of this lascivious king, and lamented his wretched end not through respect but out of vile greed that fed on his vices,"[86] Gaimar's dearly loved king Rufus is sincerely mourned by all of his most noble subjects, religious and lay equally: "The barons assembled there in the church of Saint Swithun, with the clergy of the city and the bishop and the abbot. The good bishop Walkelin kept vigil over the king until morning; with him were monks, clerks and abbots. He was well-served and sung for. The next day was such a send-off as never a man saw in his life; nor so many masses now such service will be done, until God comes in judgment. For one king, so they did this for him."[87] Rufus's funeral almost resembles the pageantry of a royal feast, with all the luminaries of his realm celebrating his life and paying their respects to his honor. By drawing parallels to contemporary romance and historiography alike, Gaimar rewrites utterly the life of William Rufus as a romance hero. Not only does this mark a radical revision of contemporary thinking about the reign of the second Norman king, but it brings to light the courtly changes being wrought in the idea of kingship of the twelfth century. The portrayal of an ideal, chivalrous king's romantic death in the forest is a courtly one, as evidenced by the parallels to other romances and *gestes* brought into the episode of William Rufus's death, and represents the idea of the forest as a courtly space, symbolic of the king's court itself and its royal pageantry.

Addicted to the Chase: Expressions of Royal Power in Marie de France's Forests

The perception of the forest as a space for the demonstration of courtly kingship would experience a significant change as the twelfth century progressed, as writers responded to political tensions that surrounded the disquiet induced by the shifting limits of the forests and the enforcement of forest laws. The conflicts over the forest would only increase over time, which served to highlight the forest and its administration and contributed to its even greater association with kingly power. Because the forest bureaucracy was so dependent on the authority of the king, the increasing breakdown of political order during Stephen's kingship was reflected in its general deterioration, which was more extensive than that of other institutions such as the Exchequer.[88] When Henry II assumed the throne in 1154, he moved quickly to assert his authority and reestablish the strong forest administration that had existed in his grandfather's time. Indeed, during the course of his reign, he afforested more territory than Henry I had acquired by the time of his death at the end of 1135.[89] He took a special interest in the forests as a juridical space, "sitting upon the eyre bench in person with his chief justices, [implementing] the forest law with a heavy hand against his barons, rebellious and loyal alike."[90] As a result, his strenuous investigations into the forest during the restoration period of the early years of his reign only heightened the association of the king's authority with the forest.

    The forest would come to new prominence in the romance literature of the period, indicating a perceptive awareness of the political and symbolic implications of this rejuvenated royal institution.⁹¹ As demonstrated by the ritualized spectacle of the hunt itself, the forest developed in romance literature as a contiguous space to the royal court, which writers would employ to explore the tensions of Carolingian-style kingship. The renewed obsession with the forest from the mid-twelfth century stemmed not only from Henry II's investigations of forest disputes, but also from his passionate interest in the forest for his own financial and personal purposes. Like his grandfather and great-grandfather before him, the new king was an avid hunter, which was seen as a shortcoming by some ecclesiastics who considered hunting a barbaric sport unbecoming a philosopher king of the civilized Anglo-Norman world.⁹² Gerald of Wales claimed, "He was addicted to the chase beyond measure."⁹³ William of Newburgh was even less complimentary and damned both Henrys in one stroke: "He delighted in the pleasure of hunting, as much as his grandfather did, and more than was right."⁹⁴ These factors, combined with the upwelling of romance literature in the second half of the twelfth century, resulted in a fresh burst of literary interpretation of the forest that established its potential as a space for the negotiation of royal power, often in ways that do not reflect well on Angevin kingship.

Much as the castle served as a symbolic space evocative of imperial authority elsewhere in Anglo-Norman England, as I demonstrated in chapter 2, the forest is used by Marie de France to suggest the idea of courtly behavior and kingship in the *Lais*, a collection of twelve short narratives written sometime in the second half of the twelfth century and derived from Breton tales. Because the *lais* are extremely short and laden with meaning, they provide excellent illustrations for examining the possibilities of the forest as a courtly space. The eponymous hero of "Eliduc" is so esteemed by his king that he is allowed to hunt in the king's forest, a rare privilege, which causes the other courtiers to become jealous of him and have him exiled from court. Guigemar's adventures toward self-actualization in love begin while hunting in the forest, through the curse of a white doe with stag's antlers. The courtly motif of hunting allows Marie to use the episode to transport the protagonist from his isolated life at the court to the forest, where he will find his destiny.⁹⁵ The hunt also functions as a metaphor for kingly behavior: Arthur goes hunting in "Lanval," which allows his queen to do some hunting of her own; and the kings' hunts in "Equitan" and "Bisclavret" are central to the structure of the poems, as noted by Glyn Burgess.⁹⁶

The space of the forest, including the activity within it, is frequently used as a crucial plot device in twelfth-century literature because, as an extension of the king and his court, it mirrors and even magnifies the social realities in which it participates. This is especially true in "Chevrefoil," for instance: Tristan exists in the forest on the periphery of society, banished from court because of his adulterous relationship with King Mark's queen, Iseut. Although Marie tells us that "he took to the forest because he wanted no man to see him,"[97] Iseut cannot pass by on her royal procession without Tristan seeing her, because the road on which she must travel cuts through the forest, which signifies the court's confluence with the forest in spite of the seeming wildness of Tristan's place of exile. In the path of the road, representing the king and his law, as discussed in chapter 2, Tristan carves his message for the queen on a hazel branch, "sun nun" (carved his name, or his message). He knows that Iseut will pass and understand his meaning, because "Autre feiz li fu avenu" (this has happened before) (l. 57).[98] Since the manuscript history is incomplete and we cannot determine a source for the material, it is not known what exactly has happened before. But the queen, recognizing the branch and comprehending its message, manages to step outside the royal procession for a moment and goes deeper into the forest, where she finds her lover and they can speak of their desires without fear.[99]

It is important to note here that, although the forest seems to represent a space in which the lovers can exist outside King Mark's court, they remain a part of his influence and are always mindful of his presence, just as the *lai* itself is a transitional moment between points in the plot of the romance as we know it. The *lai* of "Chevrefoil" exists temporarily outside the original romance story as recounted by Thomas and Béroul, and yet is completely dependent upon it for its meaning, at the same time as the lovers' sojourn in the forest seemingly exists briefly outside the courtly procession but still functions within the courtly sphere of the king's forest. This becomes especially clear when the lovers speak at their leisure of what they desire, which happens to be Tristan's return to Mark's court: "Then she spoke about in what manner he could be reconciled with the king."[100] The irony is that although the lovers think that they cannot live without each other, the fact remains that they have no purpose outside the courtly world that defines them, and indeed the parameters of their behavior are dictated and defined by their relationship to the king himself. The lovers, like the *lai* and the idea of the forest as a courtly space, are inextricably linked with the king and his court and cannot survive without them. This turn of events is not unlike the situation in the forest of Morrois episode from other versions of the legend, which precipitates the lovers' abandonment of the forest: in Thomas's courtly version, when King Mark discovers the two lovers sleeping in the forest, he veils Iseut's face with his glove, acknowledging her as his wife. In Béroul's less courtly version (although contemporary with the work of Thomas), the symbolism is even more overt: he replaces Tristan's sword with his own and places his ring on Iseut's finger and the glove on her face, thus reclaiming them as vassal and wife. Marie's use of these tropes in the forest of "Chevrefoil" evokes these other versions, and in so doing underscores the omnipresence of the king and his claim on lovers and landscape alike.

Similarly, Marie's *lai* about a courtly werewolf, "Bisclavret," further reflects the notion in "Chevrefoil" of the forest as a contiguous space to that of the court, existing outside the courtly world and at the same time as a part of it. Like the semi-lupine main character of "Bisclavret," the forest in this *lai* exists between the noble court of the wise king, who "rescues" Bisclavret while hunting in the forest and brings him to his court, and the domain of the protagonist's dishonorable wife, who condemns Bisclavret to exile in the forest in his werewolf state. Marie makes it clear from the beginning of the *lai* that this tale will *not* follow the classical tradition of monsters within the forest, explaining that she does "not wish to forget *Bisclavret*—that is its name in Breton, while the Normans call it *Garwaf*. Long ago, one could hear about it, and it often happened, that many men became werewolves and went to live in the woods. A werewolf is a savage beast which, when it is in this madness, devours men, causes great damage, and dwells and ranges in vast forests. I leave these matters now: I wish to tell you about Bisclavret."[101] Here, Marie inverts the werewolf motif of classical myths and folk tales to recount a courtly story. In the same way that the forests in her tales are not wild, violent places, but are instead an extension of the king and his court and a locus of courtly behavior, the werewolf that Marie will tell us about is a wonderful lord, a chivalrous and handsome knight of irreproachable behavior.[102] For three days a week, nearly half his life, Bisclavret disappears to the deepest parts of the forest to live as a werewolf, which emphasizes his hybridity, his existence somewhere between a monstrous state and a life as a courteous knight, undermining the classical trope of the forest as the abode of monsters.[103] Instead, the forest becomes, like Bisclavret himself, a hybrid, a space in which the characters of the courtly werewolf and the wise king can meet.

The king encounters Bisclavret in his werewolf state during one of his hunts, when his dogs have run the creature to ground. When Bisclavret begs the king for mercy by kissing his foot, the king immediately recognizes the werewolf's humanity; calling to his men, he tells them, "See the marvellous way this beast humbles itself before me! It has the intelligence of a human and is pleading for mercy. Drive back all the dogs and see that no one strikes it! The beast possesses understanding and intelligence. Hurry! Let us depart. I shall place the creature under my protection [*pes* = peace], for I shall hunt no more today."[104] The king gives his peace to Bisclavret, just as the Norman kings had extended the king's peace to include the beasts of the forest.[105] He brings Bisclavret back to his castle and sets him up among his courtiers; with the king, he is a "grant merveille" who sleeps near the king and is noble and mild-tempered, one who would not wish to harm anything.[106] Despite his outward appearance, the werewolf is in every way a noble courtier at the king's court, accentuating the king's ability to curb Bisclavret's feral instincts while in his semi-lupine form, much as the royal control of the forest recreates it as a courtly space. In spite of its outward appearance of wildness, the multiple performances of the king's peace within the forest confirm its association with the king's court: when Bisclavret pursues private vengeance by attacking his wife, the king stops him and holds an inquiry to determine the truth of the matter and dispense true justice.[107] These demonstrations of the king's justice in the forest, especially among the beasts of the forest (including Bisclavret, whose interests are protected by the king), illustrate the domesticating potential of the king's authority and claim to the forest and its beasts as an extension or representation of his peace, thus linking it to the civilization of the court.

Although the forest does not operate as a readily observable symbolic space in "Equitan," it exists on the fringes of the *lai* as a conceptual space in which the king attempts to engage in courtly behavior, especially the hunt. "Equitan" is perhaps the most obvious example of this treatment, especially because of its royal protagonist, who, like Henry II, is "addicted to the chase beyond measure": "Never, except in time of war, would the king have forsaken his hunting, his pleasures or his river sports, whatever the need might have been."[108] Corinne J. Saunders has interpreted Equitan's lack of *mésure* (self-restraint) in his pursuit of the courtly pleasures of the hunt as evidence of the forest becoming "a symbol of distance from the courtly norm."[109] Her reading, however, does not address Marie's introduction of Equitan, which describes him as a courteous lord who is secondly a king and judge.[110] The fact that Marie announces Equitan's courtliness as his first attribute is important to understanding its function within the *lai*. As Anne Rooney notes, "In secular works, the most frequent reason for appropriating the spectacle of the courtly hunt is to ennoble the figure, showing him as courtly, noble, elegant, sophisticated and civilised."[111] Rather than distancing himself from the "courtly norm" through the hunt, as Saunders suggests, Equitan attempts to embody its extreme, embracing the inversion of social roles with his seneschal that will be necessary for him to pursue a courtly lifestyle to the exclusion of all else. Indeed, Marie tells us that "Equitan enjoyed a fine reputation and was greatly loved in his land. He adored pleasure and amorous dalliance: for this reason he upheld the principles of chivalry. . . . Equitan had a seneschal, a good knight, brave and loyal, who took care of his entire territory, governing it and administering its justice."[112] In this *lai*, the hunt in the forest represents courtly behavior as much as the hunt for love and *druerie*. Moreover, the king uses the hunt as an excuse to pursue the seneschal's wife on multiple occasions, underscoring this idea even further.

The king misinterprets his role as the head of the court as the ideal of all that is "courtly," and therefore attempts to create an identity as the perfect courtly knight. In order to feed his voracious appetite for courtly activities, Equitan appropriates the seneschal's property (including his wife) in the same manner as he does his vassal's hunting rights. The king hunts in the seneschal's forests and sleeps with the seneschal's wife in his own castle, even in his own bed; the two lovers go so far as to exchange rings and vows.[113] Equitan's refusal to marry unless the seneschal is dead prompts the wife's diabolical plan to kill her own husband in a boiling bath, and the king agrees to the sordid, treacherous plot. Instead of ennobling him, Equitan's zealous pursuit of courtliness weakens him as a king, but most importantly as a lawgiver, who is supposed to protect his vassals' interests through the dispensation of justice. Instead of protecting the seneschal's rights to his property, Equitan appropriates it for his own use. Marie's moral at the end of the *lai*, "Evil can easily rebound on him who seeks another's misfortune,"[114] seems on the surface to refer to Equitan's death in the boiling water in the place of the seneschal. True justice, as the seneschal knows only too well by the end of the *lai*, is frequently not "courtly." In light of the prevailing concerns about forest laws and kingship in the late twelfth century, however, the *lai* allows Marie to highlight, in this cautionary tale, the tensions surrounding Henry II's treatment of the *forestis* and the hunt as royal spectacle imbued with imperial authority. Henry's grandfather was called the "Lion of Justice," and Henry sought to surpass his reign in many significant ways, including his forests and judicial systems. Yet it is clear in Marie's *lai* that a king who cares more for his own courtly desires than the well-being of his people risks ignoring his real purpose as king, and thus having his evils come back to haunt him. By manipulating the image of the king as lawgiver and peacemaker that Charlemagne and subsequent kings capitalized on to justify and reinforce their authority, Marie has brought the ideology of the forest full circle: she has reinforced the notion of the forest as a locus of kingly authority and behavior, but in so doing has highlighted the potential abuses inherent in such a relationship for a king who does not recognize or respect the limits of his power.

It is important for our understanding of the forest in England, therefore, to consider the source of these interpretations; the question of disenfranchisement of the nobility, secular and religious alike, caused by the creation of great forests like the New Forest and forest laws suggests a strong motive for their reactions against the forest and its administration. The abrupt process of afforestation in William I's reign initially engendered the kind of antipathy evidenced by the *Anglo-Saxon Chronicle*, because it necessitated the curtailment of local control of the forest and its revenues for the benefit of the crown. An additional political and economic motivation was the benefits to be gained from granting exemptions and modifications of forest law, profits that the Normans were most eager to exploit, especially during times of political upheaval. The anxiety caused by the uncertainty these practices engendered, aggravated by resentment toward the creation and administration of forest laws, resulted in the forest becoming a prominent subject for many twelfth-century writers. The forest, consequently, as a significant extension of royal authority in the twelfth century, became a site for exploration of the exercise and potential limitations of royal power. Because of the political and economic issues framing the rhetoric of the forest, it serves as an ideal subject through which to appreciate the Normans' ideals of kingship as exemplified by Charlemagne himself, the shadow of whose legacy haunted their imaginations as well as their history.

Epilogue

A hundred years or so after the Battle of Hastings, Wace expanded William of Malmesbury's account of the Conqueror's troops singing the *cantilena Rollandi*. Drawing on legends of the *jongleur* Taillefer, he paints a picture of the stirring heroism of one of the Norman warriors: "Taillefer, who sang exceedingly well, on a horse that swiftly galloped, went singing before the duke about Charlemagne and about Roland, and about Oliver and the vassals who died at Rencesvals."[1] This famous episode, however, which was used to emphasize the legitimacy of William's cause in England, is contained within a poem that expresses Wace's anti-French sentiment on multiple occasions, suggesting that despite growing Francophobia in certain circles, Charlemagne still carried some ideological weight for Anglo-Norman kings at the end of the twelfth century.[2] Wace's poem, in turn, influenced a romance written only slightly later, the *Roman des Franceis* of Andrew de Coutances, which David Crouch has called "virulent anti-French propaganda."[3] Although written in Angevin Normandy, its treatment of English and French legendary history makes it especially pertinent here. It is supposedly a letter from the king of Northumberland, Aldfrith (Arflet), to the English, "a little ditty" (*tirenlire*) that "shatters the spears of the Twelve Peers" in order to get revenge on the French for the slurs that they have written against the English, especially King Arthur.[4] Andrew writes of the waning of Charlemagne's France, which "was sweet, and now it is sour"[5] as a result of Arthur's conquest of their king, Frollo, which "reduced them all to the status of serf" to the English.[6]

That two nearly contemporary poems celebrating the "Anglo-Norman" past could use the Carolingian legend with such contrasting treatment calls for some consideration, especially in light of the current debate about the development of "Englishness" during the course of the twelfth century and the impact that such a legend might have on this identity. David Bates most recently claimed that "the supposed 'triumph' of Englishness was no triumph at all. This is because English identity never had to re-emerge; its continuation was made certain by the way in which the empire was created."[7] On the other hand, the appearance of disparaging commentary about Charlemagne, or about those who admire him, supports the idea that the emergence of a new "English" identity did begin late in the twelfth century, albeit one that was necessarily attenuated by the past experiences of a cross-Channel empire and the anxiety that this hybridity ultimately caused. At this time, the topos of Charlemagne's kingship was treated as "a privileged locus for questioning the nature and limits of power, including cases in which the king is in the wrong, in which the person who embodies sovereignty abuses it."[8] These writers appropriated Charlemagne's legend and demonstrated a new approach to *translatio imperii* that transferred his authority to the English past, thus legitimizing Anglo-Norman power through the Anglo-Saxons rather than the Carolingians and heralding a change in some audiences that valorized Insular over Continental culture.

Throughout this book I have tried to show that the idea of Charlemagne and Carolingian kingship could be, and was, used by the Anglo-Normans to legitimize and then expand their authority in England and elsewhere after the Norman Conquest. From the image that they projected of themselves as a civilizing influence meant to convert the barbarous British peoples, to their use of castles and roads as symbols of their imperial lordship, to their exploitation of forest laws as a means to control the economic and political landscape of England, the Normans turned to the legendary Charlemagne and his policies as a model of kingship to be emulated and adapted to their needs. Despite the countless studies that examine the influence of Charlemagne's reign on subsequent generations on the Continent, including the early Normans themselves, none have considered the profound impact of his kingship once the Normans crossed the Channel, which is surprising considering the cachet of association with Carolingian kingship that still existed into the twelfth century. We see this inclination not only in numerous literary and historiographical references to the legendary king, but also in such events as Henry II's involvement with Frederick Barbarossa in Charlemagne's canonization in 1165. Consequently, our understanding of the development of Anglo-Norman identity—especially in relation to issues such as legitimacy, imperial lordship, and cross-Channel relations—is incomplete, as is our understanding of the nature of that "Englishness" as it reasserted itself during the course of the twelfth century and especially after the events of 1204. The handling of the Charlemagne legend at this time can shed light on these ideas.

As is well known, after several years of conflict with the French king Philip II, as well as his own barons, King John lost his holdings in Normandy in 1204, in what would prove a bitter psychological blow to his kingship. By cutting the Continental umbilical cord represented by his duchy in Normandy, the losses that John suffered solidified the growing disinclination among English barons to support their king's overseas entanglements. John Gillingham attributes the political unrest and military losses to the growth of a "rising Francophobia" in England, which resulted in a renewed English resentment in late thirteenth-century literature against the events that occurred in 1066 and following.[9] But, as Gillingham acknowledges,[10] this argument is complicated by examples of English interest in French culture and learning. During John's reign and beyond, Paris was increasingly acknowledged as the intellectual center of the Christian world[11;] Bartholomaeus Anglicus, for example, praised Paris as a "new Athens," while Englishmen were studying and teaching in European schools.[12] English royal houses, especially those of queens and duchesses, would patronize ever more Continental authors than native ones for writing literature for both entertainment and edification. This could perhaps explain the continued admiration for Charlemagne in certain Anglo-Norman texts. These circumstances, however, seem to stand in direct contrast to the new habits of the baronial families and their associations with the "strongly insular nature of the Anglo-Norman romance literature."[13] John Scahill has suggested that this secular audience was also a natural one for the output of vernacular historiography, such as the Middle English poetic history Laȝamon's *Brut* and the widely circulated Anglo-Norman prose chronicle *Li rei de Engleterre*, both of which can be found in the same manuscript, the British Library MS Cotton Caligula A. ix.[14]

This period of political tension and conflict echoes in literary output as a transitional period in the first half of the thirteenth century,[15] during the reigns of John and his son, Henry III, and is frequently credited with the revitalization of interest in the pre-Conquest past and new compositions in

English. The process had begun earlier, however, with the Anglo-Normans' curiosity about their Anglo-Saxon inheritance. In rewriting Anglo-Saxon heroes and kings to reflect the mores of their courtly audience, the Anglo-Normans also participated in their survival and even made them fashionable.[16] The politically and culturally divisive opposition that threatened English society, however, equally permeated the narratives of the late twelfth and early thirteenth century. As such, it shaped the texts' internal conflicts and treatment of the "English" past,[17] creating the potential for self-contradiction contained within an antiquarian reclamation of a conquered people's past, from sources in which that past has been redefined by the conqueror, as was true in much of twelfth-century historiography. This sort of cultural ambiguity is more clearly understood, moreover, when one considers it as a negotiation between the ideologies of civilized society and kingship that still lingered from the twelfth century, on the one hand, and a new inquiry into "Englishness" of the thirteenth century, on the other. The twelfth-century models praised the courtly behavior and imperialistic ambitions that were also idealized on the Continent, but the end of the century saw a people who were increasingly defining themselves as "English" and attempting to characterize that identity, which would intensify in the wake of political upheaval and imperialistic threats from the French king in the early thirteenth century. Thus, Wace can write an anti-French praise poem of Norman history that still looks to the legend of Charlemagne to sanction the Conquest as a crusade as well as legitimize the Norman dynasty.

Andrew of Coutances's poem, however, shows us a different treatment of the Carolingian legend that is not unlike the kind of English nationalism that was becoming more evident, as can be seen in a few texts from the period. In the final lines of an early thirteenth-century Anglo-Norman poem, *La Vie de seint Josaphaz*, for instance, the poet, Chardri, severely criticizes those who would rather hear tales of Roland, Oliver, and Charlemagne's Twelve Peers than edifying stories of saints and Christ's Passion, because they are forgetting God and his own power in favor of glorifying that of men.[18] Chardri's *vie* does a couple of things: it testifies that audiences still gave currency to tales of Charlemagne in England at this time, and it reveals an anxiety about the same admiration for Charlemagne and his kingship, which could be interpreted as an anxiety about identity, as Crouch suggests about the denunciation of Charlemagne and the French in the *Roman des Franceis*.[19] His approval of English virtue over French decadence can be seen in another of Chardri's poems, the *Petit plet*, where he praises in very flattering terms the beauty and chivalry of

English women and men, in which they surpass the French because of their added attributes of loyalty, generosity, good nature, and learning.[20] Perhaps it is meant to be ironic that Chardri couches his celebration of English integrity in Anglo-Norman French;[21] certainly, there is a satiric element to the debate in the *Petit plet*, considering its unexpected reversal of the roles of Old Age and Youth, such that it is Youth who wisely comforts Old Age, who mourns the death of his *duce ami* seemingly overmuch.[22] The inversion of audience expectations allows Chardri to further criticize certain courtly values that seem to be a source of contention: Youth's practical common sense and spirited sermons ultimately trump the folly of Old Age's exaggeratedly sorrowful *courtoisie*, demonstrated by the overblown pathos of his courtly rhetoric, suggesting that these values might now be passé in the new world that is emerging. The fact that Chardri's two poems are found alongside Laȝamon's *Brut*, another poem often mined for its pro-English sympathies, indicates that one outcome of the texts in the Caligula A. ix manuscript might be to alleviate the anxiety of its audience about identities that are being redefined in the process of social and political change.

This conflict could be seen to be resolved in the Caligula A. ix manuscript via *Li rei de Engleterre*, an Anglo-Norman translation of English history from the Saxon conquest to the reign of Henry III.[23] In another extraordinary example of *translatio imperii*, *Li rei* appropriates the symbols of Charlemagne's legendary kingship for English history; what is especially striking is that these symbols are attributed to a decidedly English pre-Conquest king, thus legitimizing the authority of Anglo-Norman kings through association with the Anglo-Saxons as worthy ancestors, not the Carolingians. *Li rei* describes in detail the gift story found in William of Malmesbury's *Gesta regum Anglorum*,[24] which is purportedly from a now lost pre-Conquest Latin panegyric that he summarizes about the rich bequests offered to Athelstan by King Hugh of France for the hand of the English king's sister. *Li rei* is remarkable because the Anglo-Norman version of the story eliminates any reference to the secular gifts that are found in William's version, such as spices, jewels, and horses, to focus only on those gifts that represent religio-imperial symbols of the highest magnitude:

> The sword of the emperor Constantine with his name on the sword in letters of gold; placed in the hilt of the sword, which was made of fine gold, was one of the nails of Our Lord. The lance of Charlemagne, which was carried against the Saracens, which was the one

of which it is said that killed Our Lord. Whoever carries it in battle will not be vanquished. The gonfanon of St. Maurice, which was carried before that holy legion, which King Charles carried all his life against pagans. A piece of the True Cross enclosed in a crystal; a piece of the crown of thorns, which was placed on the head of Our Lord; a royal crown of fine gold set all about with precious stones.[25]

The author's exclusion of William's lengthy description of secular gifts serves to further draw attention to and enhance Charlemagne's presence in the catalogue of riches presented to Athelstan. William also ends the gift story with a description of the piece of the cross and crown of thorns, not the gold crown, which were given to the monastery at Malmesbury, highlighting the importance of the provenance of the relics for Malmesbury rather than the symbols of sacral kingship. Indeed, in *Li rei* the gold crown, the mark of an earthly king, is deliberately juxtaposed with the crown of thorns, the crown of the crucified Christ, which parallels the king's sacral role on earth as defender of God's law and the church, further represented by the various holy weapons that have been carried in victorious battles against pagans. The reader of the chronicle, therefore, is left with the impression that the Anglo-Saxon king has been presented with Charlemagne's greatest treasures, perhaps even his own crown, and that Athelstan has thereby acquired the status of Charlemagne, the legacy of whose reign now increases the prestige of the English king and his successors. It suggests that the Anglo-Normans, at this point in Insular history, were negotiating the stories of their hybrid past in a way that presented their newly appropriated ancestry in as formidable a light as the history they created in Normandy before the Conquest.

A critical element of Anglo-Norman unification and identity was the elimination of hostility between the two peoples. Later Anglo-Norman historians sought to reconcile the seemingly dissimilar natures of their dual heritage by revising the accounts of those predecessors to better reflect Continental and courtly ideals, but not subsuming or obliterating them. The literature of the thirteenth century, on the other hand, underscores how English ideals of kingship adapted to the political changes of England's separation from its Continental holdings and changing perceptions of English identity. I would argue that Charlemagne's kingship in texts like *Li rei* represents an ideal of Christian kingship to be emulated, but the gift story in *Li rei* implies that Charlemagne's legend, while admired by these later writers, is also firmly rooted in the past: it is now the English kings like Athelstan who have taken up the crown and sword of Christian kingship, to be carried by English kings in generations to come. There is a certain irony stemming from the inconsistency in these writers' approaches, however, revealing the fault lines of a society attempting to (re)define its identity: it suggests an ambiguous participation in—and simultaneous rejection of—the paradigms they are attempting to negotiate in order to understand what makes themselves "English" in the wake of changing cultural values and political unrest. This is especially true with regard to the ways these texts attempt to negotiate the legend of Charlemagne, a polarizing (French) figure against whom their own (English) heroes are obliquely positioned, as subsequent generations sought to assimilate and even elevate English culture and language in a world of shifting identities.

Notes

References to Bede, *Bede's Ecclesiastical History*, include book and chapter as well as page in the edition edited by Bertram Colgrave and R. A. B. Mynors.

References to Geoffrey of Monmouth, *History of the Kings of Britain*, are abbreviated HKB and include section as well as page in the edition edited by Michael D. Reeve.

References to the *Gesta Stephani* are abbreviated GS and include book and section as well as page in the edition edited by K. R. Potter.

References to Henry of Huntingdon, *Historia Anglorum*, are abbreviated HA and include book and section as well as page in the edition edited by Diana Greenway.

References to Orderic Vitalis, *The Ecclesiastical History of Orderic Vitalis*, include book and section as well as volume and page in the edition edited by Marjorie Chibnall.

References to William of Malmesbury, *Gesta pontificum Anglorum*, include book and section as well as volume and page in the edition edited by R. M. Thomson.

References to William of Malmesbury, *Gesta regum Anglorum*, include book and section as well as volume and page in the edition edited by R. A. B. Mynors, R. M. Thomson, and M. Winterbottom.

References to Symeon of Durham, *Libellus de exordio*, include book and section as well as page in the edition edited by D. W. Rollason.

References to William of Poitiers, *The "Gesta Guillelmi" of William of Poitiers*, are abbreviated GG and include book and section as well as page in the edition edited by R. H. C. Davis and Marjorie Chibnall.

Introduction

1. "Tunc cantilena Rollandi inchoata, ut martium viri exemplum pugnaturos accenderet, inclamatoque Dei auxilio" (William of Malmesbury, *Gesta regum Anglorum* 3.242 [Mynors, Thomson, and Winterbottom 1:454-55]).

2. As Melissa Furrow mentions, "From the beginning of Anglo-Norman culture, the story of Roland at Roncesvalles was cultivated in England and used to bolster Norman cultural pride, to the extent that the mythically depicted Charlemagne who

warred against the Saracens became imaginatively linked to the conqueror William" (Furrow, "Chanson de geste as Romance in England," 57). See also Sayers, "The Jongleur Taillefer at Hastings"; as well as Douglas's mention in the opening of "The *Song of Roland.*"

3. Morrissey, *Charlemagne and France*, xviii. The Other, for the Anglo-Normans, was the "barbarous" British, whose lands they would ultimately control.

4. Two excellent recent studies regarding the legendary Charlemagne and his influence on later generations' perspectives of identity and kingship are Latowsky, *Emperor of the World*, and Gabriele, *An Empire of Memory*. Unfortunately, both scholars focus primarily on the Continental experience, as that of the Anglo-Normans is outside the scope of their investigations. For more information about the influence of Carolingian kingship on pre-Conquest Normans, see below.

5. I am using the term *imperium* in the sense defined by Isidore of Seville in the *Etymologies*, meaning "rule over kingdoms," especially by right of conquest and not necessarily with any reference to the papacy or to Christianity, as clarified by James Muldoon in *Empire and Order*, 4-17, although, as Muldoon points out, there were other uses of the concept of empire throughout the Middle Ages.

6. See, for example, P. H. Sawyer's arguments, where he places the Norman need for expansion within the greater context of "violently acquisitive men in western society in the eleventh century," claiming that "the demand for land and revenue was continuous" (Sawyer, *From Roman Britain to Norman England*, 252).

7. Stoler, "Rethinking Colonial Categories," 136.

8. A similar approach to the political uses of evoking past kings for confirmation of authority can be found in Remensnyder, *Remembering Kings Past*. For excellent surveys of the development of the Charlemagne legend, see Noble, "Greatness Contested and Greatness Confirmed," and Dutton, "KAROLVS MAGNVS or KAROLVS FELIX," both in Gabriele and Stuckey, *The Legend of Charlemagne*. Other studies of the Charlemagne legend include Robert Folz's foundational work, *Le souvenir et la légende de Charlemagne*; more recently, see Kerner, *Karl der Grosse*; the collection of essays in Bastert, *Karl der Grosse*; Dutton, *The Politics of Dreaming*; Stuckey, "Charlemagne"; as well as the other essays in Gabriele and Stuckey, *The Legend of Charlemagne*.

9. Beer, *Narrative Conventions of Truth*, 10. Monika Otter has more recently shown that the truth of a work depends more on the claims of its author than on the truth value of a text: Otter, "Functions of Fiction in Historical Writing," 112.

10. Fleischman, "On the Representation of History and Fiction," 305. An example would be monastic communities' imaginative construction of foundation legends, about which Amy Remensnyder argues, "while many of these legends do seem fantastic, the monastic communities believed in them at some level. . . . Furthermore, if monasteries had not held their constructed images of the past to be true, these legends would not have had the power in the present that they did" (Remensnyder, *Remembering Kings Past*, 2).

11. Latowsky, introduction to *Emperor of the World*. On this point, also see Gabriele, *An Empire of Memory*; also refer to Fentress and Wickham, *Social Memory*, for more information on the function of collective memory in

society, especially chap. 4, "Medieval Memories," 144–72.
12. This influence has been well demonstrated, and a longer review is beyond the scope of this study, but for more examples, see Koziol, *Begging Pardon and Favor*; Goldberg, "'The Hunt Belongs to Man'"; Reuter, "Plunder and Tribute"; and Nelson, *Politics and Ritual*, as well as "The Lord's Anointed and the People's Choice."
13. Airlie, "The Palace of Memory."
14. For the Salians of the twelfth century, see Dale, "Imperial Self-Representation." For the Capetians and other French kings, see Baldwin, *The Government of Philip Augustus*, and Lambrech, "Charlemagne and His Influence."
15. Bossy, "Roland's Migration," 296.
16. Morrissey, *Charlemagne and France*, 67. On this treatment of Charlemagne in Anglo-Norman England, see my article "Taming the Wilderness."
17. See Hen, "The Uses of the Bible."
18. For a foundational study of Constantine's memory in the early medieval imagination, see Ewig, "Das Bild Constantins des Großen."
19. Benjamin Pohl has suggested that Constantine was the model for Rollo in Dudo of Saint Quentin's influential *Historia Normannorum*, although he concedes that it is difficult to prove that Dudo directly utilized the sources for Constantine's life that circulated more widely at the end of the eleventh century after Dudo composed his history (Pohl, "Translatio imperii Constantini ad Normannos"). See also Pohl, *Dudo of Saint-Quentin's "Historia Normannorum."* There are clearer borrowings from other texts, however, such as Gregory of Tours's depiction of Clovis in the *Libri Historiarum*, Roman literature, and early medieval hagiography. See, for example, Shopkow, "The Carolingian World of Dudo of Saint-Quentin"; Herrick, "Heirs to the Apostles"; and Searle, "Fact and Pattern in Heroic History."
20. Mulligan, "The British Constantine," esp. 260–63.
21. Ibid., 264.
22. See Parry, "Geoffrey of Monmouth"; Mulligan, "The British Constantine," 263.
23. Cowdrey, "Eleventh-Century Reformers' Views," 64. See also Brett, "Early Constantine Legends."
24. More recent scholarly interest, especially in cross-Channel relations, has resulted in Story, *Carolingian Connections*, as well as several collections of essays, such as McKitterick, *Carolingian Culture*, and Story, *Charlemagne: Empire and Society*.
25. As a model for kingship, Charlemagne was an important figure for pre-Conquest Normans, who made certain to emulate Charlemagne and his successors in their histories, laws, and practices, adding the patina of a Carolingian style of kingship to their authority. As Bruce O'Brien points out, "That the *reality* of Norman rule differed in degree from the Carolingian *ideal* of governance, as preserved in formularies and capitularies, is no surprise and should not lead to a rejection of the influence or attractiveness of that ideal to, for example, late-tenth- or eleventh-century Norman counts and dukes" (Bruce, *God's Peace and King's Peace*, 210n22 [emphasis in original]).
26. Davy, *Le duc et la loi*. Davy's book examines the development of ducal law in Normandy as a deliberate attempt, from Richard I through William the Conqueror's death, where he ends his study, to emulate Carolingian traditions, both legal and literary. It is important to note, however, that Davy does not argue for the slavish

preservation of past practices by the Normans; rather, ducal documents, in addition to the writing of Norman authors such as Dudo of Saint Quentin, reflect contemporary concerns in what he calls "un archétype néo-carolingien," particularly where expressions of ducal power are concerned, which are, significantly, analogous to royal images of power that also attempted to preserve Carolingian models (ibid., 51–53). See also Koziol, *Begging Pardon and Favor*, 138–59, where he discusses the Normans' use of a model of Carolingian authority for Frankish political affairs.

27. Werner, "Kingdom and Principality," 248. Jean Dunbabin has also shown that the use of regal terminology and titles in sub-Carolingian Francia "were important pillars of princely power" (Dunbabin, *France in the Making, 843–1180*, 48).

28. Nelson, "Rites of the Conqueror," 118.

29. Ibid., 117.

30. Ibid., 130. Michael Lapidge points out the 1068 *laudes* as a copy of Frankish royal acclamations adapted for William and his queen (Lapidge, "The Origin of CCCC 163," 21). For information about Anglo-Norman *laudes regiae* more generally, see Cowdrey, "The Anglo-Norman *Laudes regiae*."

31. Nelson, "Rites of the Conqueror," 130–31.

32. Turner, *The Politics of Landscape*, 2.

33. For three of the most recent assessments of continuity in post-settlement Normandy, see Hagger, "Secular Law and Custom in Ducal Normandy" (arguing strongly for continuity); Bauduin, *La première Normandie*; and Davy, *Le duc et la loi*. For a thorough overview of the scholarly discussion, see Bates, "Western Frankia." See also Le Patourel, *The Norman Empire*; Bates, *Normandy Before 1066*; Bouard, "De la Neustrie carolingienne"; Musset, "Origines et nature du pouvoir ducal"; Breese, "The Persistence of Scandinavian Connections"; Lifshitz, "La Normandie carolingienne"; Renoux, "Palais capétiens et normands"; and Webber, *The Evolution of Norman Identity*.

34. For examples, see especially Bates, *Normandy Before 1066*; Lifshitz, "La Normandie carolingienne"; and Renoux, "Palais capétiens et normands."

35. Bates, *Normandy Before 1066*, 11. On this point, François Neveux agrees: "La province possedait en premier lieu ses propres institutions. Même si celles-ci étaient en partie inspirées par le droit scandinave, le substrat carolingien semble avoir été prédominant"; moreover, "Ce modèle, avant fait ses preuves en Normandie, fut transplanté en Angleterre avant d'influencer l'Etat capétien" (Neveux, *La Normandie de ducs au rois*, 157). His view supports my argument that the Normans adapted certain useful Carolingian models alongside preexisting Anglo-Saxon institutions after the Conquest, which resulted in the development of different paradigms for rule that nevertheless exhibited Carolingian influences, such as can be seen in forest laws (chapter 3).

36. Musset, "Origines et nature du pouvoir," 50.

37. "[A]ucune rupture n'eut lieu à Rouen vers cette époque . . . en ce qui concerne la pratique administrative carolingienne" (Lifshitz, "La Normandie carolingienne," 513).

38. Musset, "Origines et nature du pouvoir," 54.

39. Hagger, "Secular Law," 866. For preservation of Carolingian legal practices in Normandy, especially during and after the duchy of Richard I, see also Davy, *Le duc et la loi*.

40. "[C]es survivances carolingiennes se laisseront mieux intégrer par l'Etat feodal que la Normandie deviendra au XIe siècle, alors que les apports nordiques seront victimes de reactions de rejet" (Musset, "Origines et nature du pouvoir," 51).
41. Bates, *Normandy Before 1066*, 36; Musset, "Les relations extérieures de la Normandie"; and Dumas-Dubourg, *Le trésor de Fécamp*, esp. 55–60.
42. Bates, *Normandy Before 1066*, 12.
43. Ibid., 38.
44. Musset, "Origines et nature du pouvoir," 50.
45. For examples, see Renoux, "Palais capétiens et normands"; Carlson, "Religious Architecture in Normandy"; and Bates, *Normandy Before 1066*.
46. In addition to Jumièges, Carolingian architectural elements were used in the construction of Notre-Dame-sous-Terre chapel at Mont Saint Michel, Saint Saturnin chapel at Saint Wandrille abbey, Saint Germain chapel at the Querqueville parish church, and the abbey church of La Trinité at Fécamp, as discussed by Carlson, "Religious Architecture," 29–31.
47. Lifshitz, "La Normandie carolingienne," 507–8.
48. See Emily Zack Tabuteau's influential work, *Transfers of Property in Eleventh Century Norman Law*, esp. 5–6, and Hagger, "Secular Law." For a complementary view of the language of charters, see Potts, "The Early Norman Charters." Potts argues that the royal language used in earlier Norman charters is reminiscent of the language of Carolingian charters and reaches a high point in the charters of Richard II's reign, illustrating a quasi-regal authority that would diminish after his death, due to the breakdown of public control in Robert the Magnificent's reign and William the Conqueror's minority, and not be regained until after 1066.
49. These changes wrought a new identity for the Normans that has been termed *Normanitas* by modern scholars, which can be defined as their self-perception as a chosen people, with an illustrious past that was distinct from that of the French, and the promise of a glorious future. The development of this identity included the creation of an origin myth that would rival that of the French, for whom they harbored a "streak of anti-French feeling" even before the conquest of England, according to Thomas, *The English and the Normans*, 35. David Bates, on the other hand, has recently called for an abandonment of the term, arguing that "it has acquired meanings that have gone far beyond the original intention [of inclusivity], and which can appear to give the word a concreteness that simply cannot be justified" (Bates, *Normans and Empire*, 183–84). For other studies of *Normanitas*, see Webber, *The Evolution of Norman Identity*; Davis, *The Normans and Their Myth*; Albu, *The Normans and Their Histories*; Bur, "Les comtes de Champagne et la 'Normanitas'"; Loud, "The 'Gens Normannorum'"; and Potts, "*Atque unum ex diversis gentibus populum effecit*."
50. Southern, *Medieval Humanism*, 158. It should be noted that Southern's assessment is not meant to be a positive one; elsewhere, he has argued that "The main reaction of men who had known pre-Conquest England was one of outrage, resentment and nostalgia," which prompted them to a "corporate monastic purpose of recreating the Old English past" (Southern, "Aspects of the European Tradition, IV," 246, 253).
51. For a lengthy study, see Le Patourel, *The Norman Empire*. Le Patourel's

work remains problematic for modern scholars, however, for his implication that England was treated as part of the duchy of Normandy, rather than as a hybrid of English and Norman customs.

52. Postcolonial approaches to the Middle Ages have received much attention in recent years, especially as a result of several influential essay collections, such as Cohen, *The Postcolonial Middle Ages*; Ingham and Warren, *Postcolonial Moves*; and Kabir and Williams, *Postcolonial Approaches*. See, further, Hoofnagle and Keller, *Other Nations*; Uebel, *Ecstatic Transformation*; Huot, *Postcolonial Fictions*; and Davis and Altschul, *Medievalisms in the Postcolonial World*. For brief surveys of the history and the multiple usages of hybridity, see Audehm and Velten, introduction to *Transgression— Hybridisierung—Differenzierung*; and Burke, *Cultural Hybridity*.

53. "Hybridisierungen sind, bezogen auf kulturelle Praktiken und Repräsentationen, in Zwischenräumen hergestellte innovative und kreative Prozesse, in denen Heterogenes verbunden und vermischt und damit unbestimmt und ambivalent gemacht wird" (Audehm and Velten, *Transgression*, 33).

54. Shortly before her death in 1980, Elizabeth Salter left a manuscript for an unfinished book provisionally entitled "An Obsession with the Continent." This book would be published posthumously as *English and International: Studies in the Literature, Art, and Patronage of Medieval England*. In the first chapter, Salter grapples with contemporary scholars' reliance on what she considers to be a fixation on discovering a strictly defined "English" achievement—which is independent of European, specifically French, influence—beyond the Conquest, existing in spite of the myriad changes that confrontation engendered. She states repeatedly that the search for English "continuities" is a futile one that ignores the cultural complexity of post-Conquest England and its long association with the Continent.

55. See, for example, the oft-cited writ to the city of London from shortly after William's coronation: "William notifies bishop William of London, Geoffrey the port-reeve, and all citizens dwelling in London that he grants them all the laws of which they were worthy in king Edward's day, and that every child shall be his father's heir after his father's death" (Will(el)m kyng gret Will(el)m bisceop ꝛ Gosfregð portirefan ꝛ ealle þa burhwaru binnan/ Londone frencisce ꝛ englisce freondlice. ꝛ ic kyðe eow [þæt] ic wylle [þæt]get beon eallra þæra/ laga weorðe þe gyt wæran on Eadwerdes dæge kynges. ꝛ ic wylle þæt ælc cyld beo his/ fæder yrfnume æfter his fæder dæge. ꝛ ic nelle geþolian [þæt] ænig man eow ænig wrang/ beode") (Bates, *Regesta regum Anglo-Normannorum*, 593).

56. See Brown, *The Normans and the Norman Conquest*, which seems to have been written in response to the effects of the "pugnacious patriotism" of scholars like E. A. Freeman, whose sentiments were echoed a century later by H. G. Richardson and G. O. Sayles in their assertion that "for half a century or so from 1066 the English way of life was not sensibly altered. The Normans had very little to teach, even in the art of war, and they had very much to learn. They were barbarians who were becoming conscious of their insufficiency" (Richardson and Sayles, *The Governance of Mediaeval England*, 27).

57. Le Patourel, *The Norman Empire*, 264.

58. Ibid., 266.

59. Ibid., 3ff.
60. In a speech early in the poem, Blancandrins calls Charlemagne a "marvellous man" who crossed the sea to England and restored the payment of Peter's pence (ll. 371-74); much later, as Roland is dying, he speaks to his sword Durendal, claiming that he used it to conquer Scotland, Ireland, Wales, and England for Charlemagne (ll. 2331-32). The two passages in question have been thought to refer to the Norman Conquest; see the overview in Douglas, "The Song of Roland," 101-2.
61. Douglas, "The Song of Roland," 108-9.
62. Ibid., 109.
63. Ibid., 113.
64. Bates, "West Francia," 416.
65. Kantorowicz, The King's Two Bodies, 45.
66. Douglas, "The Song of Roland," 113.
67. Silverman, "Ælfric's Designation of the King," 333.
68. Story, Carolingian Connections, 19-20.
69. "Cuius excellentie fama ac operum uirtutis longe lateque diffusa, etiam ad regem Francorum Pipinum peruenit, propter quod ei amicitia iunctus multa ei ac diuersa dona regalia transmisit" (Symeon of Durham, Libellus de exordio 2.3 [Rollason 80-83]).
70. William of Malmesbury, Gesta regum Anglorum 2.133 (Mynors, Thomson, and Winterbottom 1.210-13). In the General Introduction and Commentary, R. M. Thomson suggests that William did use some older verse as his source, but rewrote it to produce a version more palatable to his twelfth-century audience (Thomson, in William of Malmesbury, Gesta regum Anglorum [Mynors, Thomson, and Winterbottom 2:116-20]).
71. Thomson, in William of Malmesbury, Gesta regum Anglorum ([Mynors, Thomson, and Winterbottom 2:120]). Thomson also notes that the epitaph of Charles the Bald in particular is strikingly close to that of William's for Æthelstan.
72. Le Patourel, The Norman Empire, 238.
73. Wallach, Alcuin and Charlemagne, 32.
74. Ibid., 74.
75. Kantorowicz, The King's Two Bodies, 162.
76. Ibid., 93-94.
77. Ibid., 96.
78. Head and Landes, eds., The Peace of God, 8.
79. Bloch, Medieval French Literature and Law, 111, and The Anonymous Marie de France, 279.
80. Hudson, The Formation of the English Common Law, 82.
81. Hyams, "Common Law and the French Connection," Anglo-Norman Studies 4 (1981): 77-93, at 82.
82. Ibid., 85.
83. Wormald, The Making of English Law, 414.
84. Ibid.
85. O'Brien, "The King's Four Highways," 357.
86. O'Brien, God's Peace and King's Peace, 34.
87. "Rex autem, qui uicarius summi Regis est, ad hoc constitutus est, ut regnum et populum Domini et super omnia sanctam ecclesiam regat et defendat ab iniuriosis, maleficos autem destruat et euellat. Sin autem nomen regis perdit, testante Iohanne papa, cui Pepinus et Karolus filius eius, necdum reges sed principes sub rege Francorum stulto, scripserunt, querentes si ita deberent manere reges Francorum solo regio nomine contenti. A quo responsum est: 'Illos decet uocari reges qui uigilanter defendunt et regunt ecclesiam Dei et populum eius' imitati regem psalmigraphum dicentem: 'Non habitabit in medio domus mee qui facit superbiam' et cetera" (ibid., 174-77).
88. For more information regarding the motives of post-Conquest translators

of law codes (among others), see O'Brien, *Reversing Babel*, 123-57.

Chapter 1

1. *Sed nec in antiquis ducibus seu regibus illo*
   Omnimodis quisquam clarior enituit.
   Romani multis ducibus multisque sub annis
   Italiae populos vix sibi subdiderant:
   Unus hic in spacio perpauci temporis omnem
   Subiecit victor, disposuit dominus;
   Adde tot Europae populos, quos ipse subegit,
   Quorum Romani nomina nescierant.
   (Poeta Saxo, *Annales de gestis Caroli magni imperatoris libri quinque*, ll. 645-52, in Godman, *Poetry of the Carolingian Renaissance*, 342-43)
2. For example, see Bohn, "Der Poeta Saxo"; and Bischoff, "Das Thema des Poeta Saxo."
3. *Terrea forsan eis fuerit par gloria; sed nunc*
   Caelestis Carolus culmen honoris habet.
   Illic Daviticae pollet virtutis honore
   Cum Constantino atque Theodosio;
   Illic antiquum gaudet quod vicerit hostem
   Eripiens multos ipsius a laqueis;
   Illic congaudent illi salvata per ipsum
   Munere, Christe, tuo milia spirituum.
   Quis numeret quantas animas, dum credere fecit
   Saxonum populos, reddiderit domino?
   (Poeta Saxo, *Annales de gestis Caroli magni imperatoris libri quinque*, ll. 659-68, in Godman, *Poetry of the Carolingian Renaissance*, 344-45)
4. "Soft power" is a phrase coined by Harvard political scientist Joseph S. Nye Jr. in his book *Bound to Lead* and further developed in *Soft Power* and others. "Soft power" utilizes "intangible power resources such as culture, ideology, and institutions" as opposed to "hard power," which is usually associated with military and economic strength (*Bound to Lead*, 32). David Bates refers to this concept of "soft power" several times in his recent book *The Normans and Empire*. It strikes me as a very apt term to explain the techniques of "conversion politics" that were developed by Charlemagne and subsequent generations.
5. Numerous studies have emphasized the importance of rituals to medieval society, because of, as Philippe Buc puts it, "the importance this culture attached to solemnities," even though "rituals did not constitute the sole foci of meaning in texts, and probably not in medieval political culture, either" (Buc, *The Dangers of Ritual*, 9). In other words, rituals do not exist in and of themselves and must be read in their socio-cultural context to determine the subtext underlying the *purpose* that the ritual serves, especially for displays of royal and princely power, as demonstrated by Geoffrey Koziol in *Begging Pardon and Favor*.
6. Norbert Elias argues that "[i]n the name of the Cross, and later in that of civilization, Western society waged, during the Middle Ages, its wars of colonization and expansion. And for all its secularization, the watchword 'civilization' always retained an echo of Latin Christendom" (Elias, *The Civilizing Process*, 47).
7. Angenendt, *Kaiserherrschaft und Königstaufe*.
8. As Reinhard Schneider says, "Eingeschlossen ist damit, daß die Missionsfrage für Karl den Großen eine eminent politische Bedeutung hatte, postuliert als Annahme aber auch, daß er mit missionarischem Eifer Missions- und Ausdehnungspolitik getrieben hat—heute würde man wohl eher von missionarische außenpolitik

sprechen. . . . In der historischen Rückschau gehören die Begründung des Imperium Christianum und die Christianisierung des Sachsenstammes zu den bedeutsamsten Leistungen Karls des Großen" (Schneider, "Karl der Große," 227). Hellmut Kämpf, however, put forward an alternative view in "Reich und Mission."

9. "Inter caenandum aut aliquod acroama aut lectorem audiebat. Legebantur ei historiae et antiquorum res gestae. Delectabatur et libris sancti Augustini, praecipueque his qui de civitate Dei praetitulati sunt" ("Einhardi Vita Karoli Imperatoris," § 24, in MGH, [*Scriptores rerum Sangallensium*], trans. in Thorpe, *Two Lives of Charlemagne*, 78). For a review and a refutation of some of these statements through a careful examination of Augustine's precepts and Charlemagne's kingship, see Sidey, "The Government of Charlemagne."

10. Entry for A.D. 782, in MGH, *Annales regni Francorum*, 62.

11. It must be noted that mass conversions, even at sword point, were by no means introduced by Charlemagne's early dealings with the Saxons. Certainly Pope Gregory I, famous for his quasi-syncretic approach to conversion, was amenable to spreading Christianity by coercion, if that was what it took to convert stubborn heathens. In a letter written in 601 to Æthelberht, king of the Kentings, Gregory urges the relatively recently converted king to step up his efforts to bring the rest of England to Christianity: "So, glorious son, guard with a careful mind that grace which you have received from God; hurry to extend the Christian faith among the people subject to you; increase your righteous zeal for their conversion; suppress idolatry; throw down the buildings of shrines; strengthen the customs of [your] subjects by the outstanding excellence of [your] life, by exhorting, by terrifying, by flattering, correcting and showing an example of good works" (Et ideo, gloriose fili, eam quam accepisti divinitus gratiam sollicita mente custodi, christianam fidem in populis tibi subditis extendere festina, zelum rectitudinis tuae in eorum conversione multiplica, idolorum cultus insequere, fanorum aedificia everte, subditorum mores in magna vitae munditia exhortando, terrendo, blandiendo, corrigendo et boni operis exempla monstrando aedifica) (MGH, *Gregorii I Papae Registrum epistolarum*, vol. 2, 308-9, trans. in Higham, *The Convert Kings*, 99).

12. "Tribue ei, omnipotens deus, ut sit fortissimus protector patriae et consolator ecclesiarum atque coenobiorum sanctorum maxima cum pietate regalis munificentiae, atque et sit fortissimus regum, triumphator hostium ad oppromindas rebelles et paganas nationes, sitque inimicis suis satis terribilis proxima fortitudine regalis potentiae" (Bouman, *Sacring and Crowning*, 91-93, trans. in Nelson, "Kingship and Empire," 58).

13. MGH, *Capitularia regum Francorum*, vol. 1, 68-70.

14. Becher, *Charlemagne*, 68.

15. Alcuin was troubled about the authenticity and vigor of conversions at sword point, as evidenced by his letters to Charlemagne and others in the late 790s. In two epistles to Meginfrid and Arno dated 796, for example, he is particularly critical of the cruel punishments and extortion of the Saxons, suggesting that the Saxons be taught about the benefits of conversion instead of being forced to pay tithes and being severely punished for minor infractions.

16. This question, however, is not entirely settled and is still being discussed

by historians. For a recent evaluation of Alcuin's position on conversion, see Stofferahn, "Staying the Royal Sword." Stofferahn concludes that "the ordeals encountered with the Saxons and Avars fostered both a reorientation of missionary policy in a newly conquered province and a substantive transformation of how conversion was conceived of by Charlemagne and those many successors who would seek to emulate these achievements" (ibid., 480).

17. "Qualis erit tibi gloria, o beatissime rex, in die aeternae retributionis, quando hi omnes, qui per tuam bonam sollicitudinem ab idolatriae cultura ad cognoscendum verum Deum conversi sunt, te ante tribunal domini nostri Iesu Christi in beata sorte stantem sequentur et ex his omnibus perpetuae beatitudinis merces augetur. Ecce quanta devotione et benignitate pro dilatatione nominis Christi duritiam infelicis populi Saxonum per verae salutis consilium emollire laborasti" (MGH, *Epistolae Karolini aevi*, vol. 2, no. 110, 157, trans. in King, *Charlemagne*, 315).

18. "Gesta Karoli Magni," in MGH, *Notker der Stammler*, 90.

19. "Vita Lebuini antiqua," in MGH, [*Supplementa tomurum I-XV*], 794.

20. MGH, *Capitularia regum Francorum*, vol. 1, no. 27, 71.

21. See Nelson, "The Lord's Anointed and the People's Choice." I will discuss further in chapter 2 the importance of the *urbs Karoli* in the heart of Saxony at Paderborn, which Charlemagne rebuilt in 799 larger than before. As Julia M. H. Smith notes, the impressive size and luxury of the church and royal palace "made an unequivocal statement about the power of the Saxons' new ruler and new religion" (Smith, *Europe After Rome*, 269-70). See also Mayr-Harting, "Charlemagne, the Saxons."

22. Airlie, "Narratives of Triumph," 118.

23. Nelson, "Lord's Anointed," 169.

24. For a discussion of the poem in its literary context, see Godman, *Poets and Emperors*, 61-63; and Garrison, "The Emergence of Carolingian Latin Literature," esp. 126-29.

25. [P]roceres mundi regem venerare videntur
Ponderibus vastis ingentia dona ferentes
Inmensum argenti pondus, fulgentis et auri,
Gemmarum cumulos sacro stipante metallo
Purpura splendentes aurato tegmine vestes,
Spumantes et equos flavo stringente capistro.
(Hibernicus Exul, *Ad Karolum regem*, ll. 1-7, in Godman, *The Poetry of the Carolingian Renaissance*), 174-75.
The entire poem can be found in MGH, *Poetae Latini aevi Carolini*, vol. 1, 396-99.

26. As Bernhard Jussen notes: "Imperial godparenthood is an example of how power relations were harmonized by means of sponsorship: the fathers were usually the victors, the sons the vanquished. . . . The spiritual sonship/adoption could be interpreted as an honor, and the act of subjugation was presented as a familial celebration, so that the conquered leader could return home an honored man, a 'son' laden with gifts" (Jussen, *Spiritual Kinship as Social Practice*, 219.)

27. Nelson, "Lord's Anointed," 176.

28. Smith, *Province and Empire*, 108. See also Lynch, *Godparents and Kinship*, esp. 163-204 and 333-39.

29. Smith, *Province and Empire*, 109.

30. Nelson, "The Settings of the Gift," 116.

31. Jussen, *Spiritual Kinship*, 44.

32. Ibid., 221.

33. See my discussion of the poem *Karolus Magnus et Leo Papa* in chapter 2, where the poet challenges the standing

of the pope as Holy Father and intercessor for mankind to God and places Charlemagne in a superior position to the bishop of Rome.

34. See Higham's comment that "Bede made much of Æthelberht's decision to accept baptism, treating it as a loosening of the proverbial pebble, which set in motion a divinely predicted, sanctioned and impelled avalanche of Christianisation. It was, therefore, a cusp event in his vision of English history. Roman responsibility for it was used by Bede to sustain his vision of the God-chosen status of the English. . . . Bede's comparative understatement of the strength and significance of the early Frankish input was probably also a victim of this imperative" (Higham, *The Convert Kings*, 56). In another example from Bede, that of the Northumbrian king Oswald standing as sponsor for Cynegils, the king of the West Saxons, Oswald's prominence as godfather is diminished by his immediately becoming Cynegils's son-in-law. The two kings then *together* give the city of Dorcic to Bishop Birinus to establish as his episcopal see, which suggests some equality of authority rather than emphasizing the father-son baptismal bond.

35. Smith, *Province and Empire*, 109.

36. Dic, Herolde, precor jam nunc, quam pluris amabis
Celse fidem regis, an tua sculpta nequam?
Ferque fabricata focis auri argentique metalla,
Et tibi sive tuis inde paretur honos.
Si ferrum fuerit, fortassis ad arva colenda
Sufficit et cultros inde fabrire jube.
Plus tibi vomer opes telluri infixus habebit,
Quam Deus ille tibi conferat arte sua.
(Ermoldus Nigellus, *Carminis in honorem Ludovici*, col. 0630A)

37. Cernere namque placet Francorum regna, fidemque
Caesaris, arma, dapes, Christicolumque decus. . . .
Si Deus ille tuus nostris praefertur honore,
Et valet oranti munera plura dare,
Linquere causa monet, Christo parere juvabit,
Sculptaque flammivomis ferre metalla focis.
(Ibid., col. 0623B)

38. Ibid., col. 0634A.

39. Mox manibus junctis regi se tradidit ultro
Et secum regnum, quod sibi jure fuit.
"Suscipe, Caesar, ait, me nec non regna subacta,
Sponte tuis memet confero servitiis.
Caesar at ipse manus manibus suscepit honestis;
Junguntur Francis Danica regna piis."
(Ibid., col. 0634B)
See also Robert Levine's discussion of this poem in "Baptizing Pirates." For a discussion of the significance of the hand-having submission ritual usually related to homage, see Hyams, "Homage and Feudalism."

40. Mayr-Harting, "Charlemagne," 1118.

41. Ibid., 1123–24.

42. Ibid., 1133.

43. Ibid., 1125–30.

44. "Quis enim ignorat sub hac plaga mundi habitans, Francos ante Saxones in Christi fide atque religione fuisse, quos ipsi postmodum suae dominationi subegerunt armis, atque superiores effecti, dominorum ritu, imo magis paterno affectu, ab idolorum cultu abstrahentes, ad fidem Christi converterunt?" (Hrabanus Maurus, *Liber de Oblatione Puerorum*, col. 432A-B).

45. Airlie, "Narratives of Triumph," 109.

46. Ibid., 111–12.

47. Ibid., 113.

48. There are thirteen surviving manuscripts of all or most of the text, of which four can be dated to the eleventh century, and one of these was produced at Saint Augustine's Abbey in Canterbury; two others from the twelfth century were produced in England. For more information about the manuscripts and editions of Dudo's history, see Eric Christiansen, introduction to Dudo of Saint Quentin, *History of the Normans*, xxxiv–xxxvi.
49. Koziol, *Begging Pardon and Favor*, 67.
50. Ibid., 151.
51. The politically charged baptism of Rollo and the dynastic concerns expressed here have been noted by scholars such as François Neveux, who writes, "Le baptême de Rollon doit être rapproché du baptême d'autres fondateurs de dynastie et, en particulier, celui de Clovis" (Neveux, *La Normandie de ducs au rois*, 17).
52. Christiansen notes that Dudo emulated Carolingian writers in his history, because "there is not a theme, verse or episode in this history which is inconsistent with, if not evidently derived from, the literary culture of Carolingian Francia" (Christiansen, introduction, xviii).
53. Herrick, "Heirs to the Apostles," 24.
54. Southern, "Aspects of the European Tradition, I," 192.
55. As Christiansen notes, "A *dux*, at this period, had power over counts. *Patricius* was a title formerly given to leading Merovingian magnates, and so implied equality with the highest in the land, next to the king" (Christiansen, introduction, xxiv).
56. For a discussion of Dudo's ideological dependence upon the *Aeneid*, see Christiansen, introduction, esp. xx–xxiii; Albu, *The Normans in Their Histories*, 12–20; Searle, "Fact and Pattern in Heroic History," and *Predatory Kinship and the Creation of Norman Power, 840–1066*, 61–67.
57. Albu claims that he "gives a sinister cast to the upstart Normans he was pretending to honor" (Albu, *The Normans in Their Histories*, 14–15).
58. Ibid., 15.
59. Koziol, *Begging Pardon and Favor*, 7, 138. At this time, Koziol notes, elements such as formulas of supplication, as well as attention to emblems of authority such as formal titles and charters, "became more important in projecting a correct image of comital authority than ever before" (ibid., 139).
60. "Omnium alstignus unus pro omnibus inquit nequissimus" (Dudo of Saint Quentin, *Dudonis gesta Normannorum*, cap. 2, trans. in *History of the Normans*, 17).
61. "Si uobis non displicet romam eamus, eamque sicuti frantiam nostro dominatui subiungemus" (ibid., cap. 2, trans. in *History of the Normans*, 18).
62. "Suscipit nefarius baptismum, ad animae suae interitum" (ibid., cap. 2, trans. in *History of the Normans*, 18–19).
63. Alstignus "congratulates himself on holding sole command of the whole empire through the city" (Gratulatur tenere se monarchiam totius imperii per urbem quam putabat roman) (ibid., cap. 2, trans. in *History of the Normans*, 20).
64. "'Not for their destruction, but for their correction,' on account of their misdeeds" (qui non ad interitum sed ad correptionem propter exaggerationem scelerum francigenis acciderunt) (ibid., cap. 3, trans. in *History of the Normans*, 22).
65. "Obtain the enjoyment of the salvation that is to come" (Depromat uenturae salutis negotium) (ibid., cap. 3, trans. in *History of the Normans*, 22).
66. "Armis strenui, bellis edocti, corpore pulcherrimi, animositate robustissimi"

(ibid., cap. 5, trans. in *History of the Normans*, 26.
67. Ibid., cap. 6, trans. in *History of the Normans*, 28.
68. "Circa basim illius hinc inde et altrinsecus multa milia auium diuersorum generum uarii coloris sinistras alas, quinetiam rubicundas habentium, quarum diffuse longe lateque multitudinis inexhaustam extremitatem perspicaci" (ibid., cap. 7, trans. in *History of the Normans*, 29).
69. "Tibi homines diuersorum regnorum seruiendo accubitate obedient" (ibid., cap. 7, trans. in *History of the Normans*, 30).
70. See, for example, Dudo's poem after Rollo's battle with the Frisians:
Hinc fontis liquidi et sacri rorem
    subiturus,
Chrismate perfusus, oleique liquore
    nouatus,
Praemia perpetuae capies, cum munere
    uitae.

Thereafter to be bedewed by the sacred,
    clear-running fountain,
Anointed with chrism, made new by the
    pouring of oil,
You will receive rewards, with the gift of
    life everlasting.
(Ibid., cap. 9, trans. in *History of the Normans*, ll. 7–9, 35)
Also see especially the poem just before Rollo's dream vision of the bird empire, where his conversion is linked with earthly *and* divine *imperium*:
Perpes christicola francisca celsior aula
Patritius meritis florescens iure ualebis
Emeritam et capies condigna merce
    coronam
In summoque bono deitate mereberis
    uti.

You by right, as eternally Christian, will
    worthily enter a
Hall higher than Francia's, a patrician
    abounding in merit,
And you will receive a well-earned
    crown as a proper reward
Which you will deserve to wear in the
    Godhead of goodness supreme.
(Ibid., cap. 6, trans. in *History of the Normans*, ll. 10–14, 29)
71. "Praesenti futuraque pace poteris frui ditissimusque ac terra morari" (ibid., cap. 12, trans. in *History of the Normans*, 46).
72. Terra haec penitus desolata militibus priuata aratro non exercita, arboribus locis referta, fluuiis diuersorum genere. Piscium plenis diuisa uenatu opulenta uineis non ignara glebis cultro elaboratis fecunda mari affluentiam diuersarum rerum daturo ex una parte circumdata altera decursibus aquarum deportantium nauigio cuncta bona. Quasi frantiae regno discriminata; si fuerit frequentia hominum usitata ualde erit fertilis et uberrima, nobisque ad habitandum sufficiens et congrua. Filia quam tibi spondet utriusque progeniei semine regaliter exorta. . . . Reminiscere somnii interpretationum; mysticorumque eius intellectum. Vt remur in istis finibus uertetur nobis in prosperum.

This utterly desolated land, bereft of warriors and untilled by the plough, is full of good trees, is not unfamiliar with vines, bears fruit in soil worked by the plough, is hemmed in on one side by a sea which will afford an abundant wealth of different commodities, and on the other by the outflow of waters carrying all sorts of goods by ship. It is virtually distinct from the kingdom of Francia, and if it were occupied by a dense population it would be mightily fertile and very rich, sufficient and suitable for us to inhabit. The girl whom he is promising is lawfully born of the seed of either parent.... Remember the interpretation of the dream, and its mystical meaning. As we see it, things will turn out better for us within this territory. (Ibid., cap. 12, trans. in *History of the Normans*, 47)

73. This version of the relationship between duke Robert and Rollo may be an invention of Dudo's; Richer of Reims's slightly earlier history relates that Robert defeated the pagans in a great battle and subsequently arranged their baptism (Dudo of Saint Quentin, *History of the Normans*, 195n200).

74. "Dux idem deprecans flexis animi genibus" (Dudo of Saint Quentin, *Dudonis gesta Normannorum*, cap. 12, trans. in *History of the Normans*, 48).

75. Rollo and the duke "will be firm and inseparable friends, and no man will be able to stand against you, and he will always do you service, and make the king look ever kindly upon you" (Hinc eritis si tibi placuerit inseparabiliter fidi amici, nullusque contra uos stare poterit; facietque incessanter uestrum seruitium; regemque tibi omni tempore beneuolum) (ibid., cap. 12, trans. in *History of the Normans*, 48).

76. "Hic mihi sit paterno amore pro patre; ego filiorum dilectione ero illi pro filio. Succurrat mihi si necesse fuerit ut pater filio; ego illi ut filius patri. Gaudeat mea prosperitate; tristetur mea aduersitate. Quae meae potestati sunt sui iuris sint; et quae mei iuris suae potestati sint" (ibid., cap. 12, trans. in *History of the Normans*, 48).

77. Gisla may be another of Dudo's inventions, because there is no contemporary evidence for her existence. Christiansen notes that "the name is borrowed from the *Annals of St Vaast*, and the idea from Lavinia, daughter of king Latinus, whose predestined marriage to Aeneas symbolises the union of Latins and Trojans, which will lead to the future dominance of the Romans" (Dudo of Saint Quentin, *History of the Normans*, 195n199). By linking the Normans with the Romans in this way, Dudo further emphasizes the idea of Norman *imperium* as the "manifest destiny" of the Northmen in his history.

78. "Securitatem; omnibus gentibus in sua terra manere cupientibus fecit. Illam terram; suis fidelibus funiculo diuisit. Uniuersamque diu desertam reaedificauit, atque de suis militibus aduenisque gentibus refertam; restruxit iura et leges sempiternas; uoluntate principum sancitas et decretas plebi indixit; atque pacifica conuersatione morari simul coegit. Aecclesias funditus fusas statuit templa frequentia paganorum destructa restaurauit, muros ciuitatum et propugnacula refecit et augmentauit" (Dudo of Saint Quentin, *Dudonis gesta Normannorum*, cap. 13, trans. in *History of the Normans*, 51).

79. For an insightful discussion of the sacerdotal role of Norman dukes, supported in part by their role as the protector of the relic of the blood of Christ, "qui fut longtemps créatrice de leur pouvoir autant que symbole de celui-ci," see Beaune, "Les ducs, le roi, et le saint sang."

80. "Speciae pulchrerimus, canis praecandidis repletus, superciliis, acieque oculorum choruscus; naribus malisque splendidus, barba canifera et prolixa honoratus, statura procerus, lingua eruditus, uirtute animae et corporis plenus, bonitate diffusus, mente sagacissimus, gratia dei munitus, omnibusque erat una salus" (Dudo of Saint Quentin, *Dudonis gesta Normannorum*, cap. 58, trans. in *History of the Normans*, 166). Christiansen also notes the parallels between Richard's description and other imperial rulers: "The

penetrating and glittering eyes had been attributed by Notker to Louis the Pious (*Gesta Karoli Magni* 2, 11) and by Widukind to Otto I (*Rerum Gestarum Saxonicarum* 2, 36), who was also remarkable for his hoary hairs and for his bushy beard 'contrary to the custom of the ancients'" (Dudo of Saint Quentin, *History of the Normans*, 225n472). Einhard records an aging, wise Charlemagne as having a glorious head of gray hair, to which Paul Edward Dutton attributes the later images of Charlemagne as "an old and holy emperor with a flowing white beard" in *Charlemagne's Mustache*, 156–57. Einhard additionally describes Charlemagne as being "lofty of stature" in the *Vita Karoli Magni*, chap. 22, so it is clear here that Dudo is drawing a parallel between contemporary images of Charlemagne and Richard I.

81. For example, when we first meet Charlemagne, he is described as having a white beard and hoary white head (*blanche ad la barbe e tut flurit le chef*, l. 117; see also ll. 261, 538, and 4001).

82. Dudo of Saint Quentin, *Dudonis gesta Normannorum*, cap. 58. Jean Dunbabin has shown that the use of regal terminology and titles in territorial principalities became common during the course of the ninth and tenth centuries in sub-Carolingian Francia, arguing that "titles were important pillars of princely power" (Dunbabin, *France in the Making*, 48).

83. Nelson, "The Settings of the Gift," 146.

84. "Let the elders and the more powerful be gathered together more privately, in the evening of the night to come, and let us blind them with the very biggest gifts, and a huge grant of lands, if they should happen to look with favor on our prayers and wishes" (Conuocentur maiores natu et potentiores secretius, futurae noctis conticinio et excessemus eos muneribus praemaximis, et copioso beneficio, si forte fauerint precibus nostris et uoto) (Dudo of Saint Quentin, *Dudonis gesta Normannorum*, cap. 57, trans. in *History of the Normans*, 225n472, 157).

85. "Si uelle est uobis inherere nostris consiliis; ego faciam uos primitus baptizari, in nomine patris, et filii, et spiritus sancti; ampliorique deinde integerrimae fidei praedicatione; ab episcopis profusius erudiri; postea muneribus largissimis; beneficiisque amplissimis ditari quibus uiuere quiuiretis et in aeternum non peribitis. Sed uitae praesentis solatio, futurae remunerationis brauio; sine fine fruemini. Si integerrimae pacis quam requiro felicitatem; non abnueritis" (ibid., cap. 57, trans. in *History of the Normans*, 160).

86. "Beati mites, quoniam ipsi possidebunt terram. Quam suauis, quam mitis, quam beniuolus quamque benignissimus fuerit: qui compendiosam uitae eius seriem legerit aliquid suauitatis eius pernoscere quiuerit! Hic tetboldum comitem, aliquando deuotione, aliquando armis compescuit. Hic lotharium regem humilitatem deuicit. Hic dacos suauitate uerborum et donis cohercuit. Hic francos ceterasque gentes humillimis uerbis et muneribus sibi prouocans asscuit. Hic incolas northmannicae regionis summa deuotione protexit. Hic domigenas ut paterfamilias deuotus fouit. Beniuolus in omni negotio extitit; suauia in omni re uerba et opere sonuit. Terram namque uiuentium possidere meruit qui corporis sui terram mansueta benignitate custodiuit" (ibid., cap. 59, trans. in *History of the Normans*, 167).

87. Nelson, "Kingship and Empire," 59.

88. Although this idea is also an element clearly expressed in *Laudabiliter* for the "correction" of Christianity in Ireland, as I shall demonstrate

below in my discussion of the Anglo-Norman occupation of Ireland by Strongbow and Henry II.
89. The romance ideals of good customs and, especially, fair love for the conversion of potential enemies are deliberately vague, encompassing similar notions to those of sacral kingship, such as law-giving and peacemaking but also celebrating the king as the highest model of the qualities of courtly behavior, manners and civility (*curteisie*).
90. Gillingham, "Civilizing the English?," 36. Matthew Strickland has noted that the idea of mercy and compassion for the conquered was a new one to English politics, because by the time of the Conquest, "killing on the scale habitually seen in Anglo-Scandinavian warfare had become a remote phenomenon for the Norman knighthood" (Strickland, "Slaughter, Slavery or Ransom," 58). See also Strickland, "Killing or Clemency?"
91. Gillingham, *The English in the Twelfth Century*, 182. See the comments by Giraldus Cambrensis in the *Descriptio Kambriae*, for example, who claims that the Irish and Welsh massacre and decapitate their enemies, unlike the French, who ransom them ("Gallica tamen militia multum a Kambrica, sicut ab Hybernica, distare dignoscitur. . . . ibi capiuntur milites, hic decapitantur; ibi redimuntur, hic perimuntur" (Gerald of Wales, *Giraldi Cambrensis Opera*, vol. 6, trans. in *The Journey Through Wales*, 269).
92. Gillingham, *The English in the Twelfth Century*, 210.
93. Ibid., 228.
94. Hyams, *Rancor and Reconciliation in Medieval England* (Ithaca: Cornell University Press, 2003), esp. chap. 4, "Vengeance and Peacemaking in the Century After the Norman Conquest."
95. Gillingham, *The English in the Twelfth Century*, 184.
96. Strickland, "Killing or Clemency?," 117.
97. Hyams, *Rancor and Reconciliation*, 153.
98. Hyams, "Feud and State," 20.
99. Gillingham, "Civilizing the English?," 21.
100. William claims to include these accounts, including some from Italy and Germany, to enliven his narrative for his courtly audience, saying that "I take it that no one will object to some variety in my narrative, unless he is so clouded in mind that he imitates the critical disdain of a Cato" (nulli uarietatem relationum displicituram opinor, nisi si quis tam nubilus est ut Catonis supercilium emuletur) (William of Malmesbury, *Gesta regum Anglorum* 3.304 [Mynors, Thomson, and Winterbottom 1:538-39]). Although some of his minor works likely had a limited monastic audience, the same was not true for his two major historical works. According to Rodney Thomson in his significant study of the author, they were "probably consciously designed for a different and larger readership. Surviving copies and references in library catalogues indicate that within his own lifetime they were known throughout southern England at least. By 1200 they were read all over the country" (Thomson, *William of Malmesbury*, 39). Thomson cites the colorful stories of the Crusades in particular as evidence that William "was writing, at least in part, for a courtly audience" (ibid., 186).
101. For more information on the medieval use of this term, see Jones, "The Image of the Barbarian."
102. Davies, *The Matter of Britain*, 10.
103. Gillingham, *The English in the Twelfth Century*, 5.
104. See also Jaeger, *The Origins of Courtliness*. Although he sets 939 as his *terminus post quem*, he acknowledges

in his introduction that "the forces that produced courtly ethics were present in Carolingian court culture" (ibid., 4).
105. Gillingham, "Civilizing the English?," 41–42.
106. Gerald of Wales, *Giraldi Cambrensis Opera*, vol. 1, 302, vol. 8, lviii.
107. For longer discussions of the Anglo-Norman opinion of other British peoples as "barbarians," see Bartlett, *Gerald of Wales*, chaps. 6 and 7; Davies, "Buchedd a moes y Cymry"; and Gillingham, "The Beginnings of English Imperialism."
108. "Postquam autem Normanni, bello commisso, Anglos sibi subiugarunt, hanc etiam suo imperio terram adicientes castellis innumeris munire; propriis incolis uiriliter edomitis, constanter excoluer; ad pacem confouendam, legem et plebiscita eis indixere; adeoque terram fertilem omnibusque copiis affluentem reddidere, ut fecundissimae Britanniae nequaquam inferiorem aestimares" (*GS* 1.8 [Potter 14–15]).
109. "Wallenses more Anglicorum pene vivere inceperunt; thesaurus congregantes, et rerum damna de caetero formidantes" (Rishanger, *Willelmi Rishanger*, 148, trans. mine). Ranulf Higden echoes this notion slightly later and emphasizes that it is the cause of their now-peaceful natures: "Quas cito gens haec perderet, / Si passim nunc confligeret" (Higden, *Polychronicon*, 410–11).
110. Davies, *Domination and Conquest*, 49.
111. Recent work on medieval British postcolonial experience has brought this idea to the foreground. See, for example, the collection of essays on the conflicted relationship between England and Wales as evidenced by the literature in Kennedy and Meecham-Jones, *Authority and Subjugation*.
112. "Et haec quidem extrema iam uictoribus suis participarunt, de ceteris in eorum mores transeuntes" (William of Malmesbury, *Gesta regum Anglorum* 3.245 [Mynors, Thomson, and Winterbottom 1:458–59]).
113. "Uideas . . . recenti ritu patriam florere" (ibid., 3.246 [1:460–61]).
114. Gillingham, "Civilizing the English?," 36.
115. Davies, *The Matter of Britain*, 15.
116. "Brytland him wæs on gewealde. . . . 7 gif he moste þa gyt twa gear libban, he hæfde Yrlande mid his werscipe gewunnon 7 wiðutan ælcon wæpnon" (*The Anglo-Saxon Chronicle*, vol. 7, 97; trans. mine). John Le Patourel demonstrates the patterns of colonization in the late eleventh century as a complex process of possession by a small group of elites who were close, even related, to William I, and suggests that "it was these groups that did a great deal of the conquering and taking possession of England" (Le Patourel, "The Norman Colonization of Britain," 429). Benjamin Hudson examines William's interest in Irish affairs in "William the Conqueror and Ireland."
117. Hollister and Keefe, "The Making of the Angevin Empire," 3.
118. Ibid., 4.
119. "I would almost say, easily first among all his predecessors in England, *he preferred to do battle in the council-chamber rather than the field*, and won his victories without bloodshed if he could, and with very little if he could not" (Et pene dicam omnium antecessorum in Anglia facile primus, *libentius bellabat consilio quam gladio*: uincebat, si poterat, sanguine nullo, si aliter non poterat, pauco) (William of Malmesbury, *Gesta regum Anglorum* 5.412 [Mynors, Thomson, and Winterbottom 1:744–45]; emphasis mine).

120. Hollister and Keefe, "The Making of the Angevin Empire," 4, 5-6.
121. Jones, *Brut y Tywysogyon*, 1087, 1116, and 1157.
122. Davies, *The First English Empire*, 8.
123. "Multiplicibus exeniis muneratus inter precipuos optimates penes illum consuedit" (loaded with gifts, he sat at [Henry I's] side among the greatest of magnates) (Orderic Vitalis, *The Ecclesiastical History* 8.3 [Chibnall 4:402]).
124. "Iuuenis ceteris curialior et qui, nostrorum conuictu et familiaritate limatus a puero, omnem rubiginem Scotticae barbariei deterserat" (William of Malmesbury, *Gesta regum Anglorum* 5.400 [Mynors, Thomson, and Winterbottom 1:726-27]).
125. On the similar ideology for hostage-taking in the Roman Empire, see Allen, *Hostages and Hostage-Taking*.
126. Davies, *Domination and Conquest*, 49-50.
127. Sweetman, *Calendar of Documents*, no. 1840, vol. 1, 273.
128. Davies, *Domination and Conquest*, 6. For the many examples of submission on the part of British kings and lords, see chap. 4, "Native Submission."
129. As Davies demonstrates, "Domination is often most successfully asserted ... where it arises (as it were) out of the natural weft of political relationships" (ibid., 5). See also Davies's discussion of the cost of military occupation in contrast to the practical considerations of submission and overlordship (ibid., 60-61). Although the practicality of these methods could be seen as an end in itself for the use of nonviolent methods of subjugation, the overriding concerns of conversion and acculturation that dominate the literature reflect those of the Carolingian period.
130. Press, "The Precocious Courtesy of Geoffrey Gaimar," 270.
131. For a detailed discussion of the manuscript tradition, including what little we can determine about the author himself, see Alexander Bell's introduction to his edition of *L'Estoire des Engleis*, ix-lxxxiii; and Ian Short's introduction to his edition and translation of Gaimar's *Estoire des Engleis*.
132. Gransden, *Historical Writing in England*, 210.
133. Press, "The Precocious Courtesy of Geoffrey Gaimar," 267-69.
134. Ibid., 269.
135. "þær sæt .xiiii. niht, ⁊ þa sealde se here him gislas ⁊ mycle aðas þæt hi of his rice woldon, ⁊ him eac gehæton þæt heora cyning fulwihte onfon wolde, ⁊ hi þæt gelæs\ton/. ⁊ þæs ymbe .iii. wucan com se cyning Godrum þritiga sum þara manna þe in þam here weorþuste wæron æt Alre, ⁊ þæt is wið Æþelingaige, ⁊ his se cyning onfeng þær æt fulwihte, ⁊ his crismlising wæs æt Weþmor, ⁊ he wæs .xii. niht mid þam cyninge, ⁊ he hine mycclum ⁊ his geferan mid feo weorðode" (*The Anglo-Saxon Chronicle*, vol. 6, 27, trans. by Michael J. Swanton in *Anglo-Saxon Chronicle*, 75). Swanton notes that the "chrism-loosing" was the ceremonial removal of a white fillet bound to the head after anointing (*Anglo-Saxon Chronicle*, 76n9).
136. En quinze jurs les danta si,
    icels Daneis dunt jo vus di,
    k'il firent pleit si s'acorderent,
    e bons ostages [en] livrerent
    e jurerent, quanz k[ë] il sunt,
    ke jamés nel guerreierunt,
    e uncore plus li ont promis:
    crestïeneté li unt requis.
    (Gaimar, *Estoire des Engleis*, ll. 3199-3205; all translations of Gaimar are mine unless otherwise noted)
137. Davies, *Domination and Conquest*, 48.
138. E il vindrent a icel jor,
    si amenerent lur seignur,

> le rei Gudrun unt amenez;
> de ses parenz les plus privez
> vindrent od lui al baptizer.
> Trente en i out al primsener;
> li reis meïsmes les leva,
> nuns e bons enges lur dona:
> al baptisterie reis Gudrum
> Adelstan donc l'apela l'om,
> e les trente, ses compaignons,
> chescon par sei out enge e nuns.
> . . . .
> A Wethmore furent desalbez
> e dusze jurs ont sujurnez
> od Elveret le gentil rei
> ki par honur prist de els conrei,
> e il e ses bons compaignons
> lur donerent mult riches dons.
>
> They came on that day, and
> They brought their lord;
> King Guthorm, they brought him.
> And the nearest of his kin
> Came with him to baptism.
> Thirty there were when he was signed
>   with the cross.
> The king presented them,
> Gave them names and good angels.
> At the font, King Guthorm
> Was then called Athelstan,
> And the thirty of his companions
> Each for himself had angels and names.
> . . . .
> At Wedmore was the chrism loosing.
> And twelve days they tarried there
> With Alfred the noble king,
> Who honorably entertained them.
> And he and his good companions
> Gave them many rich gifts.
> (Gaimar, Estoire des Engleis, ll. 3211-22, 3227-32)

139. "Cil tint terre com emperere" (ibid., l. 3566).
140. En son tens amenda la terre,
     partut out pes, n'ert nule guere.
     Il sul regnout sur tuz les reis,
     e sur Escoz e sur Galeis.
     . . . .
     Li reis ama mult seint' Eglise:
     de tort, de dreit sout la devise.
     (Ibid., ll. 3567-70, 3573-74)
141. "Bones costumes alevat" (ibid., l. 3577).
142. Tuz ses veisins vers lui clinat:
     par bel amur e par supplei
     les aclinat trestuz vers sei.
     (Ibid., ll. 3578-80)
143. Ibid., lx; see especially Gillingham, *The English in the Twelfth Century*, chap. 7, "Gaimar, the Prose *Brut* and the Making of English History," 113-22.
144. Damian-Grint, *The New Historians*, 36. See also Short, "Gaimar's Epilogue," and "Gaimar et les débuts de l'historiographie en langue française," 267; and Walpole, "A New Edition."
145. Ivor Arnold certainly thought so, claiming in the introduction to his edition of Wace's *Roman de Brut* that "la ruse de Gormond pour prendre Cirencester est mentionée avant Wace par Gaimar dans son *Estoire des Engleis*; c'est peut-être par lui qu'il l'a acquise" (in Wace, *Roman de Brut*, vol. 1, lxxx). Bell, however, disputes Arnold's assessment in his edition of Gaimar (in Gaimar, *L'Estoire des Engleis*, lxiv).
146. Judith Weiss, introduction to Wace's "*Roman de Brut*," xxiii.
147. As will be discussed further below in chapter 2; see, for example, Gerould, "King Arthur and Politics."
148. Moreover, John Gillingham has shown that Arthur's position as predecessor to Anglo-Norman kings, as opposed to British kings, would not occur until much later in the twelfth century (indeed, Richard the Lionheart is the first to explicitly associate himself with Arthur). See Gillingham, *The English in the Twelfth Century*, esp. 22-23, and "The Cultivation of History," 36-39.
149. N'esteit pas tenuz pur curteis
     Escot ne Bretun ne Franceis,
     Normant, Angevin ne Flamenc
     Ni Burguinun ne Loherenc,

> *De ki que il tenist sun feu,*
> *Des occident jesqu'a Muntgeu,*
> *Ki a la curt Artur n'alout*
> *E ki od lui ne sujurnout,*
> *E ki n'en aveit vesteüre*
> *E cunuissance e armeüre*
> *A la guise que cil teneient*
> *Ki en la curt Artur serveient.*
> (Wace's "Roman de Brut," ll. 9761-72, trans. Weiss, 247)

150. *De buens homes e de richesce*
  E de plenté e de noblesce
  E de curteisie e d'enur
  Portout Engleterre la flur
  Sur tuz les regnes d'envirun
  E sur tuz cels que nus savum.
  Plus erent curteis e vaillant
  Neïs li povre païsant
  Que chevalier en alters regnes,
  E altresi erent les femes.

  . . . .

  Ja nul chevalier n'i eüst,
  De quel parage que il fust,
  Ja peüst aveir druerie
  Ne curteise dame a amie,
  Se il n'eüst treis feiz esté
  De chevalerie pruvé.
  Li chevalier mielz en valeient
  E en estur mielz en faiseient,
  E les dames meillur esteient
  E plus chastement en viveient.
  (Ibid., ll. 10493-502, 10511-20, trans. Weiss, 265)

151. *Duze ans puis cel repairement*
  Regna Artur paisiblement,
  Ne nuls guerreier ne l'osa
  Ne il alter ne guereia.
  Par sei, sens alter enseinement,
  Emprist si grant afaitement
  E se cuntint tant noblement,
  Tant bel e tant curteisement,
  N'esteit parole de curt d'ume,
  Neis de l'empereür de Rome.

  For twelve years after his return, Arthur reigned in peace. No one dared to make war on him, nor did he go to war himself. On his own, with no other instruction, he acquired such knightly skill and behaved so nobly, so finely and courteously, that there was no court so talked about, not even that of the Roman emperor.
  (Ibid., ll. 9731-43, trans. Weiss, 245)

152. *N'out remis barun des Espaine*
  Dessi al Rim vers Alemainne,
  Ki a la feste ne venist
  Pur ço kil la sumunse oïst,
  Tant pur Artur, tant pur ses duns,
  Tant pur cunustre ses baruns,
  Tant pur veeir ses mananties,
  Tant pur oïr ses curteisies,
  Tant pur amur, tant pur banie,
  Tant pur enur, tant pur baillie.
  (Ibid., ll. 10327-36, trans. Weiss, 261)

153. Ibid., l. 10373.

154. Parkes, "The Date of the Oxford Manuscript," 175. David Douglas suggests a slightly earlier period of composition, sometime from the latter half of the eleventh century and before 1124 (Douglas, "The Song of Roland," 100).

155. See Andrew Taylor's discussion of the manuscript in its social and cultural context in *Textual Situations*, 26-70.

156. "Tunc cantilena Rollandi inchoata, ut martium uiri exemplum pugnaturos accenderet, inclamatoque Dei auxilio prelium consertum bellatumque acriter, neutris in multam diei horam cedentibus" (William of Malmesbury, *Gesta regum Anglorum* 3.242 [Mynors, Thomson, and Winterbottom 1:454], trans. in *William of Malmesbury's "Chronicle of the Kings of England,"* 277). *The Carmen de Hastingae Proelio*, written shortly after the battle itself, merely mentions that a juggler (*histrio* or *mimus*) juggled a sword at the beginning of the battle and killed the first Englishman to encourage the Norman army (Guy, Bishop of Amiens, *The Carmen de Hastingae Proelio*, ll. 391-404). This story is repeated in Gaimar, *Estoire des Engleis*,

ll. 5267-5306, and briefly by Henry of Huntingdon in his *Historia Anglorum* 6.30. Wace conflates the two versions in the *Roman de Rou* so that Taillefer sings *Roland* to stir French hearts to battle:
*Taillefer, qui mult bien chantout,
sor un cheval qui tost alout,
devant le duc alout chantant
de Karlemaigne e de Rollant,
e d'Oliver e des vassals
qui morurent en Rencesvals.*
(Wace, Le Roman de Rou de Wace, vol. 3, ll. 8013-18)

157. *Des plus feluns dis en ad apelez:*
. . . .
*Dist a ses humes: "Seignurs, vos en ireiz,
Branches d'olive en voz mains portereiz,
Si me direz a Carlemagne le rei,
Pur le soen Deu qu'il ait mercit de mei.
Ja einz ne verrat passer cest premier meis
Que jel sivrai od mil de mes fedeilz,
Si recevrai la chrestïene lei,
Serai ses hom par amur a par feid.*
(Brault, La Chanson de Roland, ll. 69, 79-86 [Brault 6, trans. mine])

158. "*En la citet nen ad remés paien / Ne seit ocis u devient chretïen*" (ibid., ll. 101-2 [Brault 8], trans. Brault, 9).

159. "*Sil saluerent par amur e par bien*" (ibid., l. 121 [Brault 8], trans. mine).

160. *Quant vus serez el palais seignurill
A la grant feste seint Michel del Peril
Miz avoëz la vos sivrat, ço dit.
Enz en voz bainz que Deus pur vos i fist,
La vuldrat il chrestïens devenir.*
(Ibid., ll. 151-56 [Brault 10])

161. *Cist nostre deu sunt en recreantise.
En Rencesval malvaises vertuz firent,
Noz chevalers i unt lesset ocire.
Cest mien seignur en bataille faillirent.*
(Ibid., ll. 2715-18 [Brault 164])

162. *Dist l'amiraill: "Carles, kar te purpenses,
Si pren cunseill que vers mei te repentes!*
*Mort as mun filz, par le men escïentre,
A mult grant tort mun païs me calenges.
Deven mes hom, en fiet le te voeill render,
Ven mei servir d'ici qu'en Orïente."
Carles respunt: "Mult grant viltet me semblet,
Pais ne amor ne dei a paien rendre.
Receif la lei que Deus nos apresentet,
Chrestïentet, e pui te amerai sempres;
Puis serf e crei le rei omnipotente!"*
(Ibid., ll. 3589-99 [Brault 8], trans. Brault, slightly amended, 219)

163. *Baptizet sunt asez plus de .C. milie
Veir chrestien, ne mais sul la reïne:
En France dulce iert menee caitive,
Ço voelt li reis par amur cunvertisset.*
(Ibid., ll. 3671-74 [Brault 224], trans. mine)

164. *En ma maisun ad une caitive franche.
Tant ad oït e sermons e essamples,
Creire voelt Deu, chrestïentet demandet.
Baptizez la, pur quei Deus en ait l'anme.*
(Ibid., ll. 3978-81 [Brault 242], trans. Brault, slightly amended, 243)

165. "*Or seit faite par marrenes, / Asez cruiz e linees dames*" (ibid., ll. 3982-83 [Brault 242]).

166. *As bainz ad Ais mult sunt granz les c . . .
La baptizent la reïne d'Espaigne,
Truvee li unt le num de Juliane.
Chrestïene est par veire conoisance.*
(Ibid., ll. 3984-87 [Brault 242], trans. Brault, 243)

167. Davies, *The First English Empire*, 73.

168. Anne J. Duggan refers to several examples of Henry's interest in her examination of *Laudabiliter*'s possible legitimacy: Robert of Torigni's record of a council in Winchester in 1155; a charter of Count John of Eu, stating that it was made at Winchester at the same time a conquest of Ireland was discussed; and a Flemish chronicle entry, which mentions that Henry took an army to France that "he

had prepared to lead into Ireland in order to subjugate it to his lordship" (Duggan, "The Making of a Myth," 128–30).
169. Davies, *The First English Empire*, 72.
170. "Ad preces meas illustri regi Anglorum, Henrico secundo, concessit et dedit Hiberniam iure hereditario possidendam, sicut litterae ipsius testantur in hodiernam diem. Nam omnes insulae de iure antiquo ex donatione Constantini, qui eam fundauit et dotauit, dicuntur ad Romanam Ecclesiam pertinere" (John of Salisbury, *Metalogicon*, iv. 42, 183). Even if *Laudabiliter* is not authentic, as several scholars claim, and is instead a spurious invention of Giraldus Cambrensis, its sentiment remains of crucial importance to my discussion. See F. X. Martin's analysis of the dubious authenticity of of all eight texts that are presented by Giraldus: Martin, *Expugnatio Hibernica*, 280; as well as Duggan, "*Totius christianus caput*," 148–52.
171. Duggan's convincing argument stems from a comparison with another mid-twelfth-century bull, *Satis laudabiliter*, containing "an extremely diplomatic refusal of papal support" for Henry II and Louis VII's desire for a crusade in Spain. See Duggan, "The Making of a Myth," 137–43, as well as Duggan, "The Power of Documents."
172. Duggan, "The Making of a Myth," 157–58. Although it is significant that Henry himself was able to put a religious spin on his actions, according to J. A. Watt in *The Church and the Two Nations*, 36–38.
173. Laudabiliter satis et fructuose de glorioso nomine propagando in terris et eterne felicitatis premio cumulando in celis tua magnificencia cogitat, dum ad dilatandos ecclesie terminos, ad declarandam indoctis et rudibus populis Christiane fidei veritatem, et viciorum plantaria de agro Dominico exstirpanda, sicut catholicus princeps intendis. . . . Significasti siquidem nobis, fili in Christo carissime, te Hibernie insulam ad subdendum illum populum legibus et viciorum plantaria inde exstirpanda velle intrare. . . . Nos itaque pium et laudabile desiderium tuum cum favore congruo prosequentes, et peticioni tue benignum impendentes assensum, gratum et acceptum habemus ut pro dilatandis ecclesie terminis, pro viciorum restringendo decursu, pro corrigendis moribus et virtutibus inserendis, pro Christiane religionis augmento, insulam illam ingrediaris et que ad honorem Dei et salutem illius terre spectaverint exequaris, et illius terre populus honorifice te recipiat et sicut dominum veneratur. . . . Si ergo quod concepisti animo effectu duxeris prosequente complendum, stude gentem illam bonis moribus informare. (Gerald of Wales, *Expugnatio hibernica*, 142–49)
174. There exists strong ecclesiastical precedent for the moral justification of war in the mid-twelfth century. As Anthony Carty notes,
It is to the contemporary canonist Gratian that we owe the introduction of the concept of the just war into international jurisprudence. Around 1140 he put together a compilation of canon law known as *Concordia Discordantium Canonum*. In the vital Causa 23, on the question of war, he set out a justification of war simply to correct heresy. This rested on an Augustinian theory that love of enemies did not go so far as tolerating sinning with impunity; the physical punishment of sin, even by waging war, was not

incompatible with Christian patience. This goes back to imperial Roman times when Augustine had held to the right of the ecclesiastical hierarchy to insist upon imperial coercion of heretics as heretics. With Gregory the Great the persecution of barbarians and heretics went together. (Carty, *Was Ireland Conquered?*, 22-23)

What is most interesting about *Laudabiliter* in this context is not simply its justification of war against the Irish, therefore, but its formulation of the blessing of Henry II's enterprise in terms of civilizing barbarians.

175. Duggan, "The Making of a Myth," 156. For an examination of the Merlin prophecies in *Expugnatio*, see McCauley, "Giraldus 'Silvester' of Wales."
176. Flanagan, *Irish Society*, 79.
177. Ibid., 120-21.
178. Ibid., 122-23.

Chapter 2

1. "Proinde quia divae recordationis imperator, avus scilicet noster Karolus, cui divina providentia monarchiam totius hujus imperii conferre dignata est, in palatio Aquensi cappellam in honore beate Dei genetricis et virginis Mariae construxisse . . . nos quoque morem illius imitari ceterorumque regum et imperatorum, decessorum scilicet nostrorum, cupientes, cum pars illa regni nobis sorte divisionis nondum contigerit, infra tamen potestatis nostre dicionem in palatio videlicet Compendio . . . cui regium vocabulum dedimus" (Giry, Prou, and Tessier, *Recueil des Actes*, qtd. in Airlie, "The Palace of Memory," 15).
2. Airlie, "The Palace of Memory," 16. For more information about the influence of Aachen on later generations and architecture more generally, see Zotz, "Carolingian Tradition and Ottonian-Salian Innovation"; and Sieffert, "Les imitations de la chapelle palatine."
3. "Non multo post accepit sedem illam Rotbertus Lotharingus, qui ibi aecclesiam tereti edificauit scemate, Aquensam basilicam pro modo imitatus suo" (William of Malmesbury, *Gesta pontificum Anglorum* 458-59).
4. Most recently, see McClendon, *The Origins of Medieval Architecture*, esp. chap. 6. See also Greenhalgh, *Marble Past, Monumental Present*, esp. 333-44; and Kinney, "Roman Architectural Spolia," esp. 147-49.
5. D. W. Meinig, *The Interpretation of Ordinary Landscapes* (New York: Oxford University Press, 1979), 165.
6. Ibid., 164.
7. McClendon, *Origins of Medieval Architecture*, 35.
8. Tilley, "The Powers of Rocks," 167.
9. Ibid., 173-74.
10. Howe, "Anglo-Saxon England and the Postcolonial Void," 39.
11. Harbison, *Eccentric Spaces*, 46.
12. Howe, *Writing the Map of Anglo-Saxon England*, 83.
13. Muir, *The New Reading the Landscape*, 100.
14. Wallach, *Alcuin and Charlemagne*, 67-68.
15. Ibid., 67.
16. The precedent had been set before Charlemagne ascended the throne of the Franks, when, in a letter to Pepin the Short arguing for the king's support of the papacy, Pope Paul likens Charlemagne's father to David, "rege et propheta" (*Codex Carolinus*, no. 33, in MGH, *Epistolae Merowingici et Karolini aevi*, vol. 1, 540).
17. Wallach, *Alcuin and Charlemagne*, 70.
18. Barbero, *Charlemagne*, 86.
19. Wallace-Hadrill, "The *Via regia* of the Carolingian Age," 23.
20. Cooper, "The Rise and Fall," 39-40.

21. Lucien Musset, "Voie publique," 100–101.
22. Cooper, "The Rise and Fall," 42.
23. Bede, for example, writes that the peace of Edwin of Northumbria's reign was so great that a woman with a newborn infant could walk from one side of the island to the other without fear of molestation, and Cooper points out elsewhere that the Continental laws were likewise concerned with the safety of travelers on the highway, especially women: "The laws of the Salian Franks, the Burgundian Laws and the Alamannian Laws all contain similar and largely straightforward prohibitions against waylaying women on the highway" (ibid., 43).
24. Ibid., 48.
25. Cooper, "Extraordinary Privilege," 1181.
26. Cooper, "The Rise and Fall," 49.
27. Musset discusses one reference from Louis the Pious's reign, in an act for the monks of Noirmoutier that grants them the right to move the "viam regiam quam stratam sive calciatam dicunt" (Musset, "Voie publique," 103). Musset also notes the curious wording of the formula, which to him indicates that the legal terminology of *via regia* was not in current usage. Although this is likely, considering that it is generally believed that Smaragdus wrote the *Via regia* for Louis the Pious, it is also possible that Louis was using the term deliberately in a precocious example of the kind of usage that would emerge in England and Normandy several centuries later, which stresses the royal prerogative of justice on the highway as an example of strong kingship that unifies the land.
28. Boeft, "Some Etymologies," 255.
29. Wallach, *Alcuin and Charlemagne*, 69. In this vein, Smaragdus of St. Mihiel called his treatise on kingship *Via regia*.
30. Jong, "The Empire as *Ecclesia*," esp. 195–96.
31. Wallach, *Alcuin and Charlemagne*, 32.
32. Alcuin, in MGH, *Epistolae Karolini aevi*, vol. 2, 292–93.
33. Kershaw, *Peaceful Kings*, 178.
34. "Sollicite et diligenter custodias ejus praecepta . . . , Pater et Filius et Spiritus sanctus ad te venient . . . , pax tua feliciter multiplicabitur, et gaudium sicut flumen in aeternum complebitur" (Smaragdus of St. Mihiel, *Via regia*, in *Opera omnia*, bk. 1, cap. 2, col. 939). Smaragdus's statement is evocative of Isaiah 48:18, where God chastises the Israelites by telling them, "O that thou hadst hearkened to my commandments! Then had thy peace been as a river and thy righteousness as the waves of the sea," suggesting what will happen if the king does not uphold his sacred duty.
35. Cooper, "The Rise and Fall," 68.
36. As the twelfth century progressed, the liturgical concept of kingship, emphasized by Carolingian writers like Alcuin, would be replaced by a more secularized, juristical idea of government, which, as Ernst Kantorowicz argues, "became manifest in the king's new relationship to Law and Justice, which replaced his former status in regard to Sacrament and Altar," such that the king's twin body becomes literally an embodiment of the law, "the very Idea of Justice" (Kantorowicz, *The King's Two Bodies*, 93–94, 96).
37. Daniels and Cosgrove, introduction to *The Iconography of Landscape*, 1.
38. Henry wrote six different versions of his chronicle, with endings at 1129, 1138, 1146, 1149, and 1154, which represent his complex process of composition and revision. According to Diana Greenway, about forty-five manuscripts preserve for the most part the whole of these six versions and show that his work was being copied well

into the sixteenth century. Two manuscripts from the seventeenth century, currently at the Vatican Library, belonged to Queen Christina of Sweden (see Greenway's introduction to HA, especially section II.ii., "Chronology of Composition, lxvi-lxxvii, and section III, "The Manuscripts and the Text," cxvii-clx).

39. Alan Cooper traces Henry of Huntingdon's creation of the myth of the Four Highways and its impact on the twelfth-century law codes as well as subsequent generations of writers, including Geoffrey of Monmouth, Wace, Laȝamon, and Matthew Paris (Cooper, "The King's Four Highways").

40. See Bede's *Ecclesiastical History of the English People* 1.1.

41. Howe, "Medieval Development of Sacred Space," 212-13.

42. Glacken, *Traces on the Rhodian Shore*, 144-49, esp. 148-49.

43. "Est autem Walonia terra siluestris et pascuosa, . . . ceruorum quidem et piscium, lactis et armentorum uberrima; sed hominum nutrix bestialium, natura uelocium, consuetudine bellantium, fide semper et locis instabilium" (GS 1.8 [Potter 14-15]).

44. "Postquem autem Normanni, bello commisso, Anglos sibi subiugarunt, hanc etiam suo imperio terram adicientes castellis unnumeris munire; propriis incolis uiriliter edomitis, constanter excoluer; ad pacem confouendam, legem et plebiscita eis indixere; adeoque terram fertilem omnibusque copiis affluentem reddidere, ut fecundissimae Britanniae nequaquam inferiorem aestimares" (ibid.).

45. "Hibernia autem et latitudine sui status et salubritate ac serenitate aerum multum Brittaniae praestat" (*Bede's Ecclesiastical History* 1.1 [Colgrave and Mynors 18-19]). Furthermore, "The island abounds in milk and honey, nor does it lack vines, fish, and birds" (Diues lactis et mellis insula nec uinearum expers, piscium uolucrumque et ceruorum caprearumque uenatu insignis) (ibid. [20-21]; see below for Henry's use of Bede's statements in a praise-poem for England).

46. "Vrbes autem predicte amenis insite locis super flumina choruscant fertilia et pulcherrima" (HA 1.6 [Greenway 18-19]).

47. "Two rivers are more celebrated than the rest, the Thames and the Severn, like the two arms by which Britain brings out and carries in both its own wealth and that of foreigners. A particular characteristic of Britain is that its natives, when traveling abroad, are more splendid in their dress and manner of living, whence they may be distinguished from other peoples" (Sunt tamen duo flumina ceteris clariora, Tamasis et Sabrina, quasi duo brachia Britannie, per que sibi suas et alienas effert et infert diuicias. Proprie uero proprium Britannie est, ut incole eius in peregrinationem tendentes, omnibus gentibus cultu et sumptu clariores ex hoc unde sint dinosci possint) (ibid., 18-21).

48. The *Leis Willelme* also record four roads upon which travelers can expect to have the benefit of the king's special peace (¶ 26). Although it is generally attributed to the late eleventh century, Patrick Wormald tentatively dates this French law book to the mid-twelfth century (Wormald, *The Making of English Law*, vol. 1, 408). He claims that its reference to the peace of the four great roads is an overlap with *Leges Edwardi Confessoris* (ibid., 409). Alan Cooper attributes the *Leges Edwardi*'s usage to Geoffrey of Monmouth's use of the HA and concludes that Henry of Huntingdon invented the idea (Cooper, "The King's

Four Highways," 357–60, 364–65, esp. 365).

49. Tante autem gracie inhabitantibus fuit Britannia, quod quatuor in ea calles a fine in finem construerent, regia sullimatos auctoritate, ne aliquis in eis inimicum inuadere auderet. Primus est ab oriente in occidentem, et uocatur Ichenild. Secundus est ab austro in aquilonem et uocatur Erningestrate. Tercius est ex transuerso a Dorobernia in Cestriam, scilicet ab euroaustro in zephirum septentrionalem, et uocatur Watlingestrate. Quartus maior ceteris incipit in Catenes et desinit in Totenes, scilicet a principio Cornugallie in finem Scocie. Et hic callis uadit ex transuerso a zephiro australi in eurum septentrionalem, et uocatur Fossa, tenditque per Lincoliam. Hii sunt quatuor principales calles Anglie, multum quidem spaciose, sed nec minus speciose, sanciti edictis regum scriptisque uerendis legum (HA 2.7 [Greenway 22–23]).
50. Cooper, "The King's Four Highways," 365.
51. HA 8.1 (epilogue) (Greenway 502).
52. Rouse, *The Idea of Anglo-Saxon England*, 109.
53. HA 8.1 (epilogue) (Greenway 494, 502–3).
54. Ibid., 4.23 (Greenway 250), slightly emended. It should be noted that Greenway translates Henry's statement as "a change *in* the right hand of the Most High," which suggests Charlemagne's role as *vicarii Christi* even more forcefully; even still, Henry's claim has significant implications for interpreting the arrival of William the Bastard and the impact of the Normans upon England (see below).
55. Sayles, *The Medieval Foundations of England*, 276.
56. For example, Rouse erroneously claims that Henry II named one of his sons Arthur to lend "a royal seal of approval to an English Arthurian history" (Rouse, *The Idea of Anglo-Saxon England*, 12). It was Geoffrey of Brittany's son, born in 1187 after his death, who was named Arthur by Brittany's barons to defy Henry II, according to William of Newburgh. For an alternative view of Arthur's influence in the course of the twelfth century, see Gillingham, *The English in the Twelfth Century*, esp. 22–23, and "The Cultivation of History," 36–39).
57. Koeppler, "Frederick Barbarossa," 578. Barbarossa's imperial decree, dated 8 January 1166 (the canonization was actually celebrated 29 December 1165), reads in part: "This is why, having been so confidently disposed on account of the merits and glorious deeds of this most saintly emperor Charles, and having been persuaded by the earnest appeal of our very dear friend Henry, the illustrious king of England, we celebrated a solemn feast at Aachen at Christmastime for the purpose of exhibiting, consecrating, and canonizing his most blessed body" (Inde est quod nos gloriosis factis et meritis tam sanctissimi imperatoris Karoli confidenter animati et sedula petitione carissimi amici nostri Heinrici illustris regis Anglie inducti . . . exaltatione atque canonizatione sanctissimi corporis eius sollempnem curiam in natali domini aput Aquisgranum celebravimus). Cf. Cain, "Charlemagne in the 1170's: Reading the Oxford *Roland* in the Context of the Becket Controversy," sec. II. It is also important to note here that Henry II had Edward the Confessor, not Arthur, canonized for purposes of enhancing the prestige of the English crown (see Scholz, "The Canonization"); Henry II's participation in Charlemagne's

canonization would have secured his imperial legitimacy on both sides of the Channel.
58. "Del mieldre curuné qui unkes fust en vie" (Fantosme, *Jordan Fantosme's Chronicle*, l. 2). Fantosme's unusual poem, a mixture of romance and epic, celebrates the miraculous victory of Henry II's forces over the Scots during the rebellion of his son, Henry the Young King. Laura Ashe argues that it is a strong example of English nationalism (Ashe, *Fiction and History in England, 1066-1200*, 81-120, which I will discuss further in the epilogue).
59. Le plus honurable e le plus cunquerant
    Que fust en nule terre puis le tens Moysant,
    Fors sulement li reis Charle, ki poeste fud grant
    Par les dudze cumpaignuns, Olivier e Rodlant.
    (Fantosme, *Jordan Fantosme's Chronicle*, ll. 111-14)
60. Ibid., ll. 2043-47.
61. Innes, "Danelaw Identities," 85.
62. Howe, "Anglo-Saxon England," 30.
63. "His itaque liquido comparari poteris, an regnum istud, quod hereditario possides iure, totis animi nisibus, ut assolet, amplectendum tibi sit et retinendum, an potius longe aliud prestantius isto, congestis et coactis uiribus, querendum tibi sit et adquirendum" (*HA* 8.1 [epilogue] [Greenway, 502-3]).
64. For Cathwulf, see MGH, *Epistolae Karolini aevi*, vol. 2, no. 7, 503.
65. *HA* 1.9 (Greenway 24-25). See also, below, my discussion of the Normans' Trojan origins and their reflection of the Frankish invention of their own Trojan ancestors.
66. "Anno gratie dcclxix, Kinewlfi uero Regis anno quinto decimo, *incepit fieri mutatio dextere excelsi*. Imperium namque Romanum, quod tot annis in se precellentissimum fuerat, Karoli regi magno Francorum subiectum est, post triginta annos regni eius, quod in hoc anno inceperat, et successoribus eius usque ad hunc diem exinde contigit" (ibid., 4.22 [250-51], slightly emended).
67. "Willelmus uero tanta potitus uictoria, susceptus a Lundoniensibus pacifice, et coronatus est apud Westmunster ab Aldredo Eboracensi archiepiscopo. *Sic facta est mutatio dextere excelsi*. Quam cometa ingens in exordio eiusdem anni designauerat" (ibid., 6.30 [394-95], slightly emended [emphasis mine]).
68. "Quinque autem plagas ad exordio usque ad presens immisit diuina ultio Brittanie, que non solum uisitat fideles, sed etiam diiudicat infideles. Primam per Romanos, qui Brittaniam expugnauerunt sed postea recesserunt. Secundam per Pictos et Scotos, qui grauissime eam bellis uexauereunt, nec tamen optinuerunt. Terciam per Anglicos, qui eam debellauerunt et optinent. Quartam per Dacos, qui eam bellis optinuerunt, sed postea deperierunt. Quintam per Normannos, qui eam deuicerunt et Anglis inpresentiarum dominantutur" (ibid., 1.4 [14-15]).
69. "Lege dominantium splendide rexerunt" (ibid., 5 [prologue], [272-73]).
70. "Uictis uitam et libertatem legesque antiquas regni iure concesserunt, de quibus in antea dicendum est" (ibid.).
71. "Angliam iuste secundum ius gentium Normanni et calumpniati sunt et adepti sunt" (ibid., 6.1 [338-39]).
72. "Hoc autem Dei nutu factum esse constat, ut ueniret contra improbos malum. Genti enim Anglorum, quam sceleribus suis exigentibus disterminare proposuerat, sicut et ipsi Britones peccatis accusantibus humiliauerant, Dominus omnipotens dupplicem contricionem proposuit et quasi militares insidias adhibuit" (ibid.).
73. Specifically, these beneficial "plagues" were the Romans, Saxons, and

Normans, who ruled rightly by law; they stand in stark contrast to the Danes, for example, who were a "plague more widespread and cruel than the others" (Hec siquidem long inmanior longe crudelior ceteris fuit), who did not aim "to possess the land but to plunder it, and [desired] not to govern but to destroy everything" (eam non optinere sed predari studebant, et omnia destruere non dominari cupiebant) (ibid., 5 [prologue] [272–73]).

74. "Rex igitur secessus regni prouidentiusbr perlustrauit; et opportune loca contra excursiones hostium communiuit. Munitiones enim quas castella Galli nuncupant; Anglicis prouinciis paucissime fuerant, et ob hoc. Angli licet bellicosi fuerint et audaces; ad resistendum tamen inimicis extiterant debiliores" (Orderic Vitalis, *The Ecclesiastical History*, 4.2 [Chibnall 2:218]). See also Chibnall, "Orderic Vitalis on Castles."

75. Liddiard, *Castles in Context*, 12. On this point, see also Wheatley, *The Idea of the Castle*. For Anglo-Norman castles and architecture more generally, see also Liddiard, *Anglo-Norman Castles*; Coulson, *Castles in Medieval Society*; and Fernie, *The Architecture of Norman England*. For comparison with Normandy during the High Middle Ages, see Grant, *Architecture and Society*.

76. Liuzza, "The Tower of Babel," 5.

77. Ibid.

78. Tim Eaton points out that even this was restricted "to a select category of structures, namely the important monastic churches or *minsters*" (Eaton, *Plundering the Past*, 12). For a fuller treatment of this idea, see McClendon, *The Origins of Medieval Architecture*, chap. 4, "The Christianization of Anglo-Saxon England," 59–84. This view is also presented by Higgitt, "The Roman Background to Medieval England," esp. 1; and Hunter, "Germanic and Roman Antiquity," esp. 35–38.

79. Chris Wickham, introduction to Jong, Rhijn, and Theuws, *Topographies of Power*, 1. See also Howe, "Anglo-Saxon England."

80. Early medieval writers used Isidore of Seville's *Etymologies* as a guide to classical culture. In it, Isidore observes that the title of *imperator* originally referred to a general in command, but became a title that the senate bestowed on Augustus to distinguish him from other, ordinary, kings. See Smith, *Europe After Rome*, esp. 273–77.

81. Smith, *Europe After Rome*, 275.

82. MGH, *Cassiodori Senatoris Variae*, 10. "Regnum nostrum imitatio vestra est, forma boni propositi, unici exemplar imperii: qui quantum vos sequimur, tantum gentes alias anteimus" (trans. in Smith, *Europe After Rome*, 275). Charlemagne also removed a statue of Theodoric from Ravenna to put at Aachen.

83. McClendon, *Origins of Medieval Architecture*, 19.

84. Ibid., 42.

85. Ibid., 43.

86. Barbero, *Charlemagne*, 79.

87. Ibid., 121.

88. Ibid., 106.

89. For two complementary views on this, see ibid., especially chap. 5, "Symbols of the New Alliance," 85–104, and chap. 6, "Aachen and Rome: The Poles of an Empire," 105–27; and Lavin, "The House of the Lord."

90. McClendon, *Origins of Medieval Architecture*, 109.

91. "Omni labore et sumptu quo potui edificavi, lapidibus ex marmore preciosis adornavi" (MGH, *Die Urkunden Pippins, Karlmanns und Karls des Grossen*, no. 295, 442). David Stocker cites "iconic re-use" as one of the

three purposes for the use of spolia, explaining it as the use of stones that have particular associations, to employ "their very antiquity in a didactic or iconic way" (Stocker, "Rubbish Recycled," 93).

92. Greenhalgh, *Marble Past*, 336–40.
93. Beat Brenk, for example, argues that the use of spolia at Aachen was "to guarantee the Christian Roman imperial tradition. In contrast to Charlemagne, [earlier emperors like] Constantine and Theodoric used spolia for the purpose of protecting monuments" rather than for *translatio imperii* (Brenk, "Spolia from Constantine to Charlemagne," 109).
94. For example, Alcuin claimed in a letter that "Ecce in te solo tota salus ecclesiarum Christi inclina recumbit. Tu vindex scelerum, tu rector errantium, tu consolator maerentium, tu exaltatio bonorum" (MGH, *Epistolae Karolini aevi*, vol. 2, no. 174, 288).
95. See Sullivan, *Aix-la-Chapelle*.
96. "Caput mundi, mundi decus, aurea Roma, / Nunc remanet tantum saeva ruina tibi" ("The Destruction of Lindisfarne," ll. 37-38, in *Poetry of the Carolingian Renaissance*).
97. *Rex Karolus, caput orbis, amor populique decusque,*
  Europae venerandus apex, pater optimus, heros,
  Augustus, sed et urbe potens, ubi Roma secunda
  Flore novo, ingenti magna consurgit ad alta
  Mole tholis muro praecelsis sidera tangens.
    (*Karolus Magnus et Leo Papa*, ll. 92-96, in Godman, *Poetry of the Carolingian Renaissance*, 202)
    See also Peter Godman's discussion of the poem in *Poets and Emperors*, 82-91.
98. Godman suggests that Leo III is the suppliant to the protective Charlemagne, echoing Alcuin's assertion of the king's primacy over the pope (ibid., 91).
99. Godman, *Poetry of the Carolingian Renaissance*, 24.
100. As McClendon remarks, the description was adapted from the *Aeneid*, where Aeneas observes the construction of Carthage (*Aen.* 1.430-36) (McClendon, *Origins of Medieval Architecture*, 122).
101. Godman, *Poetry of the Carolingian Renaissance*, 24.
102. *Inclita nam superat praeclari dicta Catonis,*
  Vincit et eloquii magnum dulcedine Marcum
  Atque suis dictis facundus cedit Homerus
  Et priscos superat dialectica in arte magistros.
    (*Karolus Magnus et Leo Papa*, ll. 72-75, in Godman, *Poetry of the Carolingian Renaissance*, 200)
103. *Prospicit alta novae Romae meus arce Palemon*
  Cuncta suo imperio consistere regna triumpho,
  Rursus in antiquos mutataque secula mores.
  Aurea Roma iterum renovata renascitur orbi!
    (Moduin of Autun, *Egloga*, ll. 24-27, in Godman, *Poetry of the Carolingian Renaissance*, 192)
    William Hammer says of this work that it "makes clear how strong the concept of a restoration of Old Rome must have been among the Carolingians, be it from a political, educational or religious point of view" (Hammer, "The Concept of the New or Second Rome," 56).
104. "Cede, senex, victus dudum puerilibus armis!" (Moduin of Autun, *Ecloga*, l. 94, in Godman, *Poetry of the Carolingian Renaissance*, 196).

105. Julia M. H. Smith has commented on Charlemagne's wisdom in keeping Rome and its complex political quagmire at arm's length: "[For] a transalpine emperor, Rome was more useful as an idea than as a centre of government. As an idea, it drew on the antique past to confer a potent form of legitimacy; as a place of power, it was best left well alone, distant but powerfully evocative. Though the rhetoric of Romanness added a patina of ancient respectability to the new forms of hegemonic kingship that emerged in northern Europe from the end of the eighth century onwards, most early medieval ideologues knew very well how to distinguish 'Rome' from 'empire'" (Smith, *Europe After Rome*, 276–77).
106. Ibid., 276.
107. Ibid.
108. See Deshman, "*Christus rex et magi regis*"; and Nelson, *Politics and Ritual*.
109. There are three that we know of, in the *Anglo-Saxon Chronicle* and John of Worcester (*The Anglo-Saxon Chronicle*, vol. 7, entries for 1051 and 1052; and John of Worcester, *The Chronicle*, vol. 2, entry for 1052, 572–53, thought to be from a lost version of the *Anglo-Saxon Chronicle*).
110. Schutz, *Carolingians in Central Europe*, 325–26. See also Carlson, "Religious Architecture in Normandy"; Kleinbauer, "Charlemagne's Palace Chapel."
111. Liddiard, *Castles in Context*, 15–18. See also Creighton, *Castles and Landscapes*, 133–37, and Pounds, *The Medieval Castle*, 57–59.
112. Pounds, *The Medieval Castle*, 57. Pounds further notes here that twelve of these sites were towns with Roman origins, and eight were within Anglo-Saxon *burhs* themselves.
113. Ibid., 58.
114. Creighton, *Castles and Landscapes*, 151.
115. It should be noted that the definition of *burh* is complicated and can refer to different kinds of structures with various purposes: "Old English usage could range from a meaning of 'pre-existing earthwork', through meanings concerned with 'fortification', 'stockaded enclosure', 'walled monastic site' to 'late Anglo-Saxon town'" (Hill and Rumble, introduction to *The Defence of Wessex*, 3. As a result, some scholars prefer the use of more specific terminology such as "fortification," but for my purposes, the use of the word *burh* meaning an Anglo-Saxon lordly seat should suffice. For more information, see Williams, "A Bell-House and a Burh-Geat"; Baker and Brookes, *Beyond the Burghal Hidage*; Astill, "Community, Identity."
116. Liddiard, *Castles in Context*, 19, 28. Exceptions to this practice, however, such as at Stamford, Chester, Stafford, and others, are usually positioned to be physically more prominent than the town in the landscape, such as on a ridge, and are "a menacing presence on the horizon, visible to the townspeople and with an undoubted psychological impact" (Creighton, *Castles and Landscapes*, 147).
117. Blair, "Palaces or Minsters?," 110–13.
118. Ibid., 118–19. For more information regarding this site, see Rahtz, "The Saxon and Medieval Palaces."
119. Blair, "Palaces or Minsters?," 119.
120. For more information about Goltho, see Bassett, "Beyond the Edge of Excavation"; Davis, "Goltho—The Manorial History."
121. Liddiard, *Castles in Context*, 23.
122. Ibid., 31. See also Renn, "Burhgeat and Gonfanon."
123. Liddiard, *Castles in Context*, 33.
124. Creighton, *Castles and Landscapes*, 156–57.
125. P. J. Drury describes Colchester as a "fortress palace," with the largest

keep in England (Drury, "Aspects of the Origins and Development," 302). Drury furthermore mentions Colchester's possible "links with tenth-century, late Carolingian fortified palaces in northern France" (391). It is also interesting to note that the mid-thirteenth-century *Colchester Chronicle* claims that the castle was built "in 1076 on the foundations of the palace of Coel 'formerly king' (presumably a reference to Cunobelin, the pre-Roman king)," thereby emphasizing the castle's ancient political heritage that predates even Roman occupation, as observed by Creighton, *Castles and Landscapes*, 150. This later association with England's pre-Roman inheritance is very much in keeping with the tendency, in the thirteenth century, to look at Insular sources for legitimacy more often than Carolingian ones, as I will discuss in the epilogue.

126. Creighton, *Castles and Landscapes*, 149-50.
127. T. A. Heslop affirms this resemblance at Colchester: he claims the reuse of Roman spolia "gives the edifice a Roman fabric and thus a quasi-Roman appearance" (Heslop, "Constantine and Helena," 168). Heslop suggests that the city's connection to Helena, Constantine's mother, could indicate an additional association with the emperor himself; this affiliation, as Heslop himself admits, is not clear.
128. Eaton, *Plundering the Past*, 29.
129. Liddiard, *Castles in Context*, 20-22.
130. GS 1.16 (Potter 32-33): "Turribus Caesarianis inscissili calce confectis firmatum."
131. Liddiard, *Castles in Context*, 22.
132. Ibid., 22.
133. As Smith notes, "from a world of Roman culture within which Christianity was one element in 500, by 1000 Europe had become a Christian world of which Roman cultural attributes formed one aspect" (Smith, *Europe After Rome*, 295).
134. Later in the twelfth century, the Anglo-Norman chronicler Hugh Candidus remarks that "the monks of Peterborough were 'striving to build no commonplace structure, but a second Rome, or a daughter of Rome in England'" (qtd. in Eaton, *Plundering the Past*, 127-28).
135. Kleinbauer, "Charlemagne's Palace Chapel," 4.
136. Catherine Carver McCurrach notes that "structures have a conceptual rather than a physical similarity" (McCurrach, "'Renovatio' Reconsidered," 43).
137. Kleinbauer, "Charlemagne's Palace Chapel," 4.
138. See Peter Godman, *Poets and Emperors*, chap. 2, "New Athens and Renascent Rome," 38-92.
139. For a discussion of Notker's presentation of Charlemagne in ethical and cultural terms, see Morrissey, *Charlemagne and France*, 27-38.
140. "Omnipotens rerum dispositor ordinatorque regnorum et temporum, cum illius admirande statue pedes ferreos vel testaceos comminuisset in Romanis, alterius non minus admirabilis statue caput aureum per illustrem Karolum erexit in Francis" (MGH, *Notker der Stammler*, bk. I, § 1, trans. in Thorpe, *Two Lives of Charlemagne*, 93).
141. "Que cesar augustus imperator Karolus . . . mirifice construxit" (ibid., bk. I, § 27, trans. in Thorpe, *Two Lives of Charlemagne*, 125).
142. "Antiquis Romanorum operibus praestantiorum" (ibid., bk. I, § 28, trans. in Thorpe, *Two Lives of Charlemagne*, 125).
143. MacLean, *Kingship and Politics*, 223.
144. See R. H. C. Davis and Marjorie Chibnall, introduction to William of Poitiers, *The "Gesta Guillelmi,"* xv-xxxii.

145. The practice of clemency is among those qualities that set William apart from ordinary leaders, because "he knows that it is characteristic of wise men to temper victory" (Sed nouit esse prudentium uictoriae temperare) (William of Poitiers, GG 1.19 [Davis and Chibnall 26–27]).
146. For example, see the accounts of Augustus and Antoninus Pius in Eutropius's *Breviary of Roman History*.
147. "Quid igitur huius uiri, quem scribimus, conferendum laudibus hac uice patrauit?" (GG 2.40 [Davis and Chibnall 171]).
148. Gerould, "King Arthur and Politics," 49.
149. Loomis, "Geoffrey of Monmouth and Arthurian Origins," 16.
150. Gerould, "King Arthur and Politics," 47.
151. See Gerould's discussion of the political implications of a Charlemagne-like ancestor (ibid., esp. 49).
152. Geoffrey was in the neighborhood of Oxford from 1129–51, in fact, according to the charter evidence. See Salter, "Geoffrey of Monmouth and Oxford," esp. 383.
153. "Cumque Ratisponam venisset [Heinricus rex], insecuta est eum legatio familiarium eius, nunciantium, quod Willehelmus cognomentum Bostar rex Anglorum ab archiepiscopo Coloniensi vana pollicitatione illectus, cum magno exercitu adventaret, regni sedem Aquisgrani occupare paratus" (Lamberti Annales, in MGH, [*Annales et chronica aevi Salici*], 216).
154. "[L]'ancïen dreit de cel païs / ke i out Brenes e Belins" (Gaimar, *Estoire des Engleis*, ll. 5973–74 [Short 324]). About this time in France, Suger confirmed this rumor about William Rufus in the *Vita Ludovici Grossi regis*, claiming that it was "commonly said that this proud and headstrong king aspired to the throne of the French" (Dicebatur equidem vulgo regem illum superbum et impetuosum aspirare ad regnum Francorum) (Suger, *Vita Ludovici Grossi regis*, § 4, 10, trans. in *The Deeds of Louis the Fat*, 27).
155. It should be noted that, according to Livy, a Gallic leader named Brennus did indeed successfully invade Rome in the early fourth century B.C.
156. See Innes, "Teutons or Trojans?"; Wood, "Defining the Franks"; Gerberding, *The "Liber historiae Francorum"*; and Goffart, "Paul the Deacon's *Gesta episcoporum mettensium*."
157. "Exinde origo Francorum fuit. Priamo primo regi habuerunt; postea per historiarum libros scriptum est, qualiter habuerunt regi Friga.... Nam et illa alia pars, quae de Frigia progressa est, ab Olexa per fraude decepti, tamen non captivati, nisi exinde eiecti, per multis regionibus pervacantis cum uxores et liberos, electum a se regi Francione nomen, per quem Franci vocantur" (MGH, *Fredegarii et aliorum Chronica*, 45–46).
158. Ibid., chaps. 1–4, 241–44. Antenor was a Trojan and a counselor to Priam who argued for the return of Helen to the Greeks. In another version of his myth, Antenor was the traitorous Trojan who opened the door of Troy for the Greeks.
159. "[C]uius Anschisi nomen ab Anchise patre Aeneae, qui a Troia in Italiam olim venerat, creditur esse deductum. Nam gens Francorum, sicut a veteribus est traditum, a Troiana prosapia trahit exordium" (Paul the Deacon, *Liber de episcopis mettensibus*, in MGH, [*Scriptores rerum Sangallensium*], 264).
160. McKitterick, *History and Memory*, 125.
161. *Brute, sub occasu solis trans Gallica regna*
    insula in occeano est undique clausa mari;

    insula in occenao est habitata gigantibus olim,
    nunc deserta quidem, gentibus apta tuis.
    Hanc pete; namque tibi sedes erit illa perhennis.
    Hic fiet natis altera Troia tuis.
    Hic de prole tua reges nascentur, et ipsis tocius terrae subditus orbis erit.
    (HKB 16.21, trans. Neil Wright with slight modifications [emphasis added])

162. "Diuiso tandem regno, affectauit Brutus ciuitatem aedificare. Affectum itaque suum exequens, circuiuit tocius patriae situm ut congruum locum inueniret. Perueniens ergo ad Tamensem fluuium, deambulauit littora locumque nactus est proposito suo perspicuum. Condidit itaque ciuitatem ibidem eamque *Troiam Nouam* uocauit" (ibid., § 22, 28–31 [emphasis added]).

163. Ingledew, "The Book of Troy," 685.

164. See, for example, Geoffrey of Monmouth, *The Historia regum Britannie*, vol. 5, *Gesta regum Brittanie*, § 22, 32: "Hanc amat, hanc cingit muris; hanc turribus altis / Roborat."

165. "Fecit etiam in urbe Trinouantum ianuam mirae fabricae super ripam Tamensis, quam de nomine suo ciues temporibus istis Belinesgata uocant. Desuper uero aedificauit turrim mirae magnitudinis portumque subtus pedes applicantibus nauibus idoneum" (HKB 44.58–59).

166. Wheatley, *The Idea of the Castle*, 34.

167. The appearance of the apse has also been likened to Roman architectural styles; as Wheatley points out, however, "It has also emerged that Norman keeps in France before the Conquest show similar apsidal projections" (ibid., 129n88). To my mind, however, this fact only demonstrates further continuity with regard to the importance of Aachen and the imitation of Roman architectural style.

168. Jeremy Ashbee has pointed out the Tower's effective symbolic function "as a permanent and intrusive reminder of the Normans. . . . That this was the intention is shown by the care lavished on the elevations facing the city and the river, and in the extra height provided by the 'false' top storey" (Ashbee, "The Function of the White Tower," 139).

169. "Ad sananda uulnera sua in insulam Auallonis" (HKB 178.252–53).

170. "Nolebat enim Deus Britones in insula Britannie diutius regnare, antequam tempus illud uenniset quod Merlinus Arturo prophetauerat" (ibid., 205.278–79).

171. Faletra, "Narrating the Matter of Britain," 75–76.

172. "Barbarie etiam irrepente, iam non uocabantur Britones sed Gualenses, uocabulum siue a Gualone duce eorum siue a Galaes regina siue a barbarie trahentes" (HKB 207.280–81).

173. "At Saxones, sapientius agentes, pacem etiam et concordiam inter se habentes, agros colentes, ciuitates et oppida reaedificantes, et sic abiecto dominio Britonum iam toti Loegriae imperauerant duce Adelstano, qui primus inter eos diadema portauit. Degenerati autem a Britannica nobilitate Gualenses numquam postea monarchiam insulae recuperauerunt" (ibid., 207.280–81).

174. "Dicebat etiam populum Britonum per meritum suae fidei insulam in futuro adepturum postquam fatale tempus superueniret; nec id tamen prius futurum quam Britones, reliquiis eius potiti, illas ex Roma in Brittaniam asportarent" (ibid., 205.278–79).

Chapter 3

1. As W. L. Warren notes, the Forest was not "an area under the direct rule of royal officers administering forest law

to the exclusion of the shire and hundred: on the contrary, to be subject to forest law was to be subject of an additional, not a different, form of law and government" (Warren, *Henry II*, 391).

2. "Betwyx oðrum þingum nis na to forgytane þet gode frið þe he macode on þisan lande, swa þet an man þe him sylf aht wære mihte faran ofer his rice mid his bosum full goldes ungederad. ⁊ nan man ne dorste slean oðerne man, næfde he næfre swa mycel yfel gedon wið þone oðerne" (Among other things, the good order he made in this land is not to be forgotten, so that a man who was of any account could travel over his kingdom with his bosom full of gold, unmolested; and no man dare kill another man, however great a wrong he might have done the other) (*The Anglo-Saxon Chronicle*, vol. 6, 97, trans. by Michael J. Swanton in *Anglo-Saxon Chronicle*, entry for 1087, 220).

3. He wæs on gitsunge befeallan, ⁊
   grædinæsse he lufode mid ealle.
He sætte mycel deorfrið, ⁊ he lægde
   laga þærwið
þet swa hwa swa sloge heort oððe hinde,
   þæt hine man sceolde blendian.
He forbead þa heortas swylce eac þa
   baras;
swa swiðe \he/ lufode þa headeor swilce
   he wære heora fæder.
Eac he sætte be þam haran þæt hi
   mosten freo faran.
His rice men hit mændon, ⁊ þa earme
   men hit beceorodan.
Ac he <wæs> swa stið þæt he ne rohte
   heora eallra nið,
ac hi moston mid ealle þes cynges wille
   folgian,
gif hi woldon libban, oððe land habban,
land oððe eahta, oððe wel his sehta.
Walawa, þet ænig man sceolde modigan swa,

hine sylf upp ahebban ⁊ ofer ealle men tellan.
   (Ibid., trans. by Michael J. Swanton in *Anglo-Saxon Chronicle*, 221)

4. Ibid., 96.

5. Jurasinski, "The *Rime of King William*."

6. This lack of distinction between lay and ecclesiastical property may be surprising, but as Janet Nelson observes, ecclesiastical estates were also considered among the major royal assets of the Carolingian kings, "given the Carolingians' control of the church's material resources" (Nelson, "Literacy in Carolingian Government," 275). Hans J. Hummer points out that "Carolingian rulers systematically co-opted the most prestigious monasteries" within two generations and "developed mechanisms of control focused on monasteries" (Hummer, *Politics and Power*, 61). Thus, the control and disposition of church lands should be seen as one aspect of the expression of royal power, as Janet Nelson demonstrates about Charles the Bald's reign (Nelson, "Charles the Bald and the Church"). Similarly, on the question of Carolingian continuity in Normandy, Karl Werner also notes that the duke of Normandy had "a particularly extensive power over the Church in his territory" (Werner, "Kingdom and Principality," 253).

7. One of the most influential studies on the side of Scandinavian influence is Eleanor Searle's groundbreaking survey, *Predatory Kingship and the Creation of Norman Power, 840–1066*; for a foundational discussion of continuity, see Bates, *Normandy Before 1066*, which he reiterates in "West Francia." More recently, however, the argument for continuity has been put on a new footing by Bauduin, *La première Normandie*, and Hagger, "Secular Law and Legal Custom."

8. Davy, *Duc et la loi*, 53. See also Werner's comment that the French *princeps*, such as the Norman dukes, took over royal power, at first "as a representative of the king; later by princes acting on their own account" (Werner, "Kingdom and Principality," 248).
9. Lemarignier, *Étude sur les privilèges*, 292.
10. Hen, "Clovis, Gregory of Tours," 273.
11. Davy, *Duc et la loi*, 81.
12. Ibid., 135.
13. For more information, see McKitterick, *The New Cambridge Medieval History*, vol. 2, C. 700–c. 900.
14. Ganshof, *The Carolingians*, 97.
15. Marvin, *Hunting Law and Ritual*, 20–27.
16. Ganshof, *The Carolingians*, 67, although he concedes, "We can probably assume that permission was quite often granted" (ibid., 82n141). To better understand this departure from the general oath of fidelity taken by Carolingian kings, see Nelson, "Kingship and Royal Government."
17. "Ut in forestes nostras feramina nostra nemine furare audeat, quod iam multis vicibus fieri contradiximus; et nunc iterum banniamus firmiter, ut nemo amplius faciat, sicut fidelitatem nobis promissa unusquisque conservare cupiat, ita sibi caveat. Si quis autem comis vel centenarius aut bassus noster aut aliquis de ministerialibus nostris feramina nostra furaverit, omnino ad nostra presentia perducantur ad rationem. Caeteris autem vulgis, qui ipsum furtum de feraminibus fecerit, omnino quod iustum est componat, nullatenusque eis exinde aliquis relaxetur. Si quis autem hoc sciente alicui perpetratum, in ea fidelitate conservatum quam nobis promiserunt et nunc promittere habent, nullus hoc celare audeat" (*Capitulare missorum generale*, in MGH, *Capitularia regum Francorum*, vol. 1, no. 33, cap. 39, 98).
18. Ganshof, *The Carolingians*, 58–59 and 112–13.
19. "Volumus ut villae nostrae, quas ad opus nostrum serviendi institutas habemus, sub integritate partibus nostris deserviant et non aliis hominibus" (We wish that our estates, which we have arranged to attend our needs, serve zealously to our profit and not that of other men) (*Capitulare de villis*, in MGH, *Capitularia regum Francorum*, vol. 1, no. 32, cap. 1 [hereafter cited as CV; all translations mine unless otherwise indicated]).
20. "Si familia nostra partibus nostris aliquam fecerit fraudem de latrocinio aut alio neglecto, illud in caput componat; de reliquo vero pro lege recipiat disciplinam vapulando" (ibid., cap. 4).
21. "Ad reliquos autem homines iustitiam eorum, qualem habuerint, reddere studeant, sicut lex est; pro fauda vero nostra, ut diximus, familia vapuletur. Franci autem qui in fiscis aut villis nostris commanent, quicquid commiserint, secundum legem eorum emendare studeant, et quod pro frauda dederint, ad opus nostrum veniat, id est" (ibid., cap. 4).
22. Dolly Jørgensen mentions the CV along with some other Carolingian documents that could be interpreted as being ancestors to Anglo-Norman forest law, citing the CV as the document that first discusses the right to hunt as part of royal forest privileges (Jørgensen, "The Roots of the English Royal Forest," 118).
23. "Ut silvae vel forestes nostrae bene sint custoditae; et ubi locus fuerit ad stirpandum, stirpare faciant, et campos de silva increscere non permittant: et ubi silvae debent esse, non eas permittant nimis capulare atque damnare; et feramina nostra intra forestes bene custodiant; similiter acceptores et

spervarios ad nostrum profectum praevideant; et censa nostra exinde diligenter exactent. Et iudices, si eorum porcos ad saginandum in silvam nostram miserint vel maiores nostri aut homines eorum, ipsi primi illam decimam donent ad exemplum bonum proferendum, qualiter in postmodum ceteri homines illorum decimam pleniter persolvent" (CV, cap. 36).

24. Ibid., cap. 42.
25. Nelson, "Kingship and Royal Government," 394-95.
26. Another capitulary from Charlemagne discussing the protection of the forest more generally is the *Capitulare Aquisgranense* (dated 801-13), cap. 18. Louis the Pious also claimed in the *Capitulare per se Scribenda* of 818-19 that he would establish the forests as did his father (cap. 7), and he issued the *Capitulare missorum* in 819, which further discusses the forest in cap. 22. See MGH, *Capitularia regum Francorum*.
27. Petit-Dutaillis and Lefebvre, *Studies and Notes*, 166. According to F. W. M. Vera, "There is some agreement that the concept 'forestis' applies to the wilderness in general, and to trees, forest, shrubs, wild animals, water and fish in particular. In other words, in a 'forestis,' every individual tree, as well as every wild animal, belonged to the king" (Vera, *Grazing Ecology*, 104). For more general information regarding the history of the use of wilderness and forest terminology in the Middle Ages, see ibid., 102-88.
28. Petit-Dutaillis and Lefebvre, *Studies and Notes*, 166-67. Jørgensen also discusses the ducal appropriation of this royal privilege during the waning of late Carolingian and Ottonian power (Jørgensen, "The Roots of the English Royal Forest," 119-21). For another, more detailed examination of the pre-Conquest Norman development of Forest Law, see Petit-Dutaillis, "Les origines."
29. Vera, *Grazing Ecology*, 107.
30. Petit-Dutaillis's seminal study on the Norman French origins of the English forest system confirms the lack of any strong forest administration in pre-Conquest England. He states, "A l'époque anglo-saxonne, nous n'apercevons encore aucun des traits caractéristiques de ce régime [de la Forêt des normands]: ni 'bêtes de la Forêt' d'espèce déterminée, ni droit special, ni administration, ni tribunaux" (Petit-Dutaillis, "Les origines," 61). For more detailed information about charters and woodland in Anglo-Saxon England, see Hooke, "Pre-Conquest Woodland."
31. For example, Chris Wickham stresses that "[t]here was, indeed, so little woodland in the eleventh century that it must have needed protection from informal assarting in all but the largest tracts; Ine's law-code of c. 700 had already specified fines for uncontrolled tree-felling, which were higher for the timber trees in pig runs. And much of it must have needed formal resource management" (Wickham, "European Forests," esp. 507).
32. Rackham, "Trees and Woodland," 10.
33. "Forgá ælc man minne huntnoð, locehwær ic hit gefriðod wylle habban, be fullan wite" (II Cnut 80.1, in *Die Gesetze der Angelsachsen*, vol. 1, 366-67). "Everyone is to avoid trespassing on my hunting, wherever I wish to have it preserved, on pain of full fine" (Douglas and Greenaway, *English Historical Documents*, vol. 2, 1042-1189, 430).
34. Hooke, "Pre-Conquest Woodland," 122. Jørgensen clarifies this further, saying that "*Constitutiones de Foresta* was not, however, a genuine Anglo-Saxon text but one written by a Norman scribe reflecting Anglo-Norman practice of

the late twelfth century" (Jørgensen, "The Roots of the English Royal Forest," 117).
35. Rackham, "Trees and Woodland," 10.
36. In the *Capitulare Carisiacense* of 877, Charles the Bald forbids his son Louis to hunt in certain specified areas (cap. 32), and requires Adelelmus to provide an account of all the animals he took in the hunt (cap. 33). A charter from Lothaire in 974 confirmed a donation from Louis the Pious of a royal forest to the monastery of Sainte-Colombe de Sens (Petit-Dutaillis, "Les origines," 62n5), and in 969, he gave Dirk II, count of Friesland, the forest of Wasda (ibid., 62n6). See also Goldberg, "'The Hunt Belongs to Man.'"
37. Marvin, *Hunting Law*, 140.
38. See Goldberg, "Louis the Pious and the Hunt," for more on this important Carolingian development.
39. Nelson, "The Lord's Anointed," 168-69.
40. Ibid; 169.
41. Godman, *Poets and Emperors*, 88.
42. "A la cour franque, [la chasse] est de surcroît *élevée au rang d'institution*" (emphasis in original) (Hennebicque, "Espaces sauvages," 37).
43. "[M]ontrer aux aristocrats la supériorité et la puissance royales," "[procurer] au roi victorieux une aura quasi-magique," "[assurer] au roi une supériorité matérielle indispensable à sa puissance politique" (ibid.).
44. Petit-Dutaillis, "Les origines," 67.
45. For a detailed discussion of the monastic attitude toward their disenfranchisement, see Marvin, *Hunting Law*, esp. 48-67.
46. See Young, *The Royal Forests*, esp. 12-13, for a discussion of the pipe roll fines and pardons.
47. Warren, *Henry II*, 140; Young, *The Royal Forests*, 16.
48. Warren, *Henry II*, 390.
49. Bates, *Regesta regum*, no. 18, 144-46.

50. Young, *The Royal Forests*, 15-16.
51. Ibid., 15.
52. The influence of this idea can be seen in England in the tenth century: for example, Alan Harding notes a meeting of the bishops and reeves in London to decide an ordinance for the running of their "peace-gild" (friðgegyldum), where any thief older than twelve years of age who stole property valuing more than 12d. was to be killed and his goods confiscated; moreover, "everybody was to be 'of one friendship and one enmity' in pursuing thieves," indicating again the idea that fidelity had changed to mean more than simply not doing harm (Harding, *Medieval Law*, 79).
53. Richardson and Sayles, *The Governance of Mediaeval England*, 446-47. See also the discussion in Poole, *Domesday Book to Magna Carta, 1087-1216*, 32-34, and Short, "Forest and Wood-Pasture," esp. 134-35.
54. Douglas and Greenaway, *English Historical Documents*, 400-402.
55. "Some fifty men, who in those days seemed still blessed with some traces of wealth from the old English nobility, were apprehended and falsely accused of having taken, killed and eaten the king's deer" (Quinquaginta circiter viri, quibus adhuc illis diebus ex antiqua Anglorum ingenuitate divitiarum quaedam vestigia arridere videbantur, capti sunt et calumniati quod cervos regis ceperint, mactaverint, manducaverint) (*Historia Novorum*, 102 [1098], in Caenegem, *English Lawsuits*, 122).
56. As Viktor Pöschl states, "Vergil's landscape does not exist for its own sake. Nor is it all setting and background. Above all, it is symbolic of mood. It is a part and a reflection of the inner action" (Pöschl, *The Art of Vergil*, 143). When, in book 4, Dido and Aeneas go hunting in the forest and make love in

a cave where they had sought shelter from a storm wrought by Juno, their passion is reflected by the tempest raging throughout the forest.
57. Marvin, *The Hunting Law*, 96.
58. Rooney, *Hunting in Middle English Literature*, 98.
59. Gomes, *The Making of a Court Society*, 13.
60. A notable exception to this view is Frank Barlow's illuminating work on the king's life, *William Rufus*, which attempts to reverse much of the bad press that William has received over the centuries by showing him to be a far more generous and capable king than many medieval writers would have one believe.
61. Kantorowicz, *The King's Two Bodies*.
62. See especially Orderic Vitalis, *The Ecclesiastical History* 10.14 (Chibnall 5:284-85).
63. "Totum corpus maculatur multiformis lepra nequitae, et a capite usque ad pedes occupauit illud languor maliciae. . . . Quibus auditis rex in cachinnum resolutus est" (ibid., 10.14-15 [Chibnall 5:284-87]).
64. "Deinde iv. non. Augusti [2 Aug.], feria v., inclictione VIII., rex Anglorum Willelmus junior, dum in Nova Foresta, quae lingua Anglorum Ytene nuncupatur, venatu esset occupatus, a quodam Franco, Waltero, cognomento Tirello, sagitta incaute directa percussus, vitam finivit. . . . Nec mirum, ut populi rumor affirmat, hanc proculdubio magnam Dei virtutem esse et vindictam. Antiquis enim temporibus, Eadwardi scilicet regis, et aliorum Angliae regum praedecessorum ejus, eadem regio incolis Dei cultoribus et ecclesiis nitebat uberrime; sed, jussu regis Willelmi senioris, hominibus fugatis, domibus semirutis, ecclesiis destructis, terra ferarum tantum colebatur habitatione, et inde, ut creditur, causa erat infortunii" (Florence of Worcester, *Florentii Wigorniensis monachi Chronicon*, vol. 2, 44-45).
65. These romances are the Robin Hood legends, as well as the precursors to them such as *Fouke le Fitz Waryn*, which Maurice Keen has dubbed "the matter of the Greenwood" (as opposed to the other three traditional divisions of romances, the matter of Britain, the matter of France, and the matter of Greece and Rome), where "the forest background was essential" (Keen, *The Outlaws of Medieval Legend*, 1-2).
66. See Campbell and Darby, *The Domesday Geography*, 342: "The evidence of the soil is clear enough. The greater part of the area is covered by the most infertile Tertiary sands and gravels which cannot ever have supported a flourishing agriculture and a large population. In the middle of the Forest there are great stretches that seem always to have been virtually uninhabited. The evidence of the Domesday Book likewise shows that the making of the Forest involved no such violent upheaval as that described by the medieval chronicles."
67. Nunc de silua ubi prefatus tiro periit. uide lector cur "noua" vocitata sit. Ab antiquis temporibus ibi populosa regio erat, et uillis humanae habitationi competentibus abundabat. Copiosa uero plebs Suthhamtonae pagum sollerti cura obnixe colebat. unde australis prouincia Guentanae urbi multipliciter campestri ubertate seruiebat. Guillelmus autem primus postquam regnum Albionis optinuit, amator nemorum plusquam lx parrochias ultro deuastauit, ruricolas ad alia loca transmigrare compulit, et siluestris feras pro hominibus ut uoloptatem uenandi haberet ibidem constituit. Ibi duos filios Ricardum et Guillelmum Rufum nepotemque suum ut

dictum est Ricardum perdidit, et multiformis uisio quibusdam terribiliter apparuit, quibus consecrates aedes pro educatione ferarum derelictas Dominus sibi displicere palam ostendit. (Orderic Vitalis, *The Ecclesiastical History* 10.14 [Chibnall 5:282-85])

68. "Porro aecclesiastici doctores et prelati sordidam eius uitam et tetrum finem considerantes tunc iudicare ausi sunt. et aecclesiastica ueluti biothanatum absolutione indignum censuerunt, quem uitales auras carpentem salubriter a nequitiis castigare nequiuerunt" (ibid., 10.89-90 [Chibnall 292-93]).

69. In this account, Rufus's death is directly linked to his own offenses: "When the fame and terror of the power of King William, son of the great William, were increasing everywhere, it happened that this king by chance went hunting in the forest which, when he established it, he wished to be called 'New.' There it was that, while fully absorbed and delighting in his activity, by a secret and incomprehensible judgement of God, he was accidentally wounded by an arrow shot by a knight, and died" (Cum Regis Willelmi magni Willelmi filii circumquaque uirtutis fama et terror crebresceret, contigit eundem regem in siluam, / quam ipse stabiliens 'nouam' oucitari uoluit, uenatum forte deuenisse. Quo dum suam studiose exercens delectaretur industriam, occulto Dei quo ignoratur iudicio casu, a quodam milite, . . . uita defungitur) (Searle, *The Chronicle of Battle Abbey*, fol. 40v, 106-7).

70. Alexander Bell dates the poem "towards the close of the five-year period 1135-40" (Bell, in Gaimar, *L'Estoire des Engleis*, liii). Ian Short narrows the gap even further, setting it between March 1136 and April 1137 (Short, "Gaimar's Epilogue").

71. Gillingham, "Kingship, Chivalry," 245. Gaimar's work, it will be remembered, is a revision of English secular history, with a focus on courtly and chivalric behavior—"Anglo-Saxon history as seen through the eyes of romance," according to Gransden, *Historical Writing in England*, vol. 1, 210.

72. Short, introduction to Gaimar, *Estoire des Engleis*, ix.

73. "Engleis, Normanz l'ont coruné" (The English and the Normans crowned him) (Gaimar, *Estoire des Engleis*, l. 5778).

74. "E il la tint e bel regnat, / Normanz, Engleis fort justisat" (And he held [the land] and reigned well, he ruled the English and the Normans strongly) (ibid., ll. 5781-82).

75. "Tote la tere mist en pas" (He brought peace to the entire land) (ibid., l. 5783).

76. Encontre vent la mer passat:
Li esterman lui demandat
s'il voleit contre vent aler
e periller enz en la mer.
"Frere, respunt li reis, teisez!
Unc ne veïstes reis neiez
ne jo nen ere ja le primer!
Feites voz eschipres nager!"
  (Ibid., ll. 5831-38)
Rufus also laughs with great good humor at the boasting challenge of his rebellious vassal, the count of Mortain, finding him more ludicrous than frightening: "li reis, quant l'ot, si prist a rire / par bel amur, nïent par ire" (The king, when he heard it, began to laugh, for fair love, not for anger) (ibid., ll. 5943-44).

77. Li reis idonc out Normendie
e tut le Maine en sa baillie;
par tute France les barons
le dutouent cum uns lëons.
Tresk'a Peiters ne remist ber
K'il ne feïst vers sei cliner:
par sa nobilité [si] grant
tuz ses veisins li sunt clinant,
e s'il peüst alkes regner,
a Rome alast pur chalenger

l'ancïen dreit de cel païs
ke i out Brenes e Belins.

The king therefore had Normandy and all of Maine under his authority; throughout all of France, the barons feared him as a lion. As far as Poitiers, no man remained whom he did not make subject to him. Through his great nobility, all his neighbors bowed to him. And if he had reigned a bit longer, he would have gone to Rome to claim the ancient right of that land, which Brennus and Belinus had there.
(Ibid., ll. 5963-73 [trans. mine])

About this time in France, Suger confirmed this rumor about William Rufus in the *Vita Ludovici Grossi regis*, claiming that it was "commonly said that this proud and headstrong king aspired to the throne of the French" (dicebatur equidem vulgo regem illum superbum et impetuosum aspirare ad regnum Francorum) (*Vie de Louis VI le Gros*, 10, trans. in Richard Cusimano and John Moorhead, *The Deeds of Louis the Fat*, 27).

78. Gillingham notes that "the earliest instances of the word adouber in the full 'chivalrous' sense all occur in Gaimar's English history" (*The English in the Twelfth Century*, 238-39):
Maint gentil hom i adubat.
. . . .
adubat il trente vallez. . . .
. . . .
si richement les aduba
ke tuzjorz parlé en serra.

He knighted many a nobleman there. . . . He knighted thirty youths. . . . So richly he knighted them that it will be talked about forever.
(Gaimar, *Estoire des Engleis*, ll. 6082, 6085, 6105-6)

79. *Meis quant il out piece regné*
e le païs bien apeisé,
e tel justise e drait teneit
[ke] nuls par tort rien ne perdeit
ne nuls francs hom n'ert esguaré
ne suffratus en son regné. . . .
. . . .
De l'altre part aveit asis
ses justisers par sun païs;
par ses foresz, ses foresters:
ja n'i entrast chien në archers.
(Ibid., ll. 6211-16, 6227-30)

80. "Cest rei gentil par grant baldur / teneit son regne par honur." (ibid., ll. 6249-50).

81. Ibid., l. 6306; "En sun quer tint la felunie, / purpensat sei de un' estutie" (He held the crime in his heart; he hatched a plot within his thoughts) (ibid., ll. 6307-8).

82. See, for example, the version of the story as told by Orderic Vitalis: "Henry galloped at top speed to Winchester castle where the royal treasure was, and imperiously demanded the keys from the keepers as the lawful heir" (Henricus concito cursu ad arcem Guentoniae, ubi regalis thesaurus continebatur festinauit, et claues eius ut genuinus haeres imperiali iussu ab excubitoribus exegit) (*The Ecclesiastical History*, 10.4 [Chibnall 5:290-91]); "The moment the king was dead many nobles made off from the wood to their estates, and prepared to resist the disorders they anticipated. Some of the humbler attendants covered the king's bloody body as best they might with wretched cloths and carried him like a wild boar stuck with spears from the wood to the town of Winchester" (Mortuo rege plures optimatum ad lares suos de saltu manicauerunt, et contra futuris motiones quas timebant res suas ordinauerunt. Clientuli quidam cruentatum regem uilibus utcumque pannis operuerunt, et ueluti ferocem aprum uenabulis confossum de saltu ad urbem Guentanam detulerunt) (ibid. [Chibnall 5:292-93]).

83. *Par quatre faiz s'est escrïez,*
    le corpus domini ad demandez,
    mes il ne fu ki li donast;
    loinz de muster ert en un wast.
    E nepurquant un veneür
    prist des herbes od tut la flur,
    un poi en fist al rei manger,
    issi quidat l'acomenger.
    En Deu est ço e estre deit:
    il aveit pris pain ben[ë]eit
    le di[e]maigne dedevant:
    ço li deit estre bon guarant.
    (Gaimar, *Estoire des Englels*, ll. 6335-46)
84. *Cil detir[er]ent lur chevols*
    e firent dol a desmesuré;
    unc ne fu mes tel demené.
    (Ibid., ll. 6354-56)
85. *Cil fit tel dol, tant demenat,*
    edit sovent: "Ki m'oscirat?
    Mielz voil morir ke vivre plus!"
    Donc se pasma si chaï jus;
    quant il revint, detort ses mains,
    tant par devint febles e vains
    ke pur un poi ne rechaï.
    De tutes parz grant dol oï.
    (Ibid., ll. 6359-66)
    Fainting and dying from grief is a common trope for the ladies of romance literature, however: in laisses 268-69 of *La Chanson de Roland*, for example, Alde loses color and dies at Charlemagne's feet upon hearing of Roland's death, but Charlemagne thinks she has only fainted and tries to revive her.
86. "Stipendiarii uero milites et nebulones ac uulgaria scrota questus suos in occasu moechi principis perdiderunt, eiusque miserabilem obitum non tam pro pietate quam pro detestabili flagitiorum cupiditate planxerunt" (*The Ecclesiastical History*, 10.4 [Chibnall 5:292-93]).
87. *Enz el muster [de] saint Swithun,*
    la asemblerent li baron
    od le clergié de la cité
    e li evesque e li abbé.
    Li bons eveskes Walkelin
    gueitat le rei tresk'al matin,
    od lui moignes, clers e abbez;
    bien fu serviz e purchantez.
    L'endemain funt tel departie
    tel ne vit [ainz] home de vie,
    ne tantes messes ne tel servise
    n'i ert fet tresk'en Deu juïse
    pur un sul rei cum pur li firent.
    (Gaimar, *Estoire des Englels*, ll. 6417-29)
88. Young, *Royal Forests*, 18.
89. Ibid., 19.
90. Marvin, *Hunting Law*, 67.
91. See Saunders, *The Forest of Medieval Romance*.
92. Barlow, *William Rufus*, 119.
93. Gerald of Wales, *Giraldus Cambrensis Opera*, vol. 5, 302.
94. "Venationis delicias aeque ut avus plus justo diligens" (William of Newburgh, "Historia rerum Anglicarum," in Howlett, *Chronicles and Memorials*, vol. 1, bk. III, cap. 26 [280-81]).
95. Saunders, *The Forest of Medieval Romance*, 56-57.
96. Marie de France, *The "Lais" of Marie de France*, 90, 92. See also Larmat, "La chasse dans les *Lais*"; and Saunders, *The Forest of Medieval Romance*, 48-57.
97. "En la forest tut sul se mist, / Ne voleit pas que hum le veïst" (Marie de France, *Lais*, ll. 29-30).
98. Ibid., l. 57.
99. *Del chemin un poi s'esluina,*
    Dedenz le bois celui trova
    Que plus l'amot que rien vivant:
    Entre eus eminent joie [mut] grant.
    A li parlet tut a leisir,
    E ele li dit sun pleisir.
    (Ibid., ll. 91-96)
100. *A li parlat tut a leisir,*
     E ele li dit sun pleisir;
     Puis li mustre cumfaitement
     Del rei avrat acordement.
     (Ibid., ll. 95-98)
101. *Quant de lais faire m'entremet,*
     ne voil ublïer Bisclavret:

>   *Bisclavret ad nun en bretan,*
>   *garwaf l'apelent li Norman.*
>   *jadis le poeit hume oïr*
>   *e sovent suleit avenir,*
>   *humes plusurs garual devindrent*
>   *e es boscages meisun tindrent.*
>   *Garualf, c[eo] est beste salvage:*
>   *tant cum il est en cele rage,*
>   *hummes devure, grant mal fait,*
>   *es granz forez converse e vait.*
>   *cest afere les ore ester;*
>   *del Bisclavret [vus] voil cunter.*
>   (Ibid., ll. 1-14, trans. mine)

102. "Beaus chevalers e bons esteit / e noblement se cunteneit" (ibid., ll. 17-18).
103. Saunders discusses the Celtic influences of the world of the *fée* upon the *lais*, noting that it is a parallel reality to the human world, following "its own laws of time, logic and morality" (Saunders, *The Forest of Medieval Romance*, 45-46). I would suggest that, for Marie, the trope of the supernatural Celtic forest is combined with the courtly world of humans through the presence of the king, making it a hybrid space in some of the *lais* (such as "Bisclavret").
104.   *Seignurs, fet il, avant venez!*
        ceste merveillë esgardez,
        cum ceste beste se humilie!
        Ele ad sen de hume, merci crie.
        Chacez mei tuz ces chiens arere,
        si gardez quë hum ne la fiere!
        Ceste beste ad entente e sen.
        Espleitez vus! Alum nus en!
        a la beste durrai ma pes;
        kar jeo ne chacerai hui mes.
             (Marie de France, *Lais*, ll. 145-60, trans. in *The "Lais,"* 70)
105. The eulogy for Henry I in the *Peterborough Chronicle* entry for 1135, for instance, praises him for the "pais he makede men ⁊ dær" (He made peace for men and deer). Other instances include one of Merlin's prophecies in Geoffrey of Monmouth, "Pacem habebunt fere, humanitas supplicium dolebit" (The beasts will have peace, humanity will suffer torture), and the "pax uenationis suae" (peace of his deer) from Henry II's Assize of Woodstock in 1184.
106. Marie de France, *Lais*, l. 168; "Franc e deboneire, unques ne volt a rien mesfeire" (ibid., ll. 179-80).
107. Suggesting as well the instinctive desire for bloodfeud in contrast with the civilized dispensation of justice that is a frequent motif of twelfth-century literature and one impetus for the Peace (or Truce) of God movement that began in the late tenth century.
108.   *[S]e pur ostïer ne fust,*
        Pur nul busuin ki li creüst
        Li reis ne laissast sun chacier,
        Sun deduire, sun riveier.
             (Marie de France, *Lais*, ll. 25-28, trans. in *The "Lais,"* 56)
109. Saunders, *The Forest of Medieval Romance*, 49.
110.   *Un [lai] en firent, ceo oi cunter,*
        Ki ne fet mie a ublïer,
        D'Equitan que mut fu curteis,
        Sire de Nauns, jostis e reis.

     One of [the *lais*], which I have heard recited, should not be forgotten. It concerns Equitan, a most courtly man, lord of Nantes, justiciary and king. (Marie de France, *Lais*, ll. 9-12, trans. in *The "Lais,"* 56)
111. Rooney, *Hunting in Middle English Literature*, 98.
112.   *Equitan fu mut de grant pris*
        E mut amez en sun païs;
        Deduit amout e drüerie:
        Pur ceo maintint chevalerie.

        . . . .

        Equitan ot un seneschal,
        Bon chevaler, pruz e leal;
        Tute sa tere li gardoit
        E meinteneit e justisoit.

(Marie de France, *Lais*, ll. 13-16, 21-24, trans. in *The "Lais,"* 56)
113. "Par lur anels s'entresaisirent, / Lur fiaunce[s] s'entreplevirent" (By an exchange of rings they took possession of each other and pledged their faith) (ibid., ll. 181-82, trans. in *The "Lais,"* 58).
114. "Tel purcace le mal d'autrui / Dunt le mals [tut] revert sur lui" (ibid., ll. 309-10, trans. in *The "Lais,"* 60).

Epilogue

1. Wace, *Roman de Rou*, vol. 2, ll. 8013-18. It is significant that Wace's unfinished *roman* was originally written at the behest of Henry II.
2. Gillingham, "Civilizing the English?," 29-30. See also Turville-Petre, *England the Nation*; Thomas, *The English and the Normans*, especially chap. 20, "The Intensification and Politicization of English Identity," 323-43.
3. Crouch, "The *Roman des Franceis*," 178.
4. "Et o la dousse d'al freie" (And shatters the spears of the Twelve Peers) (Andrew de Coutances, *Roman des Franceis*, ll. 377-78, trans. in Crouch, "The *Roman des Franceis*.")
5. "Douce este[it] France or est amere" (ibid., l. 58). This is meant to mock the phrase "la douce France" from the *Chanson de Roland*.
6. "Quer il [Arthur] mist toz enseruage" (ibid., l. 205). Crouch notes that it bears the signs "of the influence of an Angevin propaganda machine which had appropriated Arthur to the line of kings of the *English*, not the Britons" (Crouch, "The *Roman des Franceis*," 178 [emphasis in original]).
7. Bates, *The Normans and Empire*, 184. The ongoing debate about the emergence of an English identity still rages in recent studies, all arguing for various degrees of identification with Englishness throughout the twelfth century. In addition to Bates, see especially Ashe, *Fiction and History in England*; Bartlett, *England under the Norman and Angevin Kings*; Carpenter, *The Struggle for Mastery*; Gillingham, *The English in the Twelfth Century*; Thomas, *The English and the Normans*, and *The Norman Conquest*; and Williams, *The English and the Norman Conquest*.
8. Morrissey, *Charlemagne and France*, 67. For an unusually precocious treatment of Charlemagne in this manner from Anglo-Norman England, see my recent article "Taming the Wilderness."
9. Gillingham, "Civilizing the English?," 29-30.
10. Ibid., 30n71. See also Matthew, *The English and the Community of Europe*.
11. Salter, *English and International*, 30. See also Matthew, *The English and the Community of Europe*, 316.
12. Matthew, *The English and the Community of Europe*, 12.
13. Salter, *English and International*, 77. See also Ridyard, "Condigna Veneratio"; and Crane, *Insular Romance*. For a similar situation in later thirteenth-century France, see Spiegel, *Romancing the Past*.
14. Scahill, "The Audiences of Medieval Chronicles."
15. See Thomas, *The English and the Normans*, esp. pt. III (in particular, 316-43), where he expands on this idea more fully, pointing especially to the events of 1215-17 and hostilities with the French as an explanation for the increasing redefinition of English identity. Matthew, *The English and the Community of Europe*, downplays this notion, however, and insists that the English were still very much invested in continental affairs and intellectual culture, and minimizes the focus on

English insularity beginning in the thirteenth century. Of course, both are correct in their arguments: although the inhabitants remaining in England after the events of 1204 were renegotiating their Englishness in light of the changes in English-French relations, there remained a concern to be a part of the flourishing culture on the continent and be seen as a civilized society as well. Ian Short traces this change to the late twelfth century in "*Tam Angli quam Franci.*"

16. See Geoffrei Gaimar's treatment of Anglo-Saxon kings, and Edgar in particular, in *Estoire des Engleis*, ll. 3565-975. For a discussion of Gaimar's courtly approach to recounting Anglo-Saxon history, see Press, "The Precocious Courtesy of Geoffrey Gaimar." A generation later, Marie de France would claim in her epilogue to the *Fables* to be translating from King Alfred's English translation of Aesop (ll. 11-19), intended for a courtly audience (*Les Fables: Édition critique*, edited by Charles Brucker).

17. Daniel Donoghue called this phenomenon "ambivalence," in which "two sides are at an equilibrium, a tension pulling in two directions" (Donoghue, "Laʒamon's Ambivalence," 558). Alternative or complementary views have been offered by Saux, *Laʒamon's "Brut*," esp. 162-75; Johnson, "Reading the Past in Laʒamon's *Brut*"; and Noble, "Laʒamon's 'Ambivalence' Reconsidered."

18. *Dunt avez oi ça avant*
    Nel fesum pas, car la folie
    Amum tant de ceste vie
    Ke plus tost orrium chanter
    De Rolant u d'Oliver,
    E les batailles des duze pers
    Orrium mut plus volenters,
    Ke ne frium, si cum jeo quit,
    La passiun de Jhesu Crist:
    Tant sumes feinz k'en ubliance
    Mettum tut deu e sa pussance.
    (Chardri, *Chardry's Josaphaz*, ll. 2930-40)

    See also Neil Cartlidge's discussion of the poem in "The Composition and Social Context of Oxford," esp. 254-55, and Rutledge, "A Critical Edition of *La Vie de Seint Josaphaz*."

19. Crouch, "The *Roman des Franceis*," 182-83.

20. *Dunt jo vei aukunes en terre,*
    De bunté pleines e de franchise,
    De naturesce e de bele aprise,
    E grant leauté unt eles en sei,
    Ceo vus pus jo affier, par fei.
    E mar en seit nul en dutance,
    En Engletere sunt plus ke en France.
    Nekedent par tut luist la lune,
    En France poet l'en aver aucune.
    Chescune terre, coment ke seit,
    Ke aucun ben eit, est reisun e dreit.
    Mes de celes en est flurie
    Engletere cum bele praerie
    Tuz les reames ke ore sunt
    Passe Engletere, e savez dunt?
    De tuz deduz e de franchise.
    Si femmes i sunt de bele aprise,
    Ne devez pas esmerveiller,
    Si sunt assez li chevaler,
    E tuz li autre ki sunt aprés
    Sunt pruz, gentiz e francs adés.
    (Chardri, *Le Petit plet*, ll. 1250-70)

21. Cartlidge writes, "Although it now seems paradoxical that he should have expressed his Francophobia in the language of the French, it is perhaps a good illustration of the complexity between language and nationality in England during the thirteenth century" (Cartlidge, "Composition and Social Context," 255).

22. Chardri, *Le Petit plet*, ll. 1182, 1290, 1421.

23. Ker, introduction to *The Owl and the Nightingale*, xi.

24. William of Malmesbury, *Gesta regum Anglorum* 2.135 (Mynors, Thomson, and Winterbottom 1:218-21). R. M.

Thomson suggests that William did use some older, tenth-century verse as his source, but he revised it to produce a version more palatable to his twelfth-century audience (in ibid. [2:116-20]).

25. Le espeie Costantin al empereur; e sun nun en l'espeie a lettres de or; el chaple de l'espeie ke fu de fin or; un des clous dunt Nostre Sires fu fiche en la croiz; la lance de Charlemaine k'il suleit porter cuntre Sarazins; ke lem quidat ke fust cele dunt Nostre Sire fu feru (car unkes ne fu levee en bataille, ke ne fust vencue); le gunfanun seint Moriz k'il suleit porter devant cele seinte legiun, ki li rei Charles porta tute sa vie encuntre pains; une partie de la veraie croiz enclos en un crystal; une partie de la curune de espine ke fu mise al chef Nostre Seignur; une curune reale de fin or, u tant aveit peres preciuses. (Loomis, "The Athelstan Gift Story," 523-24)

This article also contains more information on the Caligula version of the episode as well as a transcription of the gift story.

Bibliography

Primary Sources

Monumenta Germaniae historica
[Annales et chronica aevi Salici.] Edited by Georg Heinrich Pertz. Monumenta Germaniae historica, Scriptores (in Folio), 5. Hanover: Hahn, 1844. (MGH, [Annales et chronica aevi Salici])

Annales regni Francorum inde ab a. 741 usque ad a. 829, qui dicuntur Annales Laurissenses maiores et Einhardi. Edited by F. Kurze. Monumenta Germaniae historica, Scriptores, Scriptores rerum Germanicarum in usum scholarum separatim editi, 6. Hanover: Hahn, 1895. (MGH, Annales regni Francorum)

Capitularia regum Francorum. Edited by Alfred Boretius. 2 vols. Monumenta Germaniae historica, Leges, sec. 2. Hanover: Hahn, 1883-97. (MGH, Capitularia regum Francorum)

Cassiodori Senatoris Variae. Edited by Theodor Mommsen. Monumenta Germaniae historica, Auctores antiquissimi, 12. Berlin: Weidmann, 1894. (MGH, Cassiodori Senatoris Variae)

Epistolae Karolini aevi. Edited by Ernst Dümmler et al. 6 vols. Monumenta Germaniae historica, Epistolae, 3-8. Berlin: Weidmann, 1892-1939. (MGH, Epistolae Karolini aevi)

Epistolae Merowingici et Karolini aevi. Edited by Wilhelm Gundlach. Monumenta Germaniae historica, Epistolae, 3. Berlin: Weidmann, 1892. (MGH, Epistolae Merowingici et Karolini aevi)

Fredegarii et aliorum Chronica. Vitae sanctorum. Edited by Bruno Krusch. Monumenta Germaniae historica, Scriptores rerum Merovingicarum, 2. Hanover: Hahn, 1888. (MGH, Fredegarii et aliorum Chronica)

Gregorii I Papae Registrum epistolarum. Edited by Ludo M. Hartmann. 2 vols. Monumenta Germaniae historica, Epistolae, 1-2. Berlin: Weidmann, 1891-99. (MGH, Gregorii I Papae Registrum epistolarum)

Die Konzilien der karolingischen Teilreiche 843-859. Edited by Wilfried Hartmann. Monumenta Germaniae historica, Leges, Concilia, 3. Hanover: Hahn, 1984. (MGH, Die Konzilien der karolingischen Teilreiche 843-859)

Notker der Stammler, Taten Kaiser Karls des Grossen. Edited by Hans F. Haefele.

Monumenta Germaniae historica, Scriptores rerum Germanicarum, Nova series, 12. Berlin: Weidmann, 1959. (MGH, *Notker der Stammler*)

Poetae Latini aevi Carolini. Edited by Ernst Dümmler et al. 4 vols. Monumenta Germaniae historica, Antiquitates, Poetae Latini medii aevi. Berlin: Weidmann, 1884-1923. (MGH, *Poetae Latini aevi Carolini*)

[*Scriptores rerum Sangallensium. Annales, chronica et historiae aevi Saxonici.*] Edited by Georg Heinrich Pertz. Monumenta Germaniae historica, Scriptores (in Folio), 2. Hanover: Hahn, 1829. (MGH, [*Scriptores rerum Sangallensium*])

[*Supplementa tomurum I-XV.*] Edited by Adolf Hofmeister. Monumenta Germaniae historica, Scriptores (in Folio), 30, pt. 2. Leipzig: W. Hiersemann, 1934. (MGH, [*Supplementa tomurum I-XV*])

Die Urkunden Pippins, Karlmanns und Karls des Grossen. Edited by Engelbert Mühlbacher with Alfons Dopsch, Johann Lechner, and Michael Tangl. Monumenta Germaniae historica, Diplomatum Karolinum 1. Hanover: Hahn, 1906. (MGH, *Die Urkunden Pippins, Karlmanns und Karls des Grossen*)

Other Primary Sources

Alcuin. *Disputatio de rhetorica et de virtutibus sapientissimi Regis Karli et Albini Magistri*. The Latin Library at AD Fontes Academy. n.d. http://www.thelatinlibrary.com/alcuin/rhetorica.shtml (accessed 29 November 2007).

———. *Rhetoric*. Translated by Wilbur Howell. New York: Russell and Russell, 1965.

Anglo-Saxon Chronicle. Translated by Michael Swanton. London: Routledge, 1996.

The Anglo-Saxon Chronicle: A Collaborative Edition. Vol. 6, *MS D*. Edited by G. P. Cubbin. Cambridge: D. S. Brewer, 1996.

———. Vol. 7, *MS E*. Edited by Susan Irvine. Cambridge: D. S. Brewer, 2004.

Bede. *Bede's Ecclesiastical History of the English People*. Edited and translated by Bertram Colgrave and R. A. B. Mynors. Oxford: Clarendon Press, 1969. Reprint, 1998.

Brault, Gerald J., ed. and trans. *La Chanson de Roland*. University Park: Pennsylvania State University Press, 1984.

Capitulare de villis. Bibliotheca Augustana. http://www.hs-augsburg.de/~harsch/Chronologia/Lspost08/CarolusMagnus/kar_vill.html (accessed 12 May 2008).

Chardri. *Chardry's Josaphaz, Set dormanz und Petit plet*. Edited by John Koch. Heilbronn: Verlag von Gebr. Henninger, 1879.

———. *Le Petit plet*. Edited by Brian S. Merrilees. Oxford: Basil Blackwell for the Anglo-Norman Text Society, 1970.

Cicero. *M. Tulli Ciceronis De officiis*. Edited by M. Winterbottom. Oxford: Clarendon Press, 1994.

Crouch, David. "The *Roman des Franceis* of Andrew de Coutances: Significance, Text, and Translation." In *Normandy and Its Neighbours, 900-1250: Essays for David Bates*, edited by David Crouch and Kathleen Thompson, 175-98. Medieval Texts and Cultures of Northern Europe 14. Turnhout: Brepols, 2011.

Douglas, David C., and George W. Greenaway, eds. and trans. *English Historical Documents*, vol. 2, 1042-1189. London: Eyre and Spottiswoode, 1968.

Du Chesne, André, and François Du Chesne, eds. *Historiae Francorum scriptores coaetanei . . . Quorum plurimi nunc primum ex variis codicibus mss. in lucem prodeunt: alij vero auctiores & emendatiores. Cvm epistolis regvm, reginarvm, pontificvm . . . et aliis veteribus rerum francicarum monumentis.* 5 vols. Paris: Sumptibus S. Cramoisy, 1636-49.

Dudo of Saint Quentin. *Dudonis gesta Normannorum.* Edited by Felice Lifshitz. 1996. http://www2.fh-augsburg.de/~Harsch/Chronologia/Lspost11/Dudo/dud_n000.html (accessed 1 August 2014).

———. *History of the Normans.* Translated by Eric Christiansen. Woodbridge: Boydell Press, 1998.

Einhard. *Vita Karoli magni.* The Latin Library at AD Fontes Academy. n.d. http://www.thelatinlibrary.com/ein.html (accessed 6 March 2006).

Ermoldus Nigellus. *Carminis in honorem Ludovici christianissimi caesaris augusti.* Edited by Jacques-Paul Migne. Patrologia Latina: The Full Text Database. Chadwyck-Healey, 1996. http://pld.chadwyck.com/ (accessed 4 May 2008).

Fantosme, Jordan. *Chronicles and Memorials of Great Britain and Ireland During the Middle Ages.* Edited by Richard Howlett. Vaduz: Kraus Reprint, 1964.

———. *Jordan Fantosme's Chronicle.* Edited and translated by R. C. Johnston. Oxford: Oxford University Press, 1981.

Florence of Worcester. *Florentii Wigorniensis monachi Chronicon ex chronicis. . . .* Edited by Benjamin Thorpe. 2 vols. London: English Historical Society, 1848-49.

Gaimar, Geffrei. *L'Estoire des Engleis.* Edited by Alexander Bell. Oxford: Basil Blackwell for the Anglo-Norman Text Society, 1960.

———. *Estoire des Engleis.* Edited and translated by Ian Short. Oxford: Oxford University Press, 2009.

———. *Lestorie des Engleis solum la translacion Maistre Geffrei Gaimar.* Edited and translated by Sir Thomas Duffus Hardy and Charles Trice Martin. 2 vols. London: Eyre and Spottiswoode, 1889.

Geoffrey of Monmouth. *The Historia regum Britannie of Geoffrey of Monmouth.* Edited by Neil Wright. Cambridge: D. S. Brewer, 1984-91.

———. *History of the Kings of Britain.* Edited by Michael D. Reeve. Translated by Neil Wright. Woodbridge: Boydell Press, 2007.

Gerald of Wales. *Expugnatio hibernica.* Edited and translated by A. B. Scott and F. X. Martin. Dublin: Royal Irish Academy, 1978.

———. *Giraldi Cambrensis Opera.* 8 vols. Edited by J. S. Brewer et al. Rerum britannicarum medii aevi scriptores 21. London: Longman, 1861-91.

———. *The Journey Through Wales / The Description of Wales.* Translated by Lewis Thorpe. Harmondsworth: Penguin, 1978.

Gervase of Canterbury. *The Historical Works of Gervase of Canterbury.* Edited by W. Stubbs. 2 vols. London: Longman, 1879-80.

Giry, A., Maurice Prou, and G. Tessier, eds. *Recueil des Actes de Charles II le Chauve, roi de France.* 3 vols. Paris: Collection Chartes et Diplômes, 1943-55.

Guy, Bishop of Amiens. *The Carmen de Hastingae Proelio of Guy Bishop of Amiens.* 2nd ed. Edited and translated by Frank Barlow. Oxford: Oxford University Press, 1999.

Henry of Huntingdon. *Historia Anglorum: The History of the English People.* Edited and translated by Diana Greenway. Oxford: Clarendon Press, 1996.

Higden, Ranulf. *Polychronicon Ranulphi Higden, Monachi Cestrensis.* Vol. 1. Edited by Churchill Babington. London: Longman, Green, Longman, Roberts and Green, 1865.

Howlett, R., ed. *Chronicles and Memorials of the Reigns of Stephen, Henry II, and Richard I.* 4 vols. Chronicles and Memorials of Great Britain and Ireland During the Middle Ages 82. London: Longman, 1884–89.

Hrabanus Maurus. *Liber de Oblatione Puerorum.* Edited by Jacques-Paul Migne. Patrologia Latina: The Full Text Database. Chadwyck-Healey, 1996. http://pld.chadwyck.com/ (accessed 4 May 2008).

John of Salisbury. *Ioannis Saresberiensis, Metalogicon.* Edited by J. B. Hall and K. S. B. Keats-Rohan. Corpus Christianorum Continuatio Mediaevalis 98. Turnhout: Brepols, 1991.

John of Worcester. *The Chronicle of John of Worcester.* Edited by J. R. H. Weaver. Oxford: Oxford University Press, 1908.

Jones, Thomas, ed. and trans. *Brut y Tywysogyon or the Chronicle of Princes, Peniarth MS 20 Version.* Cardiff: University of Wales Press, 1985.

Ker, N. R., ed. *The Owl and the Nightingale, Reproduced in Facsimile from the Surviving Manuscripts Jesus College Oxford 29 and British Museum Cotton Caligula A.IX.* London: Published for the Early English Text Society by the Oxford University Press, 1963.

King, P. D., trans. and ed. *Charlemagne: Translated Sources.* Lambrigg: P. D. King, 1987.

Laʒamon. *Brut.* Edited by G. L. Brook and R. F. Leslie. 2 vols. Early English Text Society 250, 277. London: Published for the Early English Text Society by the Oxford University Press, 1963–78.

———. *Brut.* Translated by Rosamund Allen. New York: St. Martin's Press, 1992.

Marie de France. *Les Fables: Édition critique.* 2nd ed. Edited and translated by Charles Brucker. Paris: Peeters, 1998.

———. *Lais.* Edited and translated by Philippe Walter. Paris: Éditions Gallimard, 2000.

———. *The "Lais" of Marie de France.* Edited and translated by Glyn S. Burgess and Keith Busby. New York: Viking Penguin, 1986.

Migne, Jacques-Paul, ed. Patrologia Latina: The Full Text Database. Chadwyck-Healey, 1996. http://pld.chadwyck.com/ (accessed 4 May 2008).

Orderic Vitalis. *The Ecclesiastical History of Orderic Vitalis.* Edited and translated by Marjorie Chibnall. 6 vols. Oxford: Clarendon Press, 1969–80.

Rutledge, Timothy James Stuart. "A Critical Edition of La Vie de Seint Josaphaz, a Thirteenth-Century Poem by the Anglo-Norman Poet Chardri." Ph.D. diss., University of Toronto, 1973.

Skeat, Rev. Walter W., ed. *The Proverbs of Alfred.* Oxford: Clarendon Press, 1907.

Smaragdus St. Mihiel. *Opera omnia.* Edited by Jacques-Paul Migne. Patrologia cursus completus, Series latina, vol. 102. Cambridge, Mass.: Harvard University, 1865.

Suger. *The Deeds of Louis the Fat.* Translated by Richard Cusimano and John Moorhead. Washington, D.C.: Catholic University of America Press, 1992.

———. *Vie de Louis VI le Gros*. Edited and translated by Henri Waquet. Paris: H. Champion, 1929. Repr., Paris: Société d'Édition les Belles Lettres, 1964.

Symeon of Durham. *Libellus de exordio atque procursu istius, hoc est Dunelmensis, ecclesiae / Tract on the Origins and Progress of This Church of Durham*. Edited and translated by D. W. Rollason. Oxford: Oxford University Press, 2000.

Thompson, Aaron, and J. A. Giles, trans. *Six Old English Chronicles*. London: G. Bell and Sons, 1900.

Thorpe, Lewis, trans. *Two Lives of Charlemagne*. Harmondsworth: Penguin Books, 1969.

Van Houts, Elisabeth M. C., ed. and trans. *The Gesta Normannorum Ducum of William of Jumièges, Orderic Vitalis, and Robert of Torigni*. 2 vols. Oxford: Clarendon Press, 1992–95.

Wace. *The History of the Norman People: Wace's "Roman de Rou."* Translated by Glyn S. Burgess. Woodbridge: Boydell Press, 2004.

———. *Roman de Brut*. 2 vols. Edited by Ivor Arnold. Paris: Société des anciens textes français, 1938–40.

———. *Le Roman de Rou*. 3 vols. Edited by Anthony J. Holden. Société des anciens textes français. Paris: Picard, 1970–73.

———. *Wace's "Roman de Brut": A History of the British*. Edited and translated by Judith Weiss. Exeter: University of Exeter Press, 1999.

William of Malmesbury. *Gesta pontificum Anglorum: The History of the English Bishops*. 2 vols. Edited by R. M. Thomson. Oxford: Oxford University Press, 2007.

———. *Gesta regum Anglorum*. 2 vols. Edited and translated by R. A. B. Mynors, R. M. Thomson, and M. Winterbottom. Oxford: Oxford University Press, 1998.

———. *William of Malmesbury's "Chronicle of the Kings of England."* Translated by J. A. Giles. London: H. G. Bohn, 1847.

William of Poitiers. *The "Gesta Guillelmi" of William of Poitiers*. Edited and translated by R. H. C. Davis and Marjorie Chibnall. Oxford: Clarendon Press, 1998.

William Rishanger. *Willelmi Rishanger, quondam monachi S. Albani, et quorundam anonymorum, chronica et annals, regnantibus Henrico Tertio et Edwardo Primo*. Edited by Henry Thomas Riley. London: Longman, Green, Longman, Roberts and Green, 1865.

Secondary Sources

Airlie, Stuart. "Narratives of Triumph and Rituals of Submission: Charlemagne's Mastering of Bavaria." *Transactions of the Royal Historical Society*, 6th ser., 9 (1999): 93–119.

———. "The Palace of Memory: The Carolingian Court as Political Centre." In *Courts and Regions in Medieval Europe*, edited by Sarah Rees Jones, Richard Marks, and Alistair Minnis, 1–20. Woodbridge: Boydell and Brewer, 2000.

Albu, Emily. *The Normans in Their Histories: Propaganda, Myth, and Subversion*. Woodbridge: Boydell Press, 2001.

Anderson, Benedict. *Imagined Communities: Reflections on the Origin and Spread of Nationalism*. London: Verso, 1991.

Angenendt, Arnold. *Kaiserherrschaft und Königstaufe: Kaiser, Könige und Päpste als geistliche Patrone in der abendländischen*

Missionsgeschichte. Arbeiten zur Frümittelalterforschung 15. Berlin: W. de Gruyter, 1984.

Ashbee, Jeremy. "The Function of the White Tower Under the Normans." In *The White Tower*, edited by Edward Impey, 125–39. New Haven: Yale University Press in association with Historic Royal Palaces, 2008.

Ashe, Laura. *Fiction and History in England, 1066–1200*. Cambridge: Cambridge University Press, 2007.

Aspin, Isabel S. T., ed. *Anglo-Norman Political Songs*. Anglo-Norman Texts 11. Oxford: Published for the Anglo-Norman Text Society by Basil Blackwell, 1953.

Astill, Grenville. "Community, Identity and the Later Anglo-Saxon Town: The Case of Southern England." In *People and Space in the Middle Ages, 300–1300*, edited by Wendy Davies, Guy Halsall and Andrew Reynolds, 233–54. Studies in the Early Middle Ages 15. Turnhout: Brepols, 2006.

Audehm, Kathrin, and Hans Rudolf Velten, eds. *Transgression— Hybridisierung—Differenzierung: Zur Performativität von Grenzen in Sprache, Kultur und Gesellschaft*. Freiburg: Rombach, 2007.

Baker, John, and Stuart Brookes. *Beyond the Burghal Hidage: Anglo-Saxon Civil Defence in the Viking Age*. Leiden: Brill, 2013.

Baldwin, John W. *The Government of Philip Augustus: Foundations of French Royal Power in the Middle Ages*. Berkeley: University of California Press, 1986.

Barbero, Alessandro. *Charlemagne: Father of a Continent*. Translated by Allan Cameron. Berkeley: University of California Press, 2004.

Barlow, Frank. *William Rufus*. 2nd ed. New Haven: Yale University Press, 2000.

Bartlett, Robert. *England Under the Norman and Angevin Kings, 1075–1225*. Oxford: Clarendon Press, 2000.

———. *Gerald of Wales, 1146–1223*. Oxford: Clarendon Press, 1982.

Bassett, Steven. "Beyond the Edge of Excavation: The Topographical Context of Goltho." In *Studies in Medieval History Presented to R. H. C. Davis*, edited by Henry Mayr-Harting and Robert Ian Moore, 21–39. London: Hambledon, 1985.

Bastert, Bernd, ed. *Karl der Grosse in den europäischen Literaturen des Mittelalters: Konstruktion eines Mythos*. Tübingen: Max Niemeyer Verlag, 2004.

Baswell, Christopher. *Virgil in Medieval England: Figuring the Aeneid from the Twelfth Century to Chaucer*. Cambridge: Cambridge University Press, 1995.

Bates, David. *Normandy Before 1066*. New York: Longman, 1982.

———. *The Normans and Empire*. Oxford: Oxford University Press, 2013.

———, ed. and trans. *Regesta regum Anglo-Normannorum: The Acta of William I, 1066–1087*. Oxford: Clarendon Press, 1998.

———. "West Francia: The Northern Principalities." In Reuter, *The New Cambridge Medieval History*, vol. 3, c. 900–c. 1024, 398–419.

Bauduin, Pierre. *La première Normandie, Xe–XIe siècles*. Caen: Presses universitaires de Caen, 2004.

Baumgartner, Emmanuèle, and Laurence Harf-Lancner, eds. *Entre fiction et histoire: Troie et Rome au Moyen âge*. Paris: Presses de la Sorbonne Nouvelle, 1997.

Beaune, Colette. "Les ducs, le roi, et le saint sang." In *Saint-Denis et le royauté*:

Études offertes à Bernard Guenée, edited by F. Autrand, C. Gauvard, and J.-M. Moeglin, 711–32. Paris: Publications de la Sorbonne, 1999.

Becher, Matthias. *Charlemagne*. Translated by David S. Bachrach. New Haven: Yale University Press, 2003.

Beer, Jeanette. *Narrative Conventions of Truth in the Middle Ages*. Geneva: Droz, 1981.

Bell, Alexander. "Gaimar's Early 'Danish' Kings." *PMLA* 65, no. 4 (1950): 601–40.

Bennett, Matthew. "Stereotype Normans in Old French Vernacular Literature." *Anglo-Norman Studies* 4 (1981): 25–42.

Bischoff, Bernhard. "Das Thema des Poeta Saxo." In *Speculum Historiale: Geschichte im Spiegel von Geschichtsschreibung und Geschichtsdeutung, Festschrift Johannes Spörle*, edited by Clemens Bauer, Laetitia Boehm, and Max Müeller, 198–203. Freiburg: Verlag Karl Alber, 1965.

Bisson, Thomas N., ed. *Cultures of Power: Lordship, Status, and Process in Twelfth-Century Europe*. Philadelphia: University of Pennsylvania Press, 1995.

Blacker, Jean. *The Faces of Time: Portrayal of the Past in Old French and Latin Historical Narrative of the Anglo-Norman Regnum*. Austin: University of Texas Press, 1994.

Blair, John. "Palaces or Minsters? Northampton and Cheddar Reconsidered." *Anglo-Saxon England* 25 (1996): 97–121.

Bloch, R. Howard. *The Anonymous Marie de France*. Chicago: University of Chicago Press, 2003.

———. *Medieval French Literature and Law*. Berkeley: University of California Press, 1977.

Boeft, J. Den. "Some Etymologies in Augustine's *De Civitate Dei X*." *Vigiliae Christianae* 33, no. 3 (1979): 242–59.

Bohn, Jürgen. "Der Poeta Saxo in der historiographischen Tradition der 8.–10. Jahrhundert." Ph.D. diss., University of Frankfurt, 1965.

Bond, Gerald A. *The Loving Subject: Desire, Eloquence, and Power in Romanesque France*. Philadelphia: University of Pennsylvania Press, 1995.

Bossy, Michel-André. "Roland's Migration from Anglo-Norman Epic to Royal French Chronicle History." In *Epic and History*, edited by David Konstan and Kurt A. Raaflaub, 293–309. Malden, Mass.: Wiley-Blackwell, 2010.

Bouard, Michel de. "De la Neustrie carolingienne à la Normandie féodale: Continuité ou discontinuité?" *Bulletin of the Institute of Historical Research* 28 (1955): 1–14.

Bouman, C. A. *Sacring and Crowning: The Development of the Latin Ritual for the Anointing of Kings and the Coronation of an Emperor Before the Eleventh Century*. Groningen: J. B. Wolters, 1957.

Boutet, Dominique. *Charlemagne et Arthur, ou le roi imaginaire*. Paris: Champion-Slatkine, 1992.

Bradley, Richard. "Time Regained: The Creation of Continuity." *Journal of the British Archaeological Association* 140 (1987): 1–17.

Breese, Lauren Wood. "The Persistence of Scandinavian Connections in Normandy in the Tenth and Early Eleventh Centuries." *Viator* 8 (1977): 47–61.

Brenk, Beat. "Spolia from Constantine to Charlemagne: Aesthetics Versus Ideology." *Dumbarton Oaks Papers* 41, Studies on Art and Archaeology in Honor of Ernst Kitzinger on His Seventy-Fifth Birthday (1987): 103–9.

Bromwich, Rachel, and D. Simon Evans, eds. and trans. *Culhwch and Olwen: An Edition and Study of the Oldest Arthurian Tale*. 2nd ed. Aberystwyth: University of Wales, 1992.

Brooks, N. P., and S. E. Kelly, eds. "Charters of Christ Church, Canterbury." British Academy "Anglo-Saxon Charters" Series Online. The British Academy and Royal Historical Society, n.d. http://people.ds.cam.ac.uk/rjr20/details/pelteret/Ccc/CCClist.htm (accessed 6 February 2016).

Brown, R. Allen. *The Normans and the Norman Conquest*. 2nd ed. Woodbridge: Boydell Press, 1985.

Bryan, Elizabeth J. *Collaborative Meaning in Medieval Scribal Culture: The Otho Laʒamon*. Ann Arbor: University of Michigan Press, 2000.

Buc, Philippe. *The Dangers of Ritual: Between Early Medieval Texts and Social Scientific Theory*. Princeton: Princeton University Press, 2001.

Bur, Michel. "Les comtes de Champagne et la 'Normanitas': Semiologie d'un tombeau." *Anglo-Norman Studies* 3 (1980): 22–32.

Burgess, Glyn S. *The "Lais" of Marie de France: Texts and Contexts*. Atlanta: University of Georgia Press, 1987.

Burgwinkle, William E. *Sodomy, Masculinity, and Law in Medieval Literature: France and England, 1050-1230*. Cambridge: Cambridge University Press, 2004.

Burke, Peter. *Cultural Hybridity*. Cambridge: Polity Press, 2009.

Burnley, David. *Courtliness and Literature in Medieval England*. London: Addison Wesley Longman, 1998.

Caenegem, R. C. van, ed. *English Lawsuits from William I to Richard I*. London: Selden Society, 1990.

Cain, James. "Charlemagne in the 1170's: Reading the Oxford Roland in the Context of the Becket Controversy." n.d. http://people.bu.edu/bobl/cain.htm (accessed 6 February 2016).

Caldwell, Robert A. "Wace's *Roman De Brut* and the Variant Version of Geoffrey of Monmouth's *Historia Regum Britanniae*." *Speculum* 31, no. 4 (1956): 675–82.

Campbell, Alistair, ed. *Encomium Emmae Reginae*. London: Offices of the Royal Historical Society, 1949.

Campbell, James. *Essays in Anglo-Saxon History*. New York: Hambledon and London, 2003.

———. "Observations on English Government from the Tenth to the Twelfth Century." *Transactions of the Royal Historical Society*, 5th ser., 25 (1975): 39–54.

———. Review of *The New Cambridge Medieval History*, vol. 2, *C. 700-c. 900*, ed. Rosamond McKitterick. *English Historical Review* 113, no. 452 (1998): 680–84.

Cannon, Christopher. "The Style and Authorship of the Otho Revision of Laʒamon's *Brut*." *Medium Aevum* 62, no. 2 (1993): 187–210.

Carlson, Eric Gustav. "Religious Architecture in Normandy, 911–1000." *Gesta* 5 (January 1966): 27–33.

Carpenter, David. *The Struggle for Mastery: Britain, 1066-1284*. Oxford: Oxford University Press, 2003.

Cartlidge, Neil. "The Composition and Social Context of Oxford, Jesus College MS 29(II) and London, British Library MS Cotton Caligula A.IX." *Medium Aevum* 66, no. 2 (1997): 236–69.

Carty, Anthony. *Was Ireland Conquered? International Law and the Irish Question*. London: Pluto Press, 1996.

Chibnall, Marjorie. *Anglo-Norman England, 1066-1166.* Oxford: Basil Blackwell, 1986.

——. "Orderic Vitalis on Castles." In *Anglo-Norman Castles*, edited by Robert Liddiard, 119-32. Woodbridge: Boydell Press, 2003.

Clark, Cecily, ed. *The Peterborough Chronicle, 1070-1154.* 2nd ed. Oxford: Clarendon Press, 1970.

Cohen, Jeffrey Jerome. *Of Giants: Sex, Monsters, and the Middle Ages.* Medieval Cultures 17. Minneapolis: University of Minnesota Press, 1999.

——. *The Postcolonial Middle Ages.* New York: St. Martin's, 2000.

Collins, Roger. *Charlemagne.* Toronto: University of Toronto Press, 1998.

Cooper, Alan. "Extraordinary Privilege: The Trial of Penenden Heath and the Domesday Inquest." *English Historical Review* 116, no. 469 (2001): 1167-92.

——. "The King's Four Highways: Legal Fiction Meets Fictional Law." *Journal of Medieval History* 26 (2000): 351-70.

——. "The Rise and Fall of the Anglo-Saxon Law of the Highway." *Haskins Society Journal* 12 (2002): 39-69.

Cosgrove, Denis E. *Social Formation and Symbolic Landscape.* 2nd ed. Madison: University of Wisconsin Press, 1998.

Coulson, Charles. *Castles in Medieval Society: Fortresses in England, France, and Ireland in the Central Middle Ages.* Oxford: Oxford University Press, 2003.

Cowdrey, H. E. J. "The Anglo-Norman *Laudes regiae.*" *Viator* 12 (1981): 37-78.

Crane, Susan. *Insular Romance: Politics, Faith, and Culture in Anglo-Norman and Middle English Literature.* Berkeley: University of California Press, 1986.

Creighton, O. H. *Castles and Landscapes.* London: Continuum, 2002.

Cronne, H. A. "The Royal Forest in the Reign of Henry I." In *Essays in British and Irish History in Honour of James Eadie Todd*, edited by H. A. Cronne, T. W. Moody, and D. B. Quinn, 1-23. London: Frederick Muller, 1949.

Damian-Grint, Peter. *The New Historians of the Twelfth-Century Renaissance: Inventing Vernacular Authority.* Rochester, N.Y.: Boydell and Brewer, 1999.

Daniels, Stephen, and Denis Cosgrove, eds. *The Iconography of Landscape.* Cambridge Studies in Historical Geography 9. Cambridge: Cambridge University Press, 1988.

Darby, H. C., and Eila M. J. Campbell. *The Domesday Geography of South-East England.* Cambridge: Cambridge University Press, 1962.

Davies, R. R. "Buchedd a moes y Cymry: The Manners and Morals of the Welsh." *Welsh Historical Review* 5 (1992): 55-79.

——. *Domination and Conquest: The Experience of Ireland, Scotland, and Wales, 1100-1300.* Cambridge: Cambridge University Press, 1990.

——. *The First English Empire: Power and Identities in the British Isles, 1093-1343.* Oxford: Oxford University Press, 2000.

——. *The Matter of Britain and the Matter of England: Inaugural Lecture Delivered Before the University of Oxford on 29 February 1996.* Oxford: Clarendon Press, 1996.

Davis, H. W. C. *Charlemagne (Charles the Great): The Hero of Two Nations.* London: G. P. Putnam and Sons, 1900.

Davis, Kathleen, and Natalie Altschul, eds. *Medievalisms in the Postcolonial World: The Idea of the "Middle Ages" Outside Europe*. Baltimore: Johns Hopkins University Press, 2009.

Davis, R. H. C. "Goltho—The Manorial History." In *Goltho: The Development of an Early Medieval Manor, c. 850-1150*, edited by Guy Beresford, 127-30. London: Historic Buildings and Monuments Commission for England, 1987.

———. *The Normans and Their Myth*. London: Thames and Hudson, 1976.

Davy, Gilduin. *Le duc et la loi: Héritages, images et expressions du pouvoir normatif dans le duché de Normandie, des origines à la mort du Conquérant (fin du IXe siècle-1087)*. Paris: De Boccard, 2004.

Deshman, Robert. "Christus rex et magi regis: Kingship and Christology in Ottonian and Anglo-Saxon Art." *Frühmittelalterliche Studien* 10 (1976): 367-405.

Ditmas, E. M. R. "The Cult of Arthurian Relics." *Folklore* 75, no. 1 (1964): 19-33.

Donoghue, Daniel. "Laȝamon's Ambivalence." *Speculum* 65, no. 3 (1990): 537-63.

Douglas, David. "The *Song of Roland* and the Norman Conquest of England." *French Studies* 14, no. 2 (1960): 99-116.

Drury, P. J. "Aspects of the Origins and Development of Colchester Castle." *Archaeological Journal* 139 (1982): 302-419.

Duggan, Anne J., ed. *Kings and Kingship in Medieval Europe*. London: King's College, 1993.

———. "The Making of a Myth: Giraldus Cambrensis, Laudabiliter, and Henry II's Lordship of Ireland." *Studies in Medieval and Renaissance History*, 3rd ser., 4 (2007): 249-312.

———, ed. *Nobles and Nobility in Medieval Europe: Concepts, Origins, Transformations*. Woodbridge: Boydell Press, 2000.

———. "The Power of Documents: The Curious Case of *Laudabiliter*." In *Aspects of Power and Authority in the Middle Ages*, edited by Brenda Bolton and Christine Meek, 251-75. International Medieval Research Series 14. Turnhout: Brepols, 2007.

———. "*Totius christianus caput*: The Pope and the Princes." In *Adrian IV, the English Pope, 1154-1159: Studies and Texts*, edited by Anne J. Duggan, 105-56. Aldershot: Ashgate, 2003.

Dumas-Dubourg, Françoise. *Le trésor de Fécamp et le monnayage en France occidentale pendant la seconde moitié du Xe siècle*. Paris: Bibliothèque nationale, 1971.

Dunbabin, Jean. *France in the Making, 843-1180*. 2nd ed. Oxford: Oxford University Press, 2000.

Dutton, Paul Edward. *Charlemagne's Mustache: And Other Cultural Clusters of a Dark Age*. New York: Palgrave Macmillan, 2004.

———. "KAROLVS MAGNVS or KAROLVS FELIX: The Making of Charlemagne's Reputation and Legend." In Gabriele and Stuckey, *The Legend of Charlemagne*, 23-37.

———. *The Politics of Dreaming in the Carolingian Empire*. Lincoln: University of Nebraska Press, 1994.

Eaton, Tim. *Plundering the Past: Roman Stonework in Medieval Britain*. Stroud: Tempus, 2000.

Edwards, John. *Language, Society, and Identity*. Oxford: Basil Blackwell; London: A. Deutsch, 1985.

Eley, Penny, and Philip E. Bennett. "The Battle of Hastings According to Gaimar, Wace, and Benoît:

Rhetoric and Politics." *Nottingham Medieval Studies* 43 (1999): 47-78.

Elias, Norbert. *The Civilizing Process: Sociogenetic and Psychogenetic Investigations*, rev. ed. Translated by Edmund Jephcott. Edited by Eric Dunning, Johan Goudsblom, and Stephen Mennell. Malden, Mass.: Blackwell, 2000.

Ewig, Eugen. "Das Bild Constantins des Großen in den ersten Jahrhunderten des abendländischen Mittelalters." *Historisches Jahrbuch* 75 (1956): 1-46. Reprinted in *Spätantikes und fränkisches Gallien: Gesammelte Schriften, 1952-73*, edited by H. Atsma, 2 vols. Beihefte der Francia 3 (Munich: Alber, 1976-79), 1:72-113.

Faletra, Michael. "Narrating the Matter of Britain: Geoffrey of Monmouth and the Norman Colonization of Wales." *Chaucer Review* 35, no. 1 (2000): 60-85.

Fentress, James, and Chris Wickham. *Social Memory*. Oxford: Blackwell, 1992.

Fernie, Eric. *The Architecture of Norman England*. Oxford: Oxford University Press, 2002.

Field, Rosalind. "Romance as History, History as Romance." In *Romance in Medieval England*, edited by Maldwyn Mills, Jennifer Fellows, and Carole Meale, 163-73. Cambridge: D. S. Brewer, 1991.

Finke, Laurie A., and Martin B. Shichtman, eds. *King Arthur and the Myth of History*. Gainesville: University Press of Florida, 2004.

Flanagan, Marie Therese. *Irish Society, Anglo-Norman Settlers, Angevin Kingship: Interactions in Ireland in the Late 12th Century*. Oxford: Clarendon Press, 1989.

Fleischman, Suzanne. "On the Representation of History and Fiction in the Middle Ages." *History and Theory* 22 (1983): 278-310.

Folz, Robert. *Le souvenir et la légende de Charlemagne dans l'Empire germanique médiéval*. Paris: Les Belles Lettres, 1950.

Foot, Sarah. "The Making of Angelcynn: English Identity Before the Norman Conquest." In *Old English Literature: Critical Essays*, edited by Roy M. Liuzza, 51-78. New Haven: Yale University Press, 2002.

Fouracre, Paul. "Frankish Gaul to 814." In McKitterick, *The New Cambridge Medieval History*, vol. 2, C. 700-c. 900, 85-109.

Frankis, John. "Views of Anglo-Saxons in Post-Conquest Vernacular Writing." In *Orality and Literacy in Early Middle English*, edited by Herbert Pilch, 227-36. Tübingen: G. Narr, 1996.

Frantzen, Allen J. *Bloody Good: Chivalry, Sacrifice, and the Great War*. Chicago; University of Chicago Press, 2004.

———. *Desire for Origins: New Language, Old English, and Teaching the Tradition*. New Brunswick: Rutgers University Press, 1990.

Freeman, Elizabeth. "Geffrei Gaimar, Vernacular Historiography, and the Assertion of Authority." *Studies in Philology* 93, no. 2 (1996): 188-206.

———. *Narratives of a New Order: Cistercian Historical Writing in England, 1150-1220*. Turnhout: Brepols, 2002.

Fries, Maureen. "The Arthurian Moment: History and Geoffrey's *Historia regum Britannie*." *Arthuriana* 8, no. 4 (1998): 88-99.

Furrow, Melissa. "Chanson de geste as Romance in England." In *The Exploitations of Medieval Romance*, edited by Laura Ashe, Ivana Djordjević, and Judith Weiss,

57-72. Cambridge: D. S. Brewer, 2010.
Gabriele, Matthew. *An Empire of Memory: The Legend of Charlemagne, the Franks, and Jerusalem Before the First Crusade.* Oxford: Oxford University Press, 2011.
Gabriele, Matthew, and Jace Stuckey, eds. *The Legend of Charlemagne in the Middle Ages: Power, Faith, and Crusade.* New York: Palgrave Macmillan, 2008.
Ganshof, François Louis. *The Carolingians and the Frankish Monarchy: Studies in Carolingian History.* Translated by Janet Sondheimer. Ithaca: Cornell University Press, 1971.
Ganz, David. "Einhard and the Characterisation of Greatness." In *Charlemagne: Empire and Society*, edited by Joanna Story, 38-51. Manchester: Manchester University Press, 2005.
Garrison, Mary. "The Emergence of Carolingian Latin Literature and the Court of Charlemagne (780-814)." In McKitterick, *Carolingian Culture*, 111-40.
George, David. "Distinguishing Classical Tyrannicide from Modern Terrorism." *Review of Politics* 50, no. 3 (1988): 390-419.
Gerberding, Richard A. *The "Liber historiae Francorum" and the Rise of the Carolingians.* Oxford: Clarendon Press, 1987.
Gerould, Gordon Hall. "King Arthur and His Politics." *Speculum* 2, no. 1 (1927): 33-51.
———. "King Arthur and Politics Again." *Speculum* 2, no. 4 (1927): 448.
Gillingham, John. *The Angevin Empire.* 2nd ed. New York: Oxford University Press, 2001.
———. "Civilizing the English? The English Histories of William of Malmesbury and David Hume."

Historical Research 74, no. 183 (2001): 17-43.
———. "The Cultivation of History, Legend, and Courtesy at the Court of Henry II." In *Writers of the Reign of Henry II*, edited by Ruth Kennedy and Simon Meecham-Jones, 25-52. New York: Palgrave Macmillan, 2006.
———. *The English in the Twelfth Century: Imperialism, National Identity, and Political Values.* Woodbridge: Boydell and Brewer, 2000.
———. *Richard Coeur de Lion: Kingship, Chivalry and War in the Twelfth Century.* London: Hambledon and London, 2003.
———. "Thegns and Knights in Eleventh-Century England: Who Was Then the Gentleman?" *Transactions of the Royal Historical Society* 5 (1995): 129-53.
Glacken, Clarence J. *Traces on the Rhodian Shore: Nature and Culture in Western Thought from Ancient Times to the End of the Eighteenth Century.* Berkeley: University of California Press, 1967.
Godman, Peter, ed. and trans. *Poetry of the Carolingian Renaissance.* London: Gerald Duckworth, 1985.
———. *Poets and Emperors: Frankish Politics and Carolingian Poetry.* Oxford: Clarendon Press, 1987.
Goffart, Walter. "Paul the Deacon's *Gesta episcoporum mettensium* and the Early Design of Charlemagne's Succession." *Traditio* 42 (1986): 59-93.
Goldberg, Eric. "'The Hunt Belongs to Man': Some Neglected Treatises Related to Hunting and Falconry from the Court of Louis the German." In *Discovery and Distinction in the Early Middle Ages: Studies in Honor of John J. Contreni*, edited by Cullen J. Chandler and Steven Stofferahn,

31–57. Kalamazoo: Medieval Institute Publications, 2013.

———. "Louis the Pious and the Hunt." *Speculum* 88, no. 3 (2013): 613–43.

Gomes, Rita Costa. *The Making of a Court Society: Kings and Nobles in Late Medieval Portugal*. Translated by Alison Aiken. Cambridge: Cambridge University Press, 2003.

Gransden, Antonia. "Baldwin, Abbot of Bury St Edmunds, 1065–1097." *Anglo-Norman Studies* 4 (1981): 65–76.

———. *Historical Writing in England*. Vol. 1, *C. 550–c. 1307*. Ithaca: Cornell University Press, 1973.

———. *Legends, Traditions, and History in Medieval England*. New York: Hambledon and London, 1992.

———. "Prologues in the Historiography of Twelfth-Century England." In *England in the Twelfth Century: Proceedings of the 1988 Harlaxton Symposium*, edited by Daniel Williams, 55–81. Woodbridge: Boydell and Brewer, 1990.

Grant, Lindy. *Architecture and Society in Normandy, 1120–1270*. New Haven: Yale University Press, 2005.

Greenhalgh, Michael. *Marble Past, Monumental Present: Building with Antiquities in the Mediaeval Mediterranean*. Leiden: Brill, 2009.

Hagger, Mark. "Secular Law and Custom in Ducal Normandy." *Speculum* 85, no. 4 (2010): 827–67.

Hammer, William. "The Concept of the New or Second Rome in the Middle Ages." *Speculum* 19, no. 1 (1944): 50–62.

Hanning, Robert W. *The Vision of History in Early Britain: From Gildas to Geoffrey of Monmouth*. New York: Columbia University Press, 1966.

Harbison, Robert. *Eccentric Spaces*. Cambridge, Mass.: MIT Press, 2000.

Harding, Alan. *Medieval Law and the Foundations of the State*. Oxford: Oxford University Press, 2001.

Hardman, Phillipa. Introduction to *The Matter of Identity in Medieval Romance*, edited by Phillipa Hardman, 1–9. Woodbridge: Boydell and Brewer, 2002.

Harris, Stephen J. *Race and Ethnicity in Anglo-Saxon Literature*. Studies in Medieval History and Culture 24. London: Routledge, 2003.

Haskins, Charles Homer. *Norman Institutions*. Cambridge, Mass.: Harvard University Press, 1918.

Head, Thomas, and Richard Landes, eds. *The Peace of God: Social Violence and Religious Response in France Around the Year 1000*. Ithaca: Cornell University Press, 1992.

Hen, Yitzhak. "Clovis, Gregory of Tours, and Pro-Merovingian Propaganda." *Revue belge de philologie et d'histoire* 71, no. 2 (1993): 271–76.

———. "The Uses of the Bible and Perception of Kingship in Merovingian Gaul." *Early Medieval Europe* 7, no. 3 (1998): 277–89.

Heng, Geraldine. *Empire of Magic: Medieval Romance and the Politics of Cultural Fantasy*. New York: Columbia University Press, 2003.

Hennebicque, Régine. "Espaces sauvages et chasses royales dans le Nord de la Francie, VIIème–IXème siècles." *Revue du Nord* 10, no. 1 (1979): 35–57.

Herrick, Samantha Kahn. "Heirs to the Apostles: Saintly Power and Ducal Authority in Hagiography of Early Normandy." In *The Experience of Power in Medieval Europe, 950–1350*, edited by Robert K. Berkhofer, Alan Cooper, and Adam J. Kosto, 11–24. Aldershot: Ashgate, 2005.

Heslop, T. A. "Constantine and Helena: The Roman in the English Romanesque." In *Architecture* and *Interpretation: Essays for Eric Fernie*, edited by Jill A. Franklin, T. A. Heslop, and Christine Stevenson, 163–75. Woodbridge: Boydell and Brewer, 2012.

Higgitt, J. C. "The Roman Background to Medieval England." *Journal of the British Archaeological Association* 36 (1973): 1–15.

Higham, Nicholas J. *The Convert Kings: Power and Religious Affiliation in Early Anglo-Saxon England*. Manchester: Manchester University Press, 1997.

———. *King Arthur: Myth-Making and History*. London: Routledge, 2002.

Hill, Christopher. *Puritanism and Revolution*. London: Secker and Warburg, 1958.

Hill, David, and Alexander R. Rumble, eds. *The Defence of Wessex: The Burghal Hidage and Anglo-Saxon Fortifications*. Manchester: Manchester University Press, 1996.

Hodgkin, Thomas. *Charles the Great*. London: Macmillan, 1897.

Hoffman, Donald L. Review of *The Life in the Forest: The Influence of the Saint Giles Legend on the Courtly Tristan Story*, by Ülle Erika Lewes. *Speculum* 55, no. 2 (1980): 381–82.

Holdsworth, Christopher. "Peacemaking in the Twelfth Century." *Anglo-Norman Studies* 19 (1996): 1–17.

Hollister, C. Warren, ed. *Anglo-Norman Political Culture and the Twelfth-Century Renaissance: Proceedings of the Borchard Conference on Anglo-Norman History, 1995*. Woodbridge: Boydell and Brewer, 1997.

———. "The Strange Death of William Rufus." *Speculum* 48, no. 4 (1973): 637–53.

Hollister, C. Warren, and Thomas Keefe. "The Making of the Angevin Empire." *Journal of British Studies* 12, no. 2 (1973): 1–25.

Hoofnagle, Wendy Marie. "Taming the Wilderness: The Exploration of Anglo-Norman Kingship in the *Vie de Saint Gilles*." *Haskins Society Journal* 25 (2013): 165–86.

Hoofnagle, Wendy Marie, and Wolfram Keller, eds. *Other Nations: The Hybridization of Insular Mythology and Identity*. Berlin: Universitätsverlag Winter, 2011.

Hooke, Della. "Pre-Conquest Woodland: Its Distribution and Usage." *Agricultural History Review* 37, no. 2 (1989): 113–29.

Howe, John, and Michael Wolfe, eds. *Inventing Medieval Landscapes: Senses of Places in Medieval Europe*. Gainesville: University Press of Florida, 2002.

Howe, Nicholas. "Anglo-Saxon England and the Postcolonial Void." In *Postcolonial Approaches to the Middle Ages: Translating Cultures*, edited by Ananya Jaharana Kabir and Deanne Williams, 25–47. Cambridge: Cambridge University Press, 2005.

———. *Writing the Map of Anglo-Saxon England: Essays in Cultural Geography*. New Haven: Yale University Press, 2008.

Hudson, Benjamin. "William the Conqueror and Ireland." *Irish Historical Studies* 29, no. 114 (1994): 145–58.

Hudson, John. "The Abbey of Abingdon, Its Chronicle, and the Norman Conquest." *Anglo-Norman Studies* 19 (1996): 181–202.

———. *The Formation of the English Common Law: Law and Society in England from the Norman Conquest to Magna Carta*. White Plains, N.Y.: Longman, 1996.

———. *Land, Law, and Lordship in Anglo-Norman England*. Oxford: Clarendon Press, 1994.

Hudson, John, and George Garnett, eds. *Law and Government in Medieval England and Normandy: Essays in Honour of Sir James Holt.* Cambridge: Cambridge University Press, 1994.

Hume, Kathryn. *The Owl and the Nightingale: The Poem and Its Critics.* Toronto: University of Toronto Press, 1975.

Hummer, Hans J. *Politics and Power in Early Medieval Europe: Alsace and the Frankish Realm, 600–1000.* Cambridge: Cambridge University Press, 2006.

Hunter, Michael. "Germanic and Roman Antiquity and the Sense of the Past in Anglo-Saxon England." *Anglo-Saxon England* 3 (1974): 29–50.

Huot, Sylvia. *Postcolonial Fictions in the "Roman de Perceforest": Cultural Identities and Hybridities.* Cambridge: D. S. Brewer, 2007.

Hyams, Paul. "The Common Law and the French Connection." *Anglo-Norman Studies* 4 (1981): 77–92.

———. "Feud and State in Late Anglo-Saxon England." *Journal of British Studies* 40, no. 1 (2001): 1–43.

———. "Homage and Feudalism: A Judicious Separation." In *Die Gegenwart des Feudalismus*, edited by Natalie Fryde, 13–49. Göttingen: Vandenhoeck & Ruprecht, 2003.

———. *Rancor and Reconciliation in Medieval England.* Ithaca: Cornell University Press, 2003.

Ingham, Patricia Clare, and Michelle R. Warren, eds. *Postcolonial Moves: Medieval to Modern.* New York: Palgrave, 2003.

Ingledew, Francis. "The Book of Troy and the Genealogical Construction of History: The Case of Geoffrey of Monmouth's *Historia regum Britanniae*." *Speculum* 69, no. 3 (1994): 665–704.

Innes, Matthew. "Charlemagne's Government." In *Story, Charlemagne: Empire and Society*, 71–89.

———. "Danelaw Identities: Ethnicity, Regionalism, and Political Allegiance." In *Cultures in Contact: Scandinavian Settlement in England in the Ninth and Tenth Centuries*, edited by Dawn M. Hadley and Julian D. Richards, 65–88. Turnhout: Brepols, 2000.

———. "Teutons or Trojans? The Carolingians and the Germanic Past." In *The Uses of the Past in the Early Middle Ages*, edited by Yitzhak Hen and Matthew Innes, 227–49. Cambridge: Cambridge University Press, 2000.

Jaeger, C. Stephen. *The Origins of Courtliness: Civilizing Trends and the Formation of Courtly Ideals, 923–1210.* Philadelphia: University of Pennsylvania Press, 1985.

Johnson, Lesley. "Reading the Past in Laʒamon's *Brut*: A Reassessment." In Le Saux, *The Text and Tradition of Laʒamon's "Brut*," 161–70.

Johnson, Phyllis, and Brigitte Cazelles, eds. *Le Vain Siècle Guerpir: A Literary Approach to Sainthood Through Old French Hagiography of the Twelfth Century.* North Carolina Studies in the Romance Languages and Literatures 205. Chapel Hill: University of North Carolina, Department of Romance Languages, distributed by University of North Carolina Press, 1979.

Jones, W. R. "The Image of the Barbarian in Medieval Europe." *Comparative Studies in Society and History* 13, no. 4 (1971): 376–407.

Jong, Mayke de. "The Empire as Ecclesia: Hrabanus Maurus and Biblical Historia for Rulers." In *Uses of the Past in the Early Middle Ages*, edited by Matthew Innes and Yitzhak Hen, 191–226. Cambridge: Cambridge University Press, 2000.

Jong, Mayke de, Carine van Rhijn, and Frans Theuws, eds. *Topographies of Power in the Early Middle Ages*. Leiden: Brill, 2001.

Jørgensen, Dolly. "The Roots of the English Royal Forest." *Anglo-Norman Studies* 32 (2010): 114–28.

Jurasinski, Stefan. "The *Rime of King William* and Its Analogues." *Neophilologus* 88 (2004): 131–44.

Jussen, Bernhard. *Spiritual Kinship as Social Practice: Godparenthood and Adoption in the Early Middle Ages*. Translated by Pamela Selwyn. Newark: University of Delaware Press, 2000.

Kabir, Ananya Jahanara, and Deanne Williams, eds. *Postcolonial Approaches to the European Middle Ages: Translating Cultures*. Cambridge: Cambridge University Press, 2005.

Kaeuper, Richard W. *Chivalry and Violence in Medieval Europe*. Oxford: Oxford University Press, 1999.

Kämpf, Hellmut. "Reich und Mission zur Zeit Karl der Großen." *Geschichte in Wissenschaft und Unterricht* 1 (1950): 409–17.

Kantorowicz, Ernst. *The King's Two Bodies: A Study in Mediaeval Political Theology*. Princeton: Princeton University Press, 1957.

Karkov, Catherine E. *The Ruler Portraits of Anglo-Saxon England*. Woodbridge: Boydell and Brewer, 2004.

Keen, Maurice. *The Outlaws of Medieval Legend*. London: Routledge and Kegan Paul, 1961. Reprint, London: Routledge and Kegan Paul, 1979.

Kelly, J. M. *A Short History of Western Legal Theory*. Oxford: Oxford University Press, 1992.

Kennedy, Ruth, and Simon Meecham-Jones, eds. *Authority and Subjugation in Writing of Medieval Wales*. New York: Palgrave Macmillan, 2008.

———. *Writers of the Reign of Henry II*. New York: Palgrave Macmillan, 2006.

Kerner, Max. *Karl der Grosse: Entschleierung eines Mythos*. Cologne: Böhlau, 2001.

Kershaw, Paul. *Peaceful Kings: Peace, Power, and the Early Medieval Political Imagination*. Oxford: Oxford University Press, 2011.

Keynes, Simon. "The Cult of King Alfred." *Anglo-Saxon England* 28 (1999): 225–356.

Kinney, Dale. "Roman Architectural Spolia." *Proceedings of the American Philosophical Society* 145, no. 2 (2001): 138–61.

Kleinbauer, W. Eugene. "Charlemagne's Palace Chapel at Aachen and Its Copies." *Gesta* 4 (Spring 1965): 2–11.

Koeppler, H. "Frederick Barbarossa and the Schools of Bologna." *English Historical Review* 54, no. 216 (1939): 577–607.

Koziol, Geoffrey. *Begging Pardon and Favor: Ritual and Political Order in Early Medieval France*. Ithaca: Cornell University Press, 1992.

———. "England, France, and the Problem of Sacrality in Twelfth-Century Ritual." In *Cultures of Power: Lordship, Status, and Process in Twelfth-Century Europe*, edited by Thomas N. Bisson, 124–48. Philadelphia: University of Pennsylvania Press, 1995.

Laistner, M. L. W. "The Date and the Recipient of Smaragdus' *Via Regia*." *Speculum* 3, no. 3 (1928): 392–97.

Lapidge, Michael. "The Origin of CCCC 163." *Transactions of the Cambridge Bibliographical Society* 8, no. 1 (1981): 18–28.

Larmat, Jean. "La chasse dans les *Lais* de Marie de France." In *La Chasse au moyen âge: Actes du colloque du Centre d'Etudes Médiévales de Nice*, 377-84. Paris: Les Belles Lettres, 1980.

Latowsky, Anne. *Emperor of the World: Charlemagne and the Construction of Imperial Authority, 800-1225*. Ithaca: Cornell University Press, 2013.

Lavin, Irving. "The House of the Lord: Aspects of the Role of Palace Triclinia in the Architecture of Late Antiquity and the Early Middle Ages." *Art Bulletin* 44, no. 1 (1962): 1-27.

Leckie, R. William, Jr. *The Passage of Dominion: Geoffrey of Monmouth and the Periodization of Insular History in the Twelfth Century*. Toronto: University of Toronto Press, 1981.

Legge, M. Dominica. *Anglo-Norman Literature and Its Background*. London: Oxford University Press, 1963.

Lemarignier, Jean-François. *Étude sur les privilèges d'exemption et de jurisdiction ecclésiastique des abbayes normandes depuis les origines jusqu'en 1140*. Paris: Picard, 1937.

Le Patourel, John. "The Norman Colonization of Britain." In I *Normanni e la loro espansione in Europa nell'alto medioevo 16*, 409-38. Spoleto: Fondazione Centro Italiano di Studi sull'Alto Medioevo, 1969.

———. *The Norman Empire*. Oxford: Clarendon Press, 1976.

Lerer, Seth. "Old English and Its Afterlife." In *The Cambridge History of Medieval English Literature*, edited by David Wallace, 7-34. Cambridge: Cambridge University Press, 1999.

Le Saux, Françoise. *Laʒamon's "Brut": The Poem and Its Sources*. Cambridge: D. S. Brewer, 1989.

Lesne, E. *Histoire de la propriété ecclésiastique en France*. Vol. 3, *L'inventaire de la propriété; Eglises et trésors des églises, du commencement du VIIIe siècle à la fin du XIe siècle*. Lille: Facultés Catholiques, 1936.

Levine, Robert. "Baptizing Pirates: Fabula and Tri-Functionality in Norman Apology." *Mediaevistik* 4 (1991): 157-78.

Levison, W. "A Combined Manuscript of Geoffrey of Monmouth and Henry of Huntingdon." *English Historical Review* 58, no. 229 (1943): 41-51.

Leyser, Karl J. "England and the Empire in the Early Twelfth Century." *Transactions of the Royal Historical Society* 10 (1960): 61-83.

———. "Frederick Barbarossa, Henry II, and the Hand of St James." *English Historical Review* 90, no. 356 (1975): 481-506.

———. *Rule and Conflict in an Early Medieval Society: Ottonian Saxony*. London: Edward Arnold, 1979.

Liddiard, Robert, ed. *Anglo-Norman Castles*. Woodbridge: Boydell, 2003.

———. *Castles in Context: Power, Symbolism, and Landscape, 1066 to 1500*. Cheshire: Windgather Press, 2005.

Liebermann, F., ed. *Die Gesetze der Angelsachsen*. 3 vols. Halle: Max Niemayer, 1903.

Lifshitz, Felice. *The Norman Conquest of Pious Neustria*. Toronto: Pontifical Institute of Mediaeval Studies, 1995.

———. "La Normandie carolingienne: Essai sur la continuité, avec utilisation des sources negligees." *Annales de Normandie* 48 (1998): 505-24.

Liuzza, Roy. "The Tower of Babel: The Wanderer and the Ruins of

History." *Studies in the Literary Imagination* 36, no. 1 (2003): 1–35.

Loomis, Laura Hibbard. "The Athelstan Gift Story: Its Influence on English Chronicles and Carolingian Romances." *PMLA* 67, no. 4 (1952): 521–57.

Loomis, Roger Sherman. "From Segontium to Sinadon—the Legends of a *Cité Gaste*." *Speculum* 22, no. 4 (1947): 520–33.

———. "Geoffrey of Monmouth and Arthurian Origins." *Speculum* 3, no. 1 (1928): 16–33.

Loud, G. A. "The 'Gens Normannorum': Myth or Reality?" *Anglo-Norman Studies* 4 (1981): 104–16.

Lynch, Joseph H. *Godparents and Kinship in Early Medieval Europe*. Princeton: Princeton University Press, 1986.

MacLean, Simon. *Kingship and Politics in the Ninth Century: Charles the Fat and the End of the Carolingian Empire*. Cambridge: Cambridge University Press, 2003.

Magoun, Francis P., Jr. "Brutus and English Politics." *ELH* 14, no. 3 (1947): 178–80.

Marvin, William Perry. *Hunting Law and Ritual in Medieval English Literature*. Cambridge: D. S. Brewer, 2006.

Matthew, Donald J. A. *The English and the Community of Europe in the Thirteenth Century*. Reading: University of Reading, 1997.

Mayr-Harting, Henry. "Charlemagne, the Saxons, and the Imperial Coronation of 800." *English Historical Review* 111 (November 1996): 1113–33.

McCauley, Barbara Lynne. "Giraldus 'Silvester' of Wales and His 'Prophetic History of Ireland': Merlin's Role in the 'Expugnatio Hibernica.'" *Quondam et Futuris* 3, no. 4 (1993): 41–62.

McClendon, Charles. *The Origins of Medieval Architecture: Building in Europe, A.D. 600–900*. New Haven: Yale University Press, 2005.

McCurrach, Catherine Carver. "'Renovatio' Reconsidered: Richard Krautheimer and the Iconography of Architecture." *Gesta* 50, no. 1 (2011): 41–69.

McKitterick, Rosamond, ed. *Carolingian Culture: Emulation and Innovation*. Cambridge: Cambridge University Press, 1994.

———. *Carolingians and the Written Word*. Cambridge: Cambridge University Press, 1989.

———. *History and Memory in the Carolingian World*. Cambridge: Cambridge University Press, 2004.

———. ed. *The New Cambridge Medieval History*. Vol. 2, *C. 700–c. 900*. Cambridge: Cambridge University Press, 1995.

Meinig, D. W. *The Interpretation of Ordinary Landscapes*. New York: Oxford University Press, 1979.

Morris, Matthew. "The Concept of Empire and Transcendental Mission: An Augustinist Scheme in the *Chanson de Roland*." *Medieval Perspectives* 15 (2000): 82–92.

Morrissey, Robert. *Charlemagne and France: A Thousand Years of Mythology*. Translated by Catherine Tihanyi. Notre Dame: University of Notre Dame Press, 2003.

Muir, Richard. *The New Reading the Landscape: Fieldwork in Landscape History*. Exeter: University of Exeter Press, 2000.

Muldoon, James. *Empire and Order: The Concept of Empire, 800–1800*. New York: St. Martin's Press, 1999.

Mulligan, Winifred Joy. "The British Constantine: An English Historical Myth." *Journal of Medieval and Renaissance Studies* 8, no. 2 (1978): 257–79.

Musset, Lucien. "Origines et nature du pouvoir ducal en Normandie jusqu'au milieu du XIe siècle." In *Les principautés au moyen-âge: Communications du congrès de Bordeaux en 1973*, 47–59. Bordeaux: Société des historiens médiévistes de l'enseignement supérieur public, 1979.

———. "Les relations extérieures de la Normandie du IXe au XIe siècle, d'après quelques trouvailles monétaires récentes." *Annales de Normandie* 4 (1954): 31–38.

———. "Voie publique et chemin du roi en Normandie du XIe au XIIIe siècle." *Cahiers des Annales de Normandie* 17 (1985): 95–112.

Nelson, Janet L. "Aachen as a Place of Power." In *Topographies of Power in the Early Middle Ages*, edited by Mayke de Jong and Frans Theuws, 217–41. Leiden: Brill, 2001.

———. "Charles the Bald and the Church in Town and Countryside." *Studies in Church History* 16 (1979): 103–18. Reprinted in Nelson, *Politics and Ritual in Early Medieval Europe*, 75–90.

———. "Kingship and Empire in the Carolingian World." In McKitterick, *Carolingian Culture*, 52–87.

———. "Kingship and Royal Government." In McKitterick, *The New Cambridge Medieval History*, vol. 2, c. 700–c. 900, 383–430.

———. "Kingship, Law, and Liturgy in the Political Thought of Hincmar of Rheims." *English Historical Review* 92, no. 363 (1977): 241–79.

———. "Literacy in Carolingian Government." In *The Uses of Literacy in Early Medieval Government*, edited by Rosamond McKitterick, 258–96. Cambridge: Cambridge University Press, 1990.

———. "The Lord's Anointed and the People's Choice: Carolingian Royal Ritual." In *Rituals of Royalty: Power and Ceremonial in Traditional Societies*, edited by David Cannadine and Simon Price, 137–80. Cambridge: Cambridge University Press, 1987.

———. *Politics and Ritual in Early Medieval Europe*. London: Hambledon Press, 1986.

———. "Rites of the Conqueror." *Anglo-Norman Studies* 4 (1981): 117–32.

———. "The Settings of the Gift in the Reign of Charlemagne." In *The Languages of the Gift in the Early Middle Ages*, edited by Wendy Davies and Paul Fouracre, 116–48. Cambridge: Cambridge University Press, 2014.

Neveux, François. *La Normandie de ducs aux rois, Xe–XIIe siècle*. Rennes: Ouest France Université, 1998.

Nitze, W. A. "The Exhumation of King Arthur at Glastonbury." *Speculum* 9, no. 4 (1934): 355–61.

Noble, James. "Laȝamon's 'Ambivalence' Reconsidered." In Le Saux, *The Text and Tradition of Laȝamon's "Brut,"* 171–82.

Noble, Thomas F. X. "Greatness Contested and Greatness Confirmed: The Raw Materials of the Charlemagne Legend." In Gabriele and Stuckey, *The Legend of Charlemagne*, 3–21.

Nye, Joseph S., Jr. *Bound to Lead: The Changing Nature of American Power*. New York: Basic Books, 1990.

———. *Soft Power: The Means to Success in World Politics*. New York: Public Affairs, 2004.

O'Brien, Bruce R. *God's Peace and King's Peace: The Laws of Edward the Confessor*. Philadelphia: University of Pennsylvania Press, 1999.

———. "The King's Four Highways: Legal Fiction Meets Fictional Law."

Journal of Medieval History 26 (2000): 351-70.

———. *Reversing Babel: Translation Among the English During an Age of Conquests, c. 800 to c. 1200*. Newark: University of Delaware Press, 2011.

Otter, Monika. "Functions of Fiction in Historical Writing." In *Writing Medieval History*, edited by Nancy Partner, 109-32. London: Routledge, 2005.

Palmer, R. Barton. "The Narrator in *The Owl and the Nightingale*: A Reader in the Text." *Chaucer Review* 22 (1988): 305-21.

Panofsky, Erwin. *Studies in Iconology: Humanistic Themes in the Art of the Renaissance*. New York: Oxford University Press, 1939.

Parkes, Malcolm. "The Date of the Oxford Manuscript of *La Chanson de Roland* (Oxford, Bodleian Library, MS. Digby 23)." *Medioevo Romanzo* 10, no. 2 (1985): 161-76.

Parry, John J. "Geoffrey of Monmouth and the Paternity of Arthur." *Speculum* 13, no. 3 (1938): 271-77.

Partner, Nancy F. *Serious Entertainments: The Writing of History in Twelfth-Century England*. Chicago: University of Chicago Press, 1977.

Petit-Dutaillis, Charles. "Les origines franco-normandes de la 'forêt' anglaise." In *Melanges d'histoire offerts à M. Charles Bémont*, 59-76. Paris: Librairie Félix Alcan, 1913.

Petit-Dutaillis, Charles, and Georges Lefebvre. *Studies and Notes Supplementary to Stubbs' "Constitutional History."* Manchester: Manchester University Press, 1930.

Pohl, Benjamin. *Dudo of Saint-Quentin's "Historia Normannorum": Tradition, Innovation and Memory*. Woodbridge: York Medieval Press in association with the Boydell Press, 2015.

———. "Translatio imperii Constantini ad Normannos: Constantine the Great as a Possible Model for the Depiction of Rollo in Dudo of St. Quentin's *Historia Normannorum*." *Millennium* 9, no. 1 (2012): 299-342.

Poole, A. L. *Domesday Book to Magna Carta, 1087-1216*. 2nd ed. Oxford: Oxford University Press, 1955.

Pöschl, Viktor. *The Art of Vergil: Image and Symbol in the "Aeneid."* Translated by Gerda Seligson. Ann Arbor: University of Michigan Press, 1962.

Potter, K. R., ed. and trans. *Gesta Stephani*. Oxford: Clarendon Press, 1976.

Potts, Cassandra. "Atque unum ex diversis gentibus populum effecit: Historical Tradition and the Norman Identity." *Anglo-Norman Studies* 18 (1996): 139-52.

———. "The Early Norman Charters: A New Perspective on an Old Debate." In *England in the Eleventh Century: Proceedings of the 1990 Harlaxton Symposium*, edited by Carola Hicks, 25-40. Harlaxton Medieval Studies 2. Stamford: Paul Watkins, 1992.

Pounds, N. J. G. *The Medieval Castle in England and Wales: A Social and Political History*. Cambridge: Cambridge University Press, 1990.

Press, A. R. "The Precocious Courtesy of Geoffrey Gaimar." In *Court and Poet: Selected Proceedings of the Third Congress of the International Courtly Literature Society*, edited by Glyn S. Burgess, 267-76. Liverpool: Francis Cairns, 1981.

Rackham, Oliver. "Trees and Woodland in Anglo-Saxon England: The Documentary Evidence." In *Environment and Economy in Anglo-Saxon England*, edited by James Rackham, 7-11. Walmgate,

York: Council for British Archaeology, 1994.
Rahtz, Philip. "Palaces or Minsters? Northampton and Cheddar Reconsidered." *Anglo-Saxon England* 25 (1996): 97–121.
Reed, Michael. *The Landscape of Britain*. Savage, Md.: Barnes and Noble Books, 1990.
Reed, Thomas L., Jr. *Middle English Debate Poetry and the Aesthetics of Irresolution*. Columbia: University of Missouri Press, 1990.
Remensnyder, Amy G. *Remembering Kings Past: Monastic Foundation Legends in Medieval Southern France*. Ithaca: Cornell University Press, 1995.
Renn, Derek. "Burhgeat and Gonfanon: Two Sidelights from the Bayeux Tapestry." *Anglo-Norman Studies* 16 (1994): 177–86. Reprinted in Liddiard, *Anglo-Norman Castles*, 69–90.
Renoux, Annie. "Palais capétiens et normands à la fin du Xe siècle et au début du XIe siècle." In *Le roi de France et son royaume autour de l'an mil*, edited by Michel Parisse and Xavier Barral i Altet, 179–91. Paris: Picard, 1992.
Reuter, Timothy. "Plunder and Tribute in the Carolingian Empire." *Transactions of the Royal Historical Society*, 5th ser., 35 (1985): 75–94.
Richard, C. "Notice sur l'ancienne bibliothèque des Echevins de la ville de Rouen." In *Précis analytique des travaux de l'Académie royale des sciences, belles-lettres, et arts de Rouen*. Rouen: Alfred Péron, 1845.
Richardson, H. G., and G. O. Sayles. *The Governance of Mediaeval England from the Conquest to Magna Carta*. Edinburgh: Edinburgh University Press, 1963.
Ridyard, Susan J. "*Condigna Veneratio*: Post-Conquest Attitudes to the Saints of the Anglo-Saxons." *Anglo-Norman Studies* 9 (1986): 179–206.
———. *The Royal Saints of Anglo-Saxon England: A Study of West Saxon and East Anglian Cults*. Cambridge: Cambridge University Press, 1988.
Robertson, Kellie. "Geoffrey of Monmouth and the Translation of Insular Historiography." *Arthuriana* 8, no. 4 (1998): 42–57.
Roffe, David. *Domesday: The Inquest and the Book*. Oxford: Oxford University Press, 2000.
Rooney, Anne. *Hunting in Middle English Literature*. Cambridge: D. S. Brewer, 1993.
Rouse, Robert Allen. *The Idea of Anglo-Saxon England in Middle English Romance*. Cambridge: D. S. Brewer, 2005.
Said, Edward W. *Orientalism*. New York: Vintage Books, 1979.
Salter, Elizabeth. *English and International: Studies in the Literature, Art, and Patronage of Medieval England*. Edited by Derek Pearsall and Nicolette Zeeman. Cambridge: Cambridge University Press, 1988.
———. "Geoffrey of Monmouth and Oxford." *English Historical Review* 34, no. 135 (1919): 382–85.
Saunders, Corinne J. *The Forest of Medieval Romance: Avernus, Broceliande, Arden*. Cambridge: D. S. Brewer, 1993.
———, ed. *The Text and Tradition of Laʒamon's "Brut."* Cambridge: D. S. Brewer, 1994.
Sawyer, P. H. *From Roman Britain to Norman England*. 2nd ed. London: Routledge, 1998.
Sayers, William. "The Jongleur Taillefer at Hastings: Antecedents and Literary Fate." *Viator* 14 (1983): 77–88.
———. "Ships and Sailors in Geiffrei Gaimar's *Estoire des Engleis*."

Modern Language Review 98, no. 2 (2003): 299–310.
Sayles, G. O. *The Medieval Foundations of England.* Philadelphia: University of Pennsylvania Press, 1950.
Scahill, John. "The Audiences of Medieval Chronicles and of Cotton Caligula A. ix." *Geibun'Kenkyu* 80 (2001): 142–59.
Schneider, Reinhard. "Karl der Große—politisches Sendungsbewußtsein und Mission." In *Kirchengeschichte als Missionsgeschichte,* vol. 2, *Die Kirche des früheren Mittelalters,* edited by Knut Schäferdiek, 241–44. Munich: Kaiser, 1978.
Scholz, Bernhard W. "The Canonization of Edward the Confessor." *Speculum* 36, no. 1 (1961): 38–60.
Scragg, Donald, and Carole Weinberg. *Literary Appropriations of the Anglo-Saxons from the Thirteenth to the Twentieth Century.* Cambridge Studies in Anglo-Saxon England 29. Cambridge: Cambridge University Press, 2000.
Searle, Eleanor, ed. and trans. *The Chronicle of Battle Abbey.* Oxford: Clarendon Press, 1980.
———. "Fact and Pattern in Heroic History: Dudo of Saint-Quentin." *Viator* 15 (1984): 119–37.
———. *Predatory Kinship and the Creation of Norman Power, 840–1066.* Berkeley: University of California Press, 1988.
Shopkow, Leah. "The Carolingian World of Dudo of Saint-Quentin." *Journal of Medieval History* 15 (1989): 19–37.
———. *History and Community: Norman Historical Writing in the Eleventh and Twelfth Centuries.* Washington, D.C.: Catholic University of America Press, 1998.
Short, Brian. "Forest and Wood-Pasture in Lowland England." In *The English Rural Landscape,* edited by Joan Thirsk, 122–49. Oxford: Oxford University Press, 2000.
Short, Ian. "Gaimar et les débuts de l'historiographie en langue française." In *Chroniques nationales et chroniques universelles,* edited by Danielle Buschinger, 155–63. Göppingen: Kummerle, 1990.
———. "Gaimar's Epilogue and Geoffrey of Monmouth's *Liber vetustissimus.*" *Speculum* 69, no. 2 (1994): 323–43.
———. "Patrons and Polyglots: French Literature in Twelfth-Century England." *Anglo-Norman Studies* 14 (1991): 229–49.
———. "Tam Angli quam Franci: Self-Definition in Anglo-Norman England." *Anglo-Norman Studies* 18 (1996): 153–76.
Sidey, Thomas K. "The Government of Charlemagne as Influenced by Augustine's 'City of God.'" *Classical Journal* 14, no. 2 (1918): 119–27.
Sieffert, Germain. "Les imitations de la chapelle palatine de Charlemagne à Aix-la-chapelle." *Cahiers de l'art médiéval* 2 (1969): 29–70.
Silverman, M. J. "Ælfric's Designation of the King as 'Cristes Sylfes Speligend.'" *Review of English Studies* 35, no. 139 (1984): 332–34.
Simmons, Clare A. *Reversing the Conquest: History and Myth in Nineteenth-Century British Literature.* New Brunswick: Rutgers University Press, 1990.
Smith, Julia M. H. *Europe After Rome: A New Cultural History, 500–1000.* Oxford: Oxford University Press, 2005.
———. *Province and Empire: Brittany and the Carolingians.* Cambridge: Cambridge University Press, 1992.
Smyth, Alfred P. "The Emergence of English Identity, 700–1000." In *Medieval Europeans: Studies in Ethnic Identity and National Perspectives*

in *Medieval Europe*, edited by Alfred P. Smyth, 24-52. New York: St. Martin's Press, 1998.

Southern, R. W. "Aspects of the European Tradition of Historical Writing, I: The Classical Tradition from Einhard to Geoffrey of Monmouth." *Transactions of the Royal Historical Society*, 5th ser., 20 (1970): 173-96.

———. "Aspects of the European Tradition of Historical Writing, IV: The Sense of the Past." *Transactions of the Royal Historical Society*, 5th ser., 23 (1973): 243-63.

———. *Medieval Humanism and Other Studies*. Oxford: Basil Blackwell, 1970.

Spiegel, Gabrielle M. *Romancing the Past: The Rise of Vernacular Prose Historiography in Thirteenth-Century France*. Berkeley: University of California Press, 1993.

Stocker, David. "Rubbish Recycled: A Study of the Re-use of Stone in Lincolnshire." In *Stone Quarrying and Building in England, AD 43-1525*, edited by David Parsons, 83-101. Chichester: Phillimore in association with the Royal Archaeological Institute, 1990.

Stofferahn, Steven. "Staying the Royal Sword: Alcuin and the Conversion Dilemma in Early Medieval Europe." *Historian* 71, no. 3 (2009): 461-80.

Stoler, Ann Laura. "Rethinking Colonial Categories: European Communities and the Boundaries of Rule." *Comparative Studies in Society and History* 31, no. 1 (1989): 134-61.

Story, Joanna. *Carolingian Connections: Anglo-Saxon England and Carolingian Francia, c. 750-870*. Aldershot: Ashgate, 2003.

———. "Cathwulf, Kingship, and the Royal Abbey of Saint-Denis." *Speculum* 74, no. 1 (1999): 1-21.

———, ed. *Charlemagne: Empire and Society*. Manchester: Manchester University Press, 2005.

Strickland, Matthew. "Killing or Clemency? Ransom, Chivalry and Changing Attitudes to Defeated Opponents in Britain and Northern France, 7-12th Centuries." In *Krieg im Mittelalter*, edited by Hans-Henning Kortüm, 93-122. Berlin: De Gruyter, 2001.

———. "Slaughter, Slavery or Ransom: The Impact of the Conquest on Conduct in Warfare." In *England in the Eleventh Century*, edited by Carola Hicks, 41-59. Stamford: Paul Watkins, 1992.

Stuckey, Jace Andrew. "Charlemagne: The Making of an Image, 110-1300." Ph.D. diss., University of Florida, 2006.

Sullivan, Richard E. *Aix-la-Chapelle in the Age of Charlemagne*. Norman: University of Oklahoma Press, 1963.

Swan, Mary, and Elaine M. Treharne. *Rewriting Old English in the Twelfth Century*. Cambridge: Cambridge University Press, 2000.

Sweetman, H. S., ed. *Calendar of Documents Relating to Ireland, 1171-1307*. 2 vols. London: Longman, 1875.

Tabuteau, Emily Zack. *Transfers of Property in Eleventh Century Norman Law*. Chapel Hill: University of North Carolina Press, 1988.

Tatlock, J. S. P. "Geoffrey and King Arthur in 'Normannicus Draco' (Concluded)." *Modern Philology* 31, no. 2 (1933): 113-25.

———. "Geoffrey and King Arthur in 'Normannicus Draco' (Continued)." *Modern Philology* 31, no. 1 (1933): 1-18.

Taylor, Andrew. *Textual Situations: Three Medieval Manuscripts and Their Readers*. Philadelphia: University of Pennsylvania Press, 2002.

Thomas, Hugh M. *The English and the Normans: Ethnic Hostility, Assimilation, and Identity, 1066-c. 1220*. Oxford: Oxford University Press, 2003.

———. *The Norman Conquest: England After William the Conqueror*. Lanham, Md.: Rowman and Littlefield, 2008.

Thompson, Anne Booth. *Everyday Saints and the Art of Narrative in the South English Legendary*. Aldershot: Ashgate, 2003.

Thomson, Rodney M. *William of Malmesbury*. Rev. ed. Woodbridge: Boydell Press, 2003.

Tilley, Christopher. "The Powers of Rocks: Topography and Monument Construction on Bodmin Moor." *World Archaeology* 28, no. 2 (1996): 161-76.

Turner, James. *The Politics of Landscape: Rural Scenery and Society in English Poetry, 1630-1660*. Cambridge, Mass.: Harvard University Press, 1979.

Turville-Petre, Thorlac. *England the Nation: Language, Literature, and National Identity, 1290-1340*. Oxford: Clarendon Press, 1996.

Uebel, Michael. *Ecstatic Transformation: On the Uses of Alterity in the Middle Ages*. New York: Palgrave, 2005.

Ullman, Walter. *The Carolingian Renaissance and the Idea of Kingship*. London: Methuen, 1969.

———. *The Individual and Society in the Middle Ages*. Baltimore: Johns Hopkins Press, 1966.

Van Caenegem, R. C., ed. *English Lawsuits from William I to Richard I*. London: Selden Society, 1990.

Van Houts, Elisabeth M. C. *Memory and Gender in Medieval Europe, 900-1200*. Toronto: University of Toronto Press, 1999.

———. "The Memory of 1066 in Written and Oral Traditions." *Anglo-Norman Studies* 19 (1996): 167-79.

———. "The Origins of Herleva, Mother of William the Conqueror." *English Historical Review* 101, no. 399 (1986): 399-404.

Vera, F. W. M. *Grazing Ecology and Forest History*. New York: CABI, 2000.

Wallace-Hadrill, J. M. "Review of *Via Regia: Der Furstenspiegel Smaragdus von St Mihiel und seine literarische Gattung*, by Otto Eberhardt." *English Historical Review* 93, no. 369 (1978): 845-46.

———. "The *Via regia* of the Carolingian Age." In *Trends in Medieval Political Thought*, edited by Beryl Smalley, 22-41. New York: Barnes and Noble, 1965.

Wallach, Luitpold. *Alcuin and Charlemagne: Studies in Carolingian History and Literature*. Ithaca: Cornell University Press, 1959.

———. "Alcuin on Virtues and Vices: A Manual for a Carolingian Soldier." *Harvard Theological Review* 48, no. 3 (1955): 175-95.

Walpole, Ronald. "A New Edition of Geffrei Gaimar's *L'Estoire des Engleis*." *Philological Quarterly* 41 (1962): 373-85.

Warren, Michelle R. *History on the Edge: Excalibur and the Borders of Britain, 1100-1300*. Minneapolis: University of Minnesota Press, 2000.

———. "Making Contact: Postcolonial Perspectives Through Geoffrey of Monmouth's *Historia regum Britannie*." *Arthuriana* 8, no. 4 (1998): 115-34.

Warren, W. L. *Henry II*. Berkeley: University of California Press, 1973.

Watt, J. A. *The Church and the Two Nations in Medieval Ireland.* Cambridge: Cambridge University Press, 1970.

Webber, Nick. *The Evolution of Norman Identity, 911-1154.* Woodbridge: Boydell and Brewer, 2005.

Werner, Karl Ferdinand. "Kingdom and Principality in Twelfth-Century France." In *The Medieval Nobility: Studies on the Ruling Classes of France and Germany from the Sixth to the Twelfth Century,* edited and translated by Timothy Reuter, 243-90. Europe in the Middle Ages 14. Amsterdam: North Holland, 1978.

Wheatley, Abigail. *The Idea of the Castle in Medieval England.* Woodbridge: Boydell Press for the York Medieval Press, 2004.

Wickham, Chris. "European Forests in the Early Middle Ages: Landscapes and Land Clearance." *Settimane di Centro Italiano sull' Alto Medioevo* 37 (1990): 479-548.

Williams, Ann. "A Bell-House and a Burh-Geat: Lordly Residences in England before the Conquest." *Medieval Knighthood* 4 (1992): 221-40. Reprinted in Liddiard, *Anglo-Norman Castles,* 23-40.

———. *The English and the Norman Conquest.* Woodbridge: Boydell and Brewer, 1995.

Wogan-Browne, Jocelyn, Nicholas Watson, Andrew Taylor, and Ruth Evans, eds. *The Idea of the Vernacular: An Anthology of Middle English Literary Theory, 1280-1520.* University Park: Pennsylvania State University Press, 1999.

———. *Saints' Lives and Women's Literary Culture, c. 1150-1300: Virginity and Its Authorizations.* Oxford: Oxford University Press, 2001.

Wood, Ian. "Defining the Franks: Frankish Origins in Early Medieval Historiography." In *Concepts of National Identity in the Middle Ages,* edited by Simon Forde, Lesley Johnson, and Alan V. Murray, 47-57. Leeds: School of English, 1995.

Wormald, Patrick. *The Making of English Law: King Alfred to the Twelfth Century.* Vol. 1. Oxford: Blackwell, 1999.

Young, Charles R. *The Royal Forests of Medieval England.* Philadelphia: University of Pennsylvania Press, 1979.

Yver, Jean. "Les premières institutions du duché de Normandie." *Settimane di Centro Italiano sull' Alto Medioevo* 16 (1969): 299-366.

Zatta, Jane. "Gaimar's Rebels: Outlaw Heroes and the Creation of Authority in Twelfth-Century England." *Essays in Medieval Studies* 16 (1999): 27-40.

———. "Gender, Love, and Sex as Political Theory? Romance in Geffrei Gaimar's Anglo-Norman Chronicle." *Mediaevalia* 21, no. 2 (1997): 249-80.

———. "Translating the *Historia*: The Ideological Transformation of the *Historia Regum Britannie* in Twelfth-Century Vernacular Chronicles." *Arthuriana* 8, no. 4 (1998): 148-61.

Index

Aachen
    as "new Rome," 18, 72, 74-77
    palace chapel, 3, 57, 73-77, 81-82, 85
Ado of Vienne, *Chronicon*, 15
Ælfric, 12, 125
Æthelberht, 26
Æthelstan, 12-13
Æthelwold, 12
Airlie, Stuart, 24, 29
Albu, Emily, 30-31
Alcuin, 12-13, 15, 23, 28, 54-55, 61-63, 70, 75
    Rhetoric, 13, 62-63
Alfonso VI, "the Brave," 3
Alfred the Great, 5, 12, 45-47, 49, 77
Andrew de Coutances, *Roman de Franceis*, 112, 115
Angenendt, Arnold, 20
Anglo-Saxon Chronicle
    Peterborough Chronicle, 89, 160 n. 105
    "Rime of King William," 90, 96
Anglo-Saxons, 5, 10, 12, 26, 38, 44-47, 59, 62-63, 69, 72-73, 78-81
Anonymous, York or Norman, 12
Antiquity, 39, 73-77, 86
assimilation, 7-8, 19, 45-46
Assize of Woodstock (1184), 97
Athelstan (king of the Anglo-Saxons), 87, 116-17
Audehm, Kathrin, 10
Avars, 23, 43, 49, 55

Bartholomaeus Anglicus, 114
Bates, David, 7, 9, 12, 113
Battle Abbey, chronicle, 102
Battle of Hastings, 1, 5, 50, 68, 70, 112
Bauduin, Pierre, 8
Bavarians, 43, 49, 52
Becher, Matthias, 22
Bede, 26, 65-68, 83
Beer, Jeanette, 2
Béroul, *Tristan and Iseut*, 107-8
biblical models of kingship, 19, 61-63, 69
Blair, John, 79
Bloch, R. Howard, 14
bloodfeud, 14, 38, 62
Burgess, Glyn S., 106
burh, 72, 78-80
burh-geat, 79-80

Caerwent, 80
Caesar, as imperial model, 27, 80, 82
capitularies, 14, 16, 22-24, 27-28, 92-94, 96
Carloman (son of Charlemagne), 26
Cassiodorus, 73
castles, 16, 39-40
    donjon, 79
    motte-and-bailey, 80
    reuse of materials as *translatio*, 71-81, 88
    as symbols of authority, 58, 66, 71-72
Chanson de Roland, 50-53

Chardri
    Petit plet, 116
    La Vie de seint Josaphaz, 115
Charlemagne
    building program, 72-77
    canonization, 3, 68, 114
    Capitulare de villis, 92-94, 97
    Capitulare missorum generale, 92-93, 97
    Capitulatio de partibus Saxoniae, 22
    forest administration, 92-96
    as novus Constantinus, 74
    as Old Testament king, 4, 13, 19, 61
    sacral kingship, 12, 15, 23, 61-63
    use of ritual, 20, 24-29, 42, 95-96
Charles Martel, 84
Charles II the Bald (Carolingian emperor), 3, 57
Charles III the Simple (king of France), 11, 32
charters, 10, 12, 57, 90-92, 95, 97-98
Cheddar (Anglo-Saxon royal palace), 79
Chepstow Castle, 80, 87
Childeric I (king of the Salian Franks), 73-74
civilization
    Anglo-Norman views of, 2, 16, 19-20, 37-49
    Carolingian views of, 20-27
Clovis I (founder of Merovingian dynasty), 4, 74, 91
Cnut, 95
Colchester Castle, 79-80, 85
common law, 38, 89, 93
Compiègne, palace chapel, 3, 57
Constantine, 4, 19, 54, 74-75, 116
Constitutiones de Foresta, 95
continuity of Carolingian practices in early Normandy, 7-12, 91-92
conversion politics
    acculturation, 19, 25-27, 39-40, 43, 47, 136
    allurement, 20-21, 27-28, 33, 35-37, 41, 49, 53, 56
    baptismal sponsorship, 22-26, 33, 128 n. 26, 129 n. 34
    benevolence, 20, 22-23, 36, 39
    chivalry, 37-41, 44-49
    clemency, 21-23, 37-38, 47, 51
    conversion, 16, 19-30, 33-34, 36-39, 42-47, 50-51, 53-56
    cultural barbarism, 16, 21, 24, 27, 37-44, 54-56
    "fair love" (bel amur), 20-21, 37, 46-52
    forced conversions, 21-22, 50-52
    gifts, 13, 21, 25-27, 29, 31, 35-36, 42-43, 49-50
    "good customs" (bones costumes), 20, 46-49
Cooper, Alan, 64, 67
Coulson, Charles, 81
Cowdrey, John, 4
Creighton, O. H., 78

Damian-Grint, Peter, 47
Danes and conversion, 24, 27, 36, 45-46
David (Old Testament king), 4, 19, 60-62, 69
David I (king of Scotland), 42-43
Davies, R. R., 39-43, 53
Davy, Gilduin, 5, 91
Diarmait Mac Murchada (king of Leinster), 55
Domesday survey, 10-11, 17, 79, 89
Donation of Constantine, 4, 54
Douglas, David, 11
Dudo of Saint Quentin, De moribus et actis primorum Normanniae ducum, 29-36, 45-46, 50
Duggan, Anne J., 54

Eadberht (Anglo-Saxon king), 12-13
Eadmer, Historia novorum in Anglia, 98
Eaton, Tim, 75
Edgar (Anglo-Saxon king), 12, 44, 46-47, 49, 77
Edward the Confessor (Anglo-Saxon king), 78, 80, 96, 101
Einhard, Vita Caroli, 21, 24, 95
Elias, Norbert, 20
Englishness, 17, 113-15
Ermoldus Nigellus, Carminis in honorem Ludovici, 27, 74

Faletra, Michael, 86
Fantosme, Jordan, Chronique de la guerre entre les Anglois et les Ecossais, 44, 68-69
Flanagan, Marie Therese, 55

Fleischman, Suzanne, 3
forest
    abuses of royal power, 17, 90, 99-100, 111, 113
    afforestation, 90, 96, 98, 105, 111
    economic and political advantages, 92-97, 105-6, 111
    New Forest (*Nova Foresta*, Hampshire), 89, 98-103
    origins of Forest Law, 11, 89-98
    and romance literature, 105-7
    as symbol of the royal court, 91, 95-96, 98-99, 106-10
Forest of Morrois, 107-108
Franco (archbishop of Rouen), 33
Fredegar, *Chronicle*, 84
Frederick Barbarossa (Holy Roman Emperor), 3, 68, 114

Gaimar, Geoffroi, *Estoire des Engleis*, 16, 44-50, 56, 84, 90, 99, 102-5
Ganshof, François-Louis, 92
gens Karolinorum, 92
gens Ricardorum, 92
Geoffrey of Monmouth
    Historia regum Brittaniae, 4, 48-49, 71-72, 84-88
    Prophecies of Merlin (*Prophetiae Merlini*), 44, 86
Gerald of Wales (Giraldus Cambrensis), *Expugnatio Hibernica*, 39, 53-55, 106
Gerould, Gordon Hall, 83
Gesta Stephani, 39, 65-66, 80
Gift Story. See *Li rei de Engleterre*
Gillingham, John, 37-39, 41
Giraldus Cambrensis. See Gerald of Wales
Goltho, 79
Gransden, Antonia, 44
Gregory of Tours, *Libri Historiarum*, 4, 74
Guthrum (king of Danish Vikings in Danelaw), 45-46
Guy, Bishop of Amiens, *Carmen de Hastingae Proelio*, 138 n. 156

Hagger, Mark, 8
Harald (king of Denmark), 26-27
Harbison, Robert, 59
Head, Thomas, 13

Hennebicque, Régine, 96
Henry I (duke of Normandy; king of England), 14, 41-43, 46-47, 67, 69, 96-98, 110
Henry II (duke of Normandy; king of England), 14, 43, 53-56, 68-69, 105-6, 110
Henry III (king of England), 114, 116
Henry of Huntingdon, *Historia Anglorum*, 64-71
    Myth of the Four Highways, 64-68
Hereford Cathedral, 57, 81
Herrick, Samantha Kahn, 30
Hibernicus Exul, *Ad Karolum regem*, 25
Hollister, C. Warren, 41
Hooke, Della, 95
Howe, John, 65
Howe, Nicholas, 59
Hrabanus Maurus, *Liber de Oblatione Puerorum*, 28-29, 36
Hudson, John, 14
Hugh (king of France), 116
Hyams, Paul, 14, 38

imperator, classical definition, 146 n. 80
imperium, classical definition, 120 n. 5
Ingelheim (royal palace), 74
Ingledew, Francis, 85
Innes, Matthew, 69
Ireland, 40-41, 43, 53-56
Isidore of Seville, *Etymologies*, 120 n. 5, 146 n. 80

John of Salisbury, *Metalogicon*, 54
John (king of England), 114
de Jong, Mayke, 63
justice, king's or duke's, 11, 13-14, 23, 34, 38, 64, 103, 109-10

Kantorowicz, Ernst, 13, 99
Karolus Magnus et Leo Papa, 75-76, 96
Keefe, Thomas, 41
Kershaw, Paul, 63
King Arthur, 48-49, 68, 83, 86-87, 112-13
king's (or duke's) peace, 13-14, 34-35, 43, 62-66, 89-90, 102-3
king's peace for beasts of the forest, 103, 109, 160 n. 105

Kleinbauer, W. Eugene, 81
Koziol, Geoffrey, 30

Lambert of Hersfeld, *Annales*, 84
Landes, Richard, 13
landscape as symbol. *See* symbolic landscape
Latowsky, Anne, 3
Laudabiliter, 53-55
Laʒamon, *Brut*, 114, 116
Le Patourel, John, 13
Lefebvre, Georges, 95
Leges Edwardi Confessoris, 15
Leges Henrici Primi, 14, 62-63
Liber Historiae Francorum, 84
Liddiard, Robert, 72, 79, 81
Lifshitz, Felice, 8
Liuzza, Roy, 72
Loomis, Roger Sherman, 83
Losinga, Robert (bishop of Hereford), 57, 81
Louis the Pious (Carolingian emperor), 24, 26-27, 63-64

MacLean, Simon, 82
Marie de France
    "Bisclavret," 106, 108-9, 160
    "Chevrefoil," 107-8
    "Eliduc," 106
    "Equitan," 106, 109-10
    "Guigemar," 106
    "Lanval," 106
Marvin, William Perry, 98
Mayr-Harting, Henry, 28
McClendon, Charles, 58
McKitterick, Rosamond, 84
Meinig, D. W., 58
Merovingians, 4, 14, 92
Moduin, *Egloga*, 76-77
Morrissey, Robert, 1
Musset, Lucien, 8, 62

Nelson, Janet, 6, 26, 35-36, 94-95
Neustria, 7-9, 30, 91
Normanitas, 123 n. 49
Notker the Stammerer, *De Carolo Magno*, 24, 81-82

O'Brien, Bruce, 15
Old Testament models of kingship, 4, 13, 60-61, 63

Ongar Great Park (Essex), 95
Orderic Vitalis, *Historia ecclesiastica*, 71, 89, 100-104
Ottonians, 3, 12, 34, 77

Paderborn, royal palace, 74-6
Parkes, Malcolm, 50
Paul the Deacon, *Vita Arnulfi*, 84
Peace (or Truce) of God movement, 13-14
Pepin the Short (king of the Franks), 13, 15, 19, 84
Philip Augustus, 3, 114
Pippin. *See* Pepin
Pope Adrian IV, 53-54
Pope Anastasius, 91
Pope Hadrian I, 26, 74
Pope Leo III, 19, 28, 73, 76-77
Press, A. R., 44
Prophetiae Merlini. *See* Geoffrey of Monmouth, *Prophecies of Merlin*
Prospice omnipotens deus, 22

Rackham, Oliver, 95
Ranulf Higden, *Polychronicon*, 135 n. 109
Ravenna, 73-75
regio barbara, vs. *regio composita*, 39
Li rei de Engleterre, 114, 116-18
renovatio imperii, 82-83, 88
rex et sacerdos, 26, 34, 36
Richard de Clare, "Strongbow" (earl of Pembroke), 55-56
Richard I (duke of Normandy), 9, 29-30, 34-36, 52, 91-92
Richard II (duke of Normandy), 29-30, 92
Richardson, H. G., 97
Richmond Castle, 79
rituals
    anointings, 3, 73
    baptism: for cementing alliances, 26-27, 33-34; spiritual kinship, 26
    coronation and crown-wearings, 3, 6, 12, 28, 77
    feasts, 20, 24-27, 42-43
    hunting, 3, 25, 27, 42, 91, 94-99, 100, 103, 106, 108-10
    marriage, 30, 33-4, 41-42
roads, as symbol of kingship, 58-65, 69, 71
Robert Curthose (duke of Normandy), 101

Robert I, "the Magnificent" (duke of Normandy), 123 n. 48
Robert (duke of the Franks), 33
romanitas, 58, 71
Rome
    as architectural model, 58, 72–78
    as source for imperial legitimacy, 59, 70, 72–73, 80–85, 91
Rooney, Anne, 98, 109
Rougemont Castle (Exeter), 80–81, 87
Rouse, Robert Allen, 67

sacerdotal kingship, 12–13, 30, 132
sacral kingship, 2, 5, 12–13, 15, 23, 26, 56, 61, 63, 67–69, 71, 77, 88, 99, 117
Saint Albans chronicler, 40
Saint Apollinare Nuovo, church of (Ravenna), 73
Saint Augustine, *De Civitate Dei*, 21, 63
salvation, king's responsibility for, 11, 32–34, 60, 63, 68, 82, 99, 102
Saunders, Corinne J., 109–10
Saxon Poet (*Poeta Saxo*), 18–19, 29, 74
Saxons, 2, 20–29, 87
Sayles, G. O., 97
Searle, Eleanor, 7
Silverman, M. J., 12
Smaragdus St. Mihiel, *Via regia*, 62–64
Smith, Julia M. H., 26, 77
Solomon, 4, 13, 60–61, 69
Southern, R. W., 9, 30
spolia, 59, 72, 75, 78
Stephen (king of England), 43, 105
Stoler, Ann Laura, 2
Strickland, Matthew, 38
Suger, *Vita Ludovici Grossi Regis*, 150 n. 154, 158 n. 77
symbolic landscape, 16–17, 58–59, 64–66, 71–72, 77–81, 88, 91, 98–99
Symeon of Durham, *Libellus de exordio*, 12

Taillefer, 112
Tassilo (duke of Bavaria), 25, 29, 35, 43, 53
Theodoric (king of the Ostrogoths; king of Italy), 73, 81
Thomas, *Tristan and Iseut*, 107–8
translatio imperii, models, 4, 32, 59, 69–70, 75, 78, 83, 88, 113, 116

Treaty of Saint-Clair-sur-Epte, 29
Trojan origins, 30–31, 70, 84–87

urbanization, 37, 39, 41, 47, 55, 66–67, 71–72

Velten, Hans Rudolf, 10
via regia, 11, 16, 58, 59–65, 67, 69
Vikings, 7–9, 29–31, 45
Virgil, *Aeneid*
    Aeneas, 76, 84, 98
    Anchises, 84
    Antenor, 31, 84
    Dido, 98
Vita Caroli, 21
Vita Lebuini, 24
Vita Silvestri, 4

Wace, *Roman de Brut*, 12, 44, 48–50, 112, 115
Wales, 16, 39–42, 47, 49, 53, 55, 65–67, 80, 83, 87, 106
Wallace-Hadrill, J. M., 62
Wallach, Luitpold, 13, 61, 63
Wallingford (pre-Conquest high-status structure), 79
Warren, W. L., 97
Welsh, 39–40, 42–43, 65, 81, 86–87
Werner, Karl Ferdinand, 7
Wheatley, Abigail, 75
White Tower, 85–88
Widukind, 22, 26–27
William Longsword (duke of Normandy), 8–9, 11, 91
William of Malmesbury
    Gesta pontificum Anglorum, 57
    Gesta regum Anglorum, 1, 4, 13, 38–43, 50, 57, 81, 116–7
William of Newburgh, *Historia rerum Anglicarum*, 106
William of Poitiers, *Gesta Guillelmi*, 82–83
William Rishanger, chronicle of Saint Albans, 40
William II, "Rufus" (king of England), 84, 97–105
William I, "the Conqueror" (duke of Normandy; king of England), 1–2, 6, 10–11, 14, 41, 68, 70–72, 78–88, 89–90, 95–97, 100–102, 111
Wormald, Patrick, 14

Typeset by
REGINA STARACE

Printed and bound by
SHERIDAN BOOKS

Composed in
NEACADEMIA TEXT

Printed on
NATURES NATURAL

Bound in
ARRESTOX

www.ingramcontent.com/pod-product-compliance
Lightning Source LLC
Chambersburg PA
CBHW021949290426
44108CB00012B/999